Praise for *The Political Novel*

"In the very best tradition of interdisciplinary inquiry, Stuart Scheingold re-imagines the collective catastrophe of the twentieth century, offering fresh insights into the destabilization of democracies, the rise of totalitarianism, and — importantly, for both understanding our histories and anticipating our futures — our shaken faith in the promise of modernity. Deftly shifting between and among political, cultural, historical, and literary approaches to novels of political estrangement by some of the twentieth-century's most important authors, Scheingold illuminates the impact of political processes and shifting images of political agency on ordinary people, as well as the critical importance of the literary imagination for political inquiry itself."

Bill Lyons, Professor of Political Science,
University of Akron, USA

"I believe that Scheingold is the only one who could have written this book. He reads political novels with more insight into and sophistication about the way fiction works than anyone else has. The book is the product of long-term study and thinking, and I am happy to recommend it with great, great enthusiasm."

Malcolm A. Griffith, Emeritus in English,
University of Washington, USA

"Whilst the impelling concern of this unique and eloquent tour d'horizon is with novels of political estrangement, and even as a searing insight is brought to bear on them, the intense focus on what denies modern political agency also intimates what may yet fulfil it. And although that promise may lack the compelling cognates of estrangement, Scheingold's poignant evocations of the literary still give insistent voice to the possibility of fulfilment, to an inexhaustible hope."

Peter Fitzpatrick, Anniversary Professor of Law, Birkbeck,
University of London, UK

"One of the great problems of our age — the decline in political engagement — comes alive in this sobering exploration of modern literature. Demonstrating the loss of agency and of hope and commitment portrayed in novels of many nations, *The Political Novel* helps us understand the past century and maybe the one ahead."

James N. Gregory, Harry Bridges Endowed Chair of Labor Studies and
Professor of History, University of Washington, USA

The Political Novel

Re-Imagining the Twentieth Century

Stuart A. Scheingold

continuum

The Continuum International Publishing Group
80 Maiden Lane, New York, NY 10038
The Tower Building, 11 York Road, London SE1 7NX

www.continuumbooks.com

Library of Congress Cataloging-in-Publication Data
A catalog record for this book is available from the Library of Congress

ISBN: 978-1-4411-4807-0 (hardcover)
         978-1-4411-7639-4 (paperback)

Typeset by Pindar NZ, Auckland, New Zealand
Printed in the United States of America

Contents

Preface

When all is said and done, I see this project as an extension of my career-long search to look beyond the hard data of empirical social science to subtler, less quantifiable but no less real truths. The cornerstone of this search was my 1974 book, *The Politics of Rights: Lawyers, Public Policy and Political Change*. In *The Politics of Rights* I constructed a theory of rights and law rooted in their cultural resonance in the United States. I have also regularly used novels and films in my courses and in some of my research. Finally a course that I taught for many years on the ideological conflicts that pervaded and perverted the twentieth century can be seen as a kind of accidental template for *The Political Novel: Re-imagining the 20th Century*.

What distinguishes this book from all of these precursors is that the literary imagination is no longer at the periphery of my gaze but is instead its heart and soul. Little did I realize that as the project matured I would discover a new genre of political novel, *the novels of political estrangement*, These novels reveal not only multiple variants of estrangement in the best of twentieth century literature but at the same time provide a revealing new perspective into the history and politics of the twentieth century.

In short, the most gratifying element of the entire intellectual adventure was the way in which the truths of these novels unfolded and converged around the multiple and mutually constitutive prisms of literary, political and historical inquiry. I simply went where the literary imagination took me. So, this book not only enabled me to re-imagine the terrible twentieth century, it also allowed me to fully indulge my long time love affair with novels and with the literary imagination.

Through the entirety of this intellectual adventure into terra incognita, I have been blessed by dear friends and consummate scholars. They have encouraged me to plunge ahead, have provided invaluable ideas about how to proceed, and have enabled me to understand the true nature of my project and how to make the most of it.

To begin at the beginning, my fascination with political novels goes back decades to courses taught jointly with my dear friend and English

Department colleague Malcolm Griffith. He has been unfailingly supportive of this project.

I have dedicated the book in part to Michael McCann, who over and over again helped me escape from blind alleys of my own making. He knows the ins and outs of this project at least as well as I do. I will also be eternally grateful to Austin Sarat, whose deft touch and incomparable intellectual instincts have been continuously and steadfastly at my disposal. Sabine Lang's knowledge of German literature has been invaluable to my understanding of the very best of post-Nazi, post-WW II novelists. Julie Drew has helped me understand how to bridge the gap between literary and political inquiry. Gad Barzilai has given me much-needed confidence in my readings of Holocaust novels. Beth Kier has been my informant on the follies of total warfare. She and Jon Mercer have been unstinting in their friendship and a lifeline for me and for Lee through some difficult times. I have also relied on two former students, Bill Lyons and Lennie Feldman, who have become successful and talented scholars. Among others who have counseled and encouraged me are Lance Bennett, Peter Fitzpatrick, John Goldberg-Hiller and George Lovell.

Then there is Malcolm Feeley who deserves a line of his own for his struggle to bring out the best in me. Perhaps I should have followed his lead. Although I balked, he has been unstinting in his enthusiasm for this book and in his determination that I make the most out of this break-out moment in my scholarly career.

At Continuum I have had the extreme good fortune to work with accomplished professionals including my project manager, Sara-May Mallett, and my cover designer, Louise Dugdale. Most of all, however, I am profoundly grateful to my editor, Haaris Naqvi, who has done everything humanly possible to make this the best publishing experience of my life.

I cannot close these acknowledgements without expressing my admiration for, and my debt to, Tony Judt. Although we have never met, the spirit of his historical scholarship hovers over and is infused into just about every nook and cranny of this volume.

For Lee: my love, my soul mate, and my emotional strength. Only she and I know in how many ways this book is ours.

And for Michael McCann who has made certain over and over again that I have ended my career with a song in my heart.

1 Novels of Political Estrangement: Subversion of Agency in the Twentieth Century

> Literature can stop my heart and execute me for a moment, allow me to become someone else. It is another chance at history.
>
> Colum McCann[1]

> The century had cored him with its war.
>
> Mary Karr[2]

Novels of political estrangement live in and draw sustenance from cultural context filtered through the mind's eye. As such they empower us to re-imagine the twentieth century and help us to anticipate the twenty-first. Novels of political estrangement engage not with political processes and institutions but instead with those who are subjected to, but have little or no say in the decisions made by authoritative agencies on their behalf — and too often at their expense. These novels are a product of, and a window into, the dispiriting calamities of the twentieth century.

Reformers and revolutionaries alike — liberals Adam Smith and John Stuart Mill as well as socialists Karl Marx and Antonio Gramsci — *imagined* that technological innovation in combination with democratic political regimes would usher in an era of peace, prosperity and social harmony. Put another way, there was widespread faith in *modernity* as a wellspring of progress with the ever more robust democracies of the United States and Western Europe taking the lead.

It did not turn out that way. The "terrible twentieth century," as Winston Churchill put it, was contaminated by total war, the destabilization of democracy and the emergence of totalitarian regimes in which state prerogatives overrode political agency and made a mockery of accountability.[3] Not surprisingly, faith in modernity was profoundly shaken by the breathtakingly bestial and destructive forces that were unleashed and by the epic suffering that spread from Western Europe through much of the world. Inevitably, historians as well as social theorists, looking back and no longer under the spell of utopian visions, have scrutinized modernism, uncovered its intrinsic shortcomings and pondered its impact on all that went wrong in the twentieth century and its dire implications for the twenty-first.

The *literary imagination* is distinctively revealing — a counterpart, a complement, perhaps a corrective, to these other forms of scholarly inquiry. The literary imagination has long been recognized as capturing the spirit and the soul of the times. Moreover, while history and social theory have already figured prominently in the multitude of postmortems conducted on the entrails of the twentieth century, the role of political novels has been mostly neglected. Finally insofar as there has been literary engagement with the terrible twentieth century, these have been largely through novels that embrace the modernist canon. They focus on political actors and political regimes and privilege a politics of hope and struggle.

Novels of political estrangement thus constitute a new genre that resonates with the mournful legacy of the twentieth century — that is, with the futility of political struggle. As I have already indicated, novels of political estrangement shift attention from political actors and institutions to the general public — ordinary people whose agency has been appropriated by autocratic regimes, by bureaucratic institutions and by professionals with the expertise to colonize consciousness.

As will become clear from novels themselves, people are largely unaware, and in any case cannot comprehend, the forces driving the appropriation of their agency. Put in somewhat different terms, this shift is from what politics do *for* people to what they do *to* people. These novels are the work of some of the twentieth century's most distinguished and widely recognized authors — Franz Kafka, Joseph Heller, Elie Wiesel, Pat Barker, Russell Banks, Gunter Grass, Kurt Vonnegut, Imre Kertesz and the many others who constitute and sustain this book.

Whereas social scientists and historians tend to gaze down from *above* on the twentieth century, novelists peer into the shattered lives, the moral dilemmas and the emotional chaos of the century — thus viewing a collective catastrophe through the everyday lives of victims, victimizers, temporizers, opportunists, true believers and those who simply averted their eyes. In so doing, these novelists reveal, sometimes prophetically, the etiology and the aftermath of catastrophe. They both deepen our memory of the past and help us to think more clearly about what is to come — enabling us to *re-imagine the past and to remember the future*.

What follows, then, is an interdisciplinary inquiry refracted through political, cultural, historical and literary prisms. When all is said and done, however, politics drives this research and literature is deployed to tell a political, not a literary, story. In other words, the debacle of the twentieth century provides the context for my exploration of the contribution of the literary imagination to political inquiry.

My starting point is an analysis of the modern project viewed sympathetically but not uncritically from above. Aesthetically, socially and historically, it is seen in its origins and in its realization as a progressive force. This will serve as a prelude to the unmasking of the modern project by late modernists and by novels of political estrangement — beginning in this chapter with Franz Kafka's *The Trial*. Kafka is in my judgment the progenitor of the novels of political estrangement that have provided a literary window into the terrible twentieth century.

1. Modernity

"Marry nothing beneath you," her mother always said, meaning no one darker than herself . . . "Human beings should never go back. They should always go forward."

Antebellum southern black mother
and daughter. Edward P. Jones[4]

Modernity is an intellectual construct that is deployed by a variety of disciplines to make sense out of relentless sea changes in societies at the close of the nineteenth and beginning of the twentieth century. There is broad agreement on the antecedents of modernity, on its origins and on its constituent elements. Yet, because multiple disciplines chose to refract these sea changes through the prism of modernity, it is hardly surprising that countless disciplinary-based iterations of modernity have emerged over the years. Modernist readings of politics, society, literature, the fine and applied arts and so on became increasingly prominent and, indeed, dominant. While I will make passing reference to all of these iterations to clarify the context of modernity, my purposes are most directly served and organized by the socio-political and the literary. When woven together, I argue, they produce an *interdisciplinary synthesis* that enhances intellectual inquiry.

The ethos and institutions of the modern project

There is broad agreement among modernists that the *origins* of the modern project can be traced to the culture of rationality associated with the eighteenth century Enlightenment.[5] More concretely, the origins of the modern project are located in the "modes of social life and organizations which emerged in Europe from about the seventeenth century onwards and which subsequently became more or less worldwide in their influence."[6]

It was, however, not until the late nineteenth and early twentieth centuries that modernity was consolidated.

Progress, rooted in human endeavor, has been the ideal which defines and animates the modernist ethos. As Christopher Crouch puts it, "not only could humankind improve itself and its condition without supernatural assistance, but was also under a moral obligation to do so."[7] Rationality, technology and science were the mutually constitutive elements of material, moral and political progress. In the economy, capital supplanted land as the repository of wealth. Democracy increasingly became the hallmark of political legitimacy, taking the place of monarchy, aristocracy, theocracy and other forms of authoritarian rule.

The defining institutions of the modern world are, according to Anthony Giddens: the nation-state system, the world capitalist economy, the world military order and the division of labor.[8] Hall, Held and McGrew offer a more expansive summary:

> Modernity can be characterized by a cluster of institutions, each with its own pattern of change and development. Among these we would include: the nation-state and an international system of states; a dynamic and expansionist capitalist economic order based on private property; industrialism; the growth of large-scale administrative and bureaucratic systems of social organization and regulation; the dominance of secular, materialist, rationalist, and individualist cultural values; and the formal separation of the 'private' from the 'public.'[9]

Hall, Held and McGrew draw attention to the culture as well as to the institutions of modernism — and, in particular, to modernist values — that is, to "the dominance of secular, materialist, rationalist, and individualist cultural values; and the formal separation of the 'private' from the 'public'."

Giddens identifies modernity with optimism about the direction in which the world is heading — with, in other words, a belief in progress that sustains both liberal capitalism and Marxian socialism. For liberal capitalists, private property, the division of labor and industrialization produce material abundance which makes a robust democracy possible. In short, democracy and capitalism are mutually constitutive — both necessary and sufficient conditions for realizing modernity's progress towards, and its promise of, peace and prosperity. For Marxists and socialists, capitalism is readily distinguishable from, and ultimately incompatible with, democracy, peace and prosperity. While capitalism creates both material abundance and rudimentary democracy, it also generates inequalities of wealth and power, a political culture of acquisitive individualism and aggressive nationalism — all of which are incompatible with widespread prosperity, true democracy and global peace.

The modern project: second thoughts
The destructiveness of *modern* warfare was especially dispiriting for modernists. The resultant loss of innocence was experienced by artists, writers and social theorists — leading to distinct but linked reframing of the possibilities and limitations of modernism as a social force. Crouch points out that, as early as 1920, the Dada Berlin exhibit included "a number of paintings by Otto Dix of war cripples."[10] This was not art as ironic parody of modernism but art that cuts much more deeply. The pre-eminent anti-war painting of the interwar era was Picasso's "Guernica". In that painting, Picasso, as Crouch puts it, "uses Modernist form to describe the destruction of the town by Fascist forces during the Spanish Civil War."[11] For Mexican realist artists Diego Rivera, Jose Orozco and David Sequeiros, the critique of modernism went beyond war to industrial society in general and to the oppression of the working class more specifically.

Similarly, writers and social theorists associated with the Frankfurt School's critical version of Marxism also targeted the failings of modernity. Crouch calls particular attention to Bertolt Brecht and Theodor Adorno. Despite meaningful differences between them, they agreed that artists had both the capability and the responsibility to offer a searching critique of the failings of the modern project.

> Brecht focused his attention on the audience reading and acting upon the information presented to them. To achieve this Brecht talked about "distanciation" (sic). This is sometimes called more elegantly, if not more accurately, "the alienation effect": removing the art work just enough from reality to provoke questioning from the audience.[12]

Brecht was willing to settle for an art which destabilized. Adorno, however, looks for something more — that is "a continuing struggle to find an oppositional language that is never codified, that forever transgresses and refuses assimilation into cultural life."[13]

It can, however, be inferred from the identification of many of these critics of modernism with Communism and Marxism that they still believed in, and were committed to, a socialist realization of the modern project. Certainly, this was true of Marxian theorists of the Frankfurt school who continued to believe in democratic socialism and to pursue its realization through revolutionary politics. The role of literature and art in all of this was to create "a cultural dialogue not of ideological solutions, but demonstrable problems."[14] Either way, the left-wing critique of the inter-war period was about the realization of the modern project, not its rejection.

2. Literary Modernism and the Modern Political Novel

While some modern novels are political, the dominant tendency among literary modernists is to associate excellence with technical mastery — the capacity, that is, to convey the destabilizing impact of modern life on emotional equilibrium. The result is a rarefied rather than a robust engagement with the modern project — in sharp contrast not only to social and political modernism but to aesthetic modernism as well.* Put another way, the political novel is viewed virtually as an oxymoron — at odds with literary excellence. This, I will argue, is because of the mistaken belief that political novels are inevitably polemics which trump and thus subvert literary values. Certainly, there are such novels — think for example of socialist realism — but the best political novels are the work of many of the century's most distinguished novelists — whether writing from within or in rejection of modernism.

As a prelude to considering the modern political novel, I want to clarify how and why the aesthetic standards of literary modernism lead to a marginalizing of, although not suppression of, the *political*. When

---

* In the fine and applied arts, amidst a welter of competing visions, the Bauhaus stands out as a flagship of modernism not only for its aesthetic values but also for its commitment to the technology of industrial society — which *when properly deployed* was seen as serving universal and humanist values. Housing, for example, was, to use Le Corbusier's phrase, "well-designed and well-produced 'machines for living in'" (Crouch, 1999: 67). But Bauhaus aesthetics were also wedded to a collective creative process dominated by "a search for a sophisticated, anonymous form in which the individual becomes part of a much grander 'universal' scheme" (Crouch, 1999: 67). In short, the Bauhaus can be seen, and saw itself, as both a creative force and a social movement driven to realize the opportunities afforded by the materials, technologies and practices of industrialization. Bauhaus and the artists associated with the Dutch journal De Stiljl were also determined voices of a humanistic vision of the modern project — dedicated to products that were intended to serve immediate and long-term human needs. In contrast, futurism, the right wing of aesthetic modernism, identified progress with war rather than with peace. According to Crouch, F. T. Marinetti, one of Futurism's early advocates, "proposed an artistic and aesthetic sensibility based upon a love of danger, of speed and machinery, in which beauty emerges from struggle and 'no masterpiece [is] without the stamp of aggressiveness' . . . a chilling precursor of Fascism" (Crouch, 1999: 53). Not surprisingly, Futurism lost much of its artistic support in the wake of World War I which "was to disrupt the continuity of the Modern Movement, and which was itself the direct consequence of mass industrialization, and whose atrocities were those of a 'scientific', 'rational' culture" (Crouch, 1999: 48).

subsequently we turn to the modern *political* novel our guide will be Irving Howe who, writing primarily about novels of the inter-war period, was the foremost modernist literary critic to take the political novel seriously.[15]

The modern novel

To be sure, literary modernism is all about coping with a world in which the static rhythms and eternal verities of the past have been increasingly overwhelmed by what the poet Charles Baudelaire saw as "the transient, the fleeting, the contingent."[16]

> So they "took the novel and sped up its pace, or made it ebb and flow like real life; they made its sentences slippery as the movements of the human mind; they let plot go random, told their stories from changing points of view, and began and ended them abruptly.[17]

Faced with a bubbling caldron of indeterminacy, the modern novelists took it upon themselves to invent modes of expression which maximized the verisimilitude between their narratives and the tempos, dilemmas and undercurrents of the world that they portrayed. In short, the primary objective of literary modernism was to convey the emotional and psychological truths of modern lives within modern society.

Henry James is widely recognized as both innovator and master of this idiom. As Matz puts it:

> What James himself did . . . was enrich the "consciousness" of the novel. Never before had a novelist ventured so far into the heads of characters, and never had a novelist so much to report about the complexity, subtlety, and limitlessness of what he found there.[18]

However, it is one thing to venture into the heads of characters and quite another to venture into the political and social instabilities wrought by the institutions and the ethos of modernism.[19]

The modern political novel

As I have already indicated, the distinguished literary critic and public intellectual Irving Howe[20] is the most notable exception to this flight from the political. So, he will be our guide to the modern political novel. Howe constructed his conception of the political novel on the crushed hopes of the Russian Revolution.

> The central event of our century remains the Russian Revolution. For a moment, one of the most fervent in all history, it stirred the

hope among millions of people that mankind had at last begun to lift itself, however painfully, from the realm of necessity to the realm of freedom[21] (Howe, 2002: 203).

To Howe's way of thinking, World War I unleashed a new revolutionary politics, anchored in an inspiring socialist ideology and bearing the liberating message of social democracy. Accordingly, it stands to reason that for him the tragic mission of twentieth century political literature is to explain how and why the revolution went awry. So for him, the dual mission of a political novel is to illuminate the shortcomings of the prevailing political order and to identify how best to transcend them. "[T]he vision of an ultimate harmony — and *no political novel would be tolerable without it* — can gain our full assent only after the existing disharmonies have been fully explored."[*]

If, however, World War I is seen as the first of a series of twentieth century calamities — each of which was indicative of the failure of democracy and the suppression of political agency, the political becomes increasingly more suspect. In short, the seeds of the literary transformation, so unforgettably captured by Paul Fussell in his masterful *The Great War and Modern Memory*, generated an ethos of late modernity and novels of political estrangement were, I argue, sown in the blood, the tragedy and the deceptions of World War I. Put another way, novels of political estrangement express a distrust of the political derived from and in tune with World War I, the subsequent global economic turmoil and totalitarianism of the left and the right in the 1930s.

In short, the novels of political estrangement that are my focus are also political novels. They do not supplant Howe's understanding of politics

---

* Howe, 2002: 92. Italics added. Robert Boyers, who as I noted above, identifies closely with Howe, when confronted by a multitude of post-World War II political novels which prefigure and reflect a late-modern political ethos, seems to come very close to stepping outside Howe's modernist canon but does not do so. In his sensitive and searching *Atrocity and Amnesia: The Political Novel Since 1945* (New York: Oxford University Press, 1987), Boyers' conception of the political novel is much more open and eclectic with respect to the political, but he is unwilling to acknowledge alienation and cynicism as legitimate standpoints for the political novelist. Thus, Boyers says of Doris Lessing's *The Golden Notebooks*: "The common world here, as in most political fictions, is a projection of hope, a movement toward a world not yet made . . . intermittently embodied in the shared memories of struggle and the planned protests to which Jack and his friends have recourse" (1987: 14). In short, what Lessing has done, according to Boyers, and what political novelists worth their salt must do is create a fictional world in which the search for a resolution to the vexing and seemingly intractable problems of political life becomes the raison d'être of the novel.

and the novel, but are especially consonant with the convulsions of the twentieth century.

But first to Howe.

THE POLITICS OF ULTIMATE HARMONY

This emphasis on the vision of ultimate harmony leads Howe to the inspirational power of ideology, leavened by an acute awareness of the obstacles to realizing that vision. So the challenge of the novelist is to formulate a political path to overcoming those obstacles. And, as we shall see, Howe is under no illusions about how high a mountain this is for political novelists to climb.

The challenge begins with ideology itself which Howe recognizes on the basis of the experience of the Russian Revolution is a two-edged sword.

> [Ideology is not] a symptom of some alien disease but . . . both the burden and challenge of history: necessary in times of social crisis, frightening in its rigor, and precisely because it can be put to such terrible uses, a temptation as dangerous to those most in need of it. Yet . . . ideology must be confronted, history allows no alternative."[22]

Then there is the problem of bureaucratic corruption which Howe terms the "central dilemma of all political action: the only way of preventing bureaucracy is to refrain from organization, but the refusal to organize with one's fellow men can lead only to acquiescence in detested power or to isolated and futile acts of martyrdom and terrorism."[23] Howe sees all of novelists of revolution-gone-wrong as illuminating these two elements which are necessary for revolution but that also poison the revolutionary well.

Accordingly, it is not surprising that Howe is in sympathy with George Orwell's portrayal in *1984* of the grotesque politics of totalitarian states. In Howe's words, "Everything has hardened into politics, the leviathan has swallowed man . . . *1984* projects a nightmare in which politics has displaced humanity and the state has stifled society."[24]

> Orwell's profoundest insight is that in a totalitarian world man's life is shorn of dynamic possibilities . . . man becomes a function of a process he is never allowed to understand or control.[25]

Thus Howe acknowledges the authenticity of Orwell's characterization of totalitarian politics, but concludes, nonetheless, that *1984* is a "profoundly antipolitical book."[26]

Howe reaches this seemingly contradictory position, because he is unwilling to share Orwell's cynicism about politics — a cynicism based solely on totalitarian politics: politics at its very worst. In contrast, Howe believes that politics provides the only opportunity for beneficent collective action — human agency working on behalf of human welfare.[27] What then are political novelists to do when faced with these seemingly insurmountable obstacles?

He answers this question by contrasting the distinct ways in which Andre Malraux, Ignazio Silone, Arthur Koestler and George Orwell cope with the perversion of socialist revolutionary ideals in the Soviet Union. All four, he tells us, "are obsessed by the failure, or betrayal of the revolution."[28] Koestler and Orwell seem to do no more than invite us to somehow adapt, indeed capitulate, to the disastrous consequences that inevitably accompany the consolidation of "successful" revolutions; they offer only despair.

In contrast, Malraux and Silone tell us how and why to persevere even in the face of seemingly hopeless conditions. Thus for Howe the authentic political novel is constituted by its account of heroic action on behalf of ideals that are forever out of reach. He reserves his warmest praise for those novelists who grasp the essential tragedy of revolutionary political action and are able to convey how and why resisting the ultimately irresistible is truly heroic.

> For it is central to Malraux's vision of heroism in our time that the moment of trial, the gesture which defines and embodies the heroic, should come into being primarily in anticipation of defeat . . . The commitment to the impersonality of history has led, through the painful circle of paradox, to a history of personality.[29]

However, the heroic, while necessary, is for Howe insufficient if not combined with the *political* — human beings taking charge of their own destiny. Accordingly, Howe faults Malraux's heroic vision as too bound up in action leading him "to exalt the will at the expense of the mind, thereby betraying him into a dubious adventurism."[30] The result is a "paean to revolution yet a strangely nonpolitical one, for Malraux is concerned with revolution . . . not primarily as a political act but as the incarnation of human desire."[31] In contrast, Howe sees Silone as discovering the implacable capacity among the peasant classes to endure "the most profound vision of what heroism can be in the modern world."[32]

> But they are his, by adoption of blood, and he remains hopeful with a hopefulness that has nothing to do with optimism, that from the

hidden inarticulate resources of the poor, which consist neither of intelligence nor nobility, but rather of training in endurance and an education in ruse — that from all this something worthy of the human may yet emerge.[33]

Silone's vision is thus celebrated as the more political because "in some vague but indestructible way he remains a socialist, indifferent to party or dogma, yet utterly committed to poor and dispossessed."[34] In the final analysis, Howe puts his faith in politics and honors novelists who believe that in the long run political action will somehow be successful.

POLITICAL NOVELS AND LITERARY EXCELLENCE

For all of his emphasis on the political novelist as a revolutionary and the political novel as a search for an authentic politics, Howe also sees himself as a guardian of literary excellence. Indeed, he sees the literary and the political as inextricably linked to one another. Thus, he is well aware that the wedding of any ideology to literature is a two-edged sword both for both politics and for literature. Ideology is the source of political ideals — of, that is, hope and illumination — and, as such, essential to the political novel. Howe puts it this way: Ideology is "an effort to employ abstract ideas, a means of overcoming the abstractness of social life. It is the passion of men with their backs against the wall."[35] Ideology, in other words, can give meaning and purpose to the detachment and interpersonal isolation that characterizes life in modern society. But ideology is also a literary trap for the political novelist. As David Bromwich puts it his introduction to the 2002 edition of *Politics and the Novel*, the trick, and it is no mean feat, is "to imagine the life of ideology without being reduced to ideology."[36]

To be worthy as literature, a political novel must, according to Howe, negotiate the treacherous passage between the polemical and personal. If a political novel is to have literary merit and not degenerate into a polemic, it must be anchored in an authentic portrayal of the lives of its characters. Bromwich puts it this way:

> [The political novel] must be written by an artist who feels divided by the claim of justice and the claim of other values. Fully achieved, as in *The Charterhouse of Parma*, *The Possessed*, *The Bostonians*, and *Nostromo*, such a novel keeps alive an awareness of conflict — an awareness that inhibits action even as it informs the consciousness of action. The good of books that perform that work is a good that belongs to the moral imagination.[37]

Instead, Howe assesses the modern political novel by how well it conveys the dilemma of the political conditions while avoiding characters that are largely instruments of the novelist's values and aspirations. The political novel "must contain the usual representation of human behavior and feeling; yet it must also absorb into its stream of movement the hard and perhaps insoluble pellets of modern ideology."[38] Just as all novelists must endow their characters with an appropriately contingent capacity for *human agency*, political novelists must do the same with respect to *political agency*. In short, it is essential that the characters in political novels embody with verisimilitude the challenges that they face, the resources that they have available and the personal qualities that allow them to persevere against all odds. For Howe, then, respecting what is possible while pursuing something better is the burden that political novelists must bear.[39]

Bromwich notes that as the twentieth century progressed, Howe came to distrust revolutionary ideology while continuing to cling to it as the essential source of political critique and aspiration. "As the argument of *Politics and the Novel* passes into the twentieth century, ideology is portrayed more and more as a temptation, a giddy magnetism of ideas which only the greatest strength of will and conscience can resist. Ideology has now become the mass culture of political life — a distorting and narrowing discipline that absorbs the mind of the political actor, just as theology absorbs the mind of the religious fanatic."[40] More specifically Howe believed that ideology could "blind men to simple facts"[41] and that revolutionaries "cannot help being tainted by the societies they would overthrow."[42]

Still, in developing his analysis of political novelists working under the cloud of "the God that failed," Howe clings to his modernism. To do otherwise would, of course, be to abandon his modernist *ideologically derived* ideals and surrender to a politics of despair. He, therefore, ascribes to political novels a responsibility to pursue a social democratic iteration of the modern project — without wavering from a clear-eyed vision of the formidable obstacles that must be surmounted. Howe is, to my way of thinking, simply unable or unwilling to grasp the possibility that his vision of heroic struggle as the essence of politics had lost much of its explanatory power over the course of the twentieth century.[*]

---

[*] The Russian revolution and its increasingly toxic aftermath were without a shadow of a doubt a large part of what made the twentieth century so "terrible." However, the literature of repression in the Soviet Union and behind the iron curtain, while revealing profound and widespread political estrangement, is not concerned as are the other novels in this research with an escalating tide of disenchantments with

3. Late Modernity: The Subversion of Political Agency

If today we face a world in which there is no grand narrative of social prog-
ress, no politically plausible project of social justice, it is in large measure
because Lenin and his heirs poisoned the well.

Tony Judt[43]

The *late-modern* critique, like modernity itself, is multi-layered and many-faceted. It picks up, one might say, where Howe and Boyers leave off. At the risk of oversimplifying a subtle complex of explanations of how and why the modern project went so disastrously wrong, I will boil it all down to an ever-increasing suppression of agency and accountability that exposed the deficiencies of democracies in Western Europe and the United States and led to a widespread estrangement from politics. Social theorists as well as political novelists have taken part in the unmasking of modernity.[*]

The retreat from modernity began in the years just before World War I and accelerated in the postwar period.[44] During those years the contradictions of the modern project became ever clearer to artists, novelists, social theorists and literary critics. The events that most unforgettably and tragically expose the contradictions of modernity are the Holocaust

---

liberal democracy. Each of the two literatures is of equal importance for understanding the twentieth century and its impact on the emerging twenty-first century. However, given their divergent trajectories and distinctive implications, it seems imprudent to shoehorn them into a single study.

[*] For the record, I want to mention that literary theorists developed their own critique of modernism — although for them it is the postmodern not the late-modern that takes the place of modernism. Because, however, postmodern literary theory privileges narrative form it does not shed much if any light on the political. Put another way, the role of postmodern literary theorizing is to illuminate the countless variations among narrative themes and the uses to which they can be put. Postmodern literary theory thus comes off as relentlessly preoccupied with the permutations, illuminations and obfuscations of the narrative — not due to an intellectual obsession, but because narrative is deemed the quintessential agent of cognitive and affective communication. See, for example, Linda Hutcheon, *The Politics of Postmodernism* (2nd ed, London: Routledge, 2003). I choose Hutcheon because she identifies the postmodern as intrinsically political but not by any means in the way that I will be representing the political. "The postmodern," she explains, ". . . is fundamentally demystifying and critical, and among the things of which it is critical are modernism's elitist and sometimes totalitarian modes of effecting 'radical change'" (2003: 26). Thus, for her the literary is by definition political and the political is literary. In contrast, what defines the late-modern political novel is its capacity to illuminate how and why the modern project has betrayed its promises to enhance individual political agency and promote democracy, peace and prosperity.

and total war. Each presented the inhuman spectacle of the modern project consuming itself — technological expertise put at the service of gratuitously destructive and utterly futile policies.

These outrages have been subjected to searching inquiries by social theorist Zygmunt Bauman (the Holocaust) and cultural historian Tony Judt (total war). Taken together, Bauman and Judt reveal the connections between the Holocaust and total war while at the same time exposing intrinsic conflicts between democracy and modernity. Following Bauman's and Judt's social and political accounts of late modernity, the chapter will conclude with a preview of the novels of political estrangement: Franz Kafka's introduction to the late-modern literary sensibilities in his prescient novel *The Trial* (originally published in German in 1925, but begun in 1914).[45]

Unmasking modernity: the Holocaust

Zygmunt Bauman has argued persuasively that modernism is intimately associated with the Holocaust.[46] He therefore rejects the standard explanations for the Holocaust as a horrific aberration — as a stain on, rather than as a product of, modernism. In his words: "Modern civilization was not the Holocaust's *sufficient* condition; it was, however, most certainly its *necessary* condition."[47] Without modernity there have been brutal pogroms and destructive communal violence but nothing as thorough, as systematic and as dehumanizing as Hitler's vast and relentless killing machine.

It follows that Bauman does not believe, as many (perhaps most) do that the Holocaust was all about anti-Semitism — that it was, in his words, the "culminating point of European-Christian anti-Semitism."[48] He also takes exception to the claim that the Holocaust can be understood as the actualization of aggressive inclinations that are part and parcel of human life — "pre-social and immune from cultural manipulation."[49] The problem with each of these explanations is that they trace the Holocaust to the pre-modern, thus attributing the Holocaust to a failure rather than a by-product of the civilizing mission of modernity. In so doing, these explanations serve to repress "an unspoken terror permeating our collective memory . . . the gnawing suspicion that the Holocaust may be more than an aberration, more than a deviation from an otherwise straight path of *progress* . . . We suspect (even if we refuse to admit it) that the Holocaust could have merely uncovered another face of . . . modern society."[50]

To get beyond reductive explanations of the Holocaust and of modernity, Bauman draws on Max Weber to indicate the several ways in which the Holocaust was dependent on such defining elements of modernity as: "modern bureaucracy, rational spirit, principle of efficiency, scientific mentality, relegation of values to the realm of subjectivity etc."[51]

The Hobbesian world of the Holocaust arrived . . . in a factory-produced vehicle, wielding weapons only the most advanced science could supply, and following an itinerary designed by scientifically managed organization . . . The Nazi mass murder of the European Jewry was not only the technological achievement of an industrial society, but also the organizational achievement of a bureaucratic society.[52]

So, to begin with, the modern project supplied the basic, the banal, tools for organizing an efficient and massive transnational killing machine. Secondly, and just as important as the hallmark of the Holocaust's organizational attributes was the bureaucratic ethos which elevated duty and obedience into ethical principles and suppressed moral qualms.

In the opinion of [Harvard psychologist] Herbert C. Kelman,[53] moral inhibitions against violent atrocities tended to be eroded once three conditions are met, singly or together: the violence is authorized (by official orders coming from the legally entitled quarters), actions are *routinized* (by rule-governed practices and exact specification of roles), and the victims of violence are *dehumanized* (by ideological definitions and indoctrinations).[54]

In other words, most Nazis functionaries were *not* motivated by race hatred, ideological fervor; nor were they sociopaths. Quoting from Max Weber,[55]

The honor of the civil servant is vested in his ability to execute conscientiously the order of superior authorities, exactly as if the order agreed with his own convictions.[56]

Adolph Eichmann was in this sense typical — an ordinary German functioning within a bureaucratic machine and subjected to imperatives that were determined at, and imposed from, the top downward.

There is yet one more contribution of modernity to the Holocaust — what Bauman refers to as to the social production of moral invisibility by both distancing the victimizers from the victims and by dehumanizing the victims. Maximizing distance was distinctively bureaucratic.

The increase of physical and/or psychic distance between the act and its consequences achieves more than the suspension of moral inhibition; it quashes the moral significance of the act and thereby pre-empts all conflicts between personal standards of moral decency and immorality of the social consequences of the act.[57]

The hierarchically ordered chain of command insulated in one way or another all those involved in the Holocaust from its machinery of death. For those in the front line, insulation was, for example, provided by replacing the firing squads, which meant killing victims at point-blank range, with gas chambers which "reduced the role of the killer to that of the 'sanitation officer' asked to empty a sackful of 'disinfecting chemicals' through an aperture in the roof of a building the interior of which he was not prompted to visit."[58]

A second step in the production of moral invisibility was to dehumanize the victims — to both characterize and treat them as vile creatures who stand outside the boundaries of what is human.

> Hence Frank's favourite conjunction of "Jews and lice," the change in rhetoric expressed in the transplanting of the "Jewish question" from the context of racial self-defense into the linguistic universe of "self-cleansing" and "political hygiene," the typhus-warning posters on the wall of ghettos and finally the commission of the chemical for the last act from . . . the German Fumigation Company.[59]

Consider the images unmistakably revealed in the more than ample photographic record of the Holocaust. Respectable citizens rounded up en masse, delivered to overcrowded cattle cars devoid of even the most primitive opportunities for hygiene and without food or water, with those who survived transformed in appearance — no longer respectable but disreputable. Then they were further deprived of their civilized selves and their individuality by ill-fitting prison uniforms and by prison barbers.

Unmasking modernism: total war

Modernity was also a precondition for the unprecedented barbarity of twentieth-century warfare — human waves thrown against powerful armaments in World War I, the German blitzkrieg, the carpet bombing, and the use of nuclear weapons in World War II. Political historian Tony Judt detects and fears a widespread celebratory modernism that recalls World War II in triumphal terms — looking past the scourge that is total war. The result is a pronounced tendency to forget what should be remembered and to remember what is best forgotten. "The twentieth century is hardly behind us but already its quarrels and its achievements, its ideals and its fears are slipping into the obscurity of mis-memory."[60]

Judt does not deny that the institutions and ethos of modernism gave us much to celebrate. There were breathtaking advances in the natural sciences — in physics, biology, mathematics and medicine. The 1000-year Reich was limited to a decade or so, and other aggressive authoritarian and totalitarian regimes in Germany, Italy, Japan and eventually the Soviet Union were decisively defeated. Colonized peoples in Africa and in the Middle East, South Asia and the Far East were liberated. In many of these instances reasonably stable and arguably democratic states took the place of their authoritarian predecessors.

However, in choosing to privilege the achievements of modernity we ignore, at our peril, its shameful consequences. We are, in other words, remembering the twentieth century for all of the wrong reasons.

> [T]he twentieth century that we have chosen to commemorate is curiously out of focus. The overwhelming majority of places of official twentieth-century memory are either avowedly nostalgo-triumphalist — praising famous men and celebrating famous victories — or else, and increasingly, they are opportunities for the recollection of selective suffering . . . The twentieth century is thus on the path to becoming a moral memory palace: a pedagogically serviceable Chamber of Historical Horrors whose way stations are labeled "Munich" or "Pearl Harbor," "Auschwitz" or "Gulag".[61]

Judt's point is, of course, *not* that we should abandon our "moral memory." Much like Bauman, Judt sees us dwelling on what happened as human nature run amok — a shameful aberration. We make the mistake of thinking "that all of that is now behind us, that its meaning is clear, and that we may now advance — unencumbered by past errors — into a different and better era."[62]

What we fail to reflect on, especially in the United States, is the true and intrinsic destructiveness of modern warfare. For Judt it is a moral and political imperative that twentieth-century warfare be remembered for the ever-increasing grip of *total war*, ushered in by modernity. Moreover, in his view this sense of warfare without limits continues to influence both policy calculations and political discourse. As a case in point, Judt calls our attention to the lawlessness of the Bush administration's war on terrorism.[63]

> The sophistic distinctions we draw today in our war on terror — between the rule of law and "exceptional" circumstances, between citizens (who have rights and legal protections) and non-citizens to whom anything can be done, between normal people and "terrorists," between "us" and "them" . . . are the self-same distinctions

that licensed the worst horrors of the recent past: internment camps, deportation, torture and murder.[64]

In addition, he argues that "ignorance of twentieth-century history . . . leads to a misidentification of the enemy."[65] We choose to wage war on terrorism as such — deploying de-contextualized, abstract and undifferentiated labels like "Islamofascism" — thus disregarding the "contrasting and sometimes conflicting objectives" that drive terrorism and terrorists. In misremembering the past — and thus losing sight of the havoc that war inflicts on values and practices that are the foundation of democracy, human rights and law — we put the future at risk.[66]

He warns us that total war is not only a "catastrophe in its own right" but also "the crucial antecedent for conditions of mass criminality in the modern era."[67] Total war dehumanizes enemies, magnifies the threat that they pose and unleashes lawless means — such as torture, genocide and a myriad of other violations of human rights — to serve putatively imperative, but all too often exaggerated ends. Yet under the influence of celebratory modernism, total war continues to be embraced by the policy makers and the public.

4. Late-Modern Novels of Political Estrangement

Isherwood's novels are political and yet not political; rather than analyze politics, he simply observed its effect on human lives.

Brooke Allen[68]

The late-modern novels of political estrangement that constitute all that is to follow in this book track with, and give personal immediacy to, Bauman's and Judt's fears of the bitter fruits of modernity. Accordingly these novels are, as has already been indicated, directly at odds with Howe's understanding of what a political novel should and must be. Most fundamentally, novels of political estrangement abandon the search for an "ultimate harmony." In addition, Howe's iteration of the modern political novel focuses on the Sisyphus-like struggle of heroic revolutionaries for social justice and democracy — and thus on their relationship with established but illegitimate political institutions. Novels of political estrangement are still further removed from the center to the periphery of politics. Indeed, politics and politicians are largely invisible in these novels.*

---

* There is a third kind of political novel that will not be considered in this book although it is probably the most familiar and many might say more authentically

The political thus becomes an absent presence — directing attention to its consumers and casualties. Politics creates conditions and circumstances that must be borne but are opaque, incomprehensible and irresistible — thus suppressing any semblance of political agency among ordinary people. As a result, the late-modern reconstitutes our understanding of the "terrible" twentieth century from the bottom up. We learn lessons about the past century that have important implications for the twenty-first century — lessons that complement and/or correct what late-modern social theory has already taught us.

Franz Kafka: *The Trial*

Franz Kafka, I will argue, is the progenitor of both literary modernism and late-modern social theory. He is well recognized as the former but not, so far as I know, for the latter. *The Trial* provides ample evidence in support of both claims. Accordingly, I will begin with a précis of the novel's simple and straightforward plotline. I will then go on to the much more obscure and fragmented narrative to demonstrate how and why this novel reveals Kafka's modern and late-modern prescience.[69]

The plot is easily summarized. Joseph K., the chief clerk of a bank, is visited at home one morning by warders of a court that is completely unknown to K. The warders announce that they are arresting him because he has been accused of a crime. The court's authority, if any, is never clarified nor is his alleged crime specified, but K. grudgingly accepts his status as the accused. Subsequently, he is able to locate the court, which conducts its affairs in a strikingly shabby, very un-court-like setting (pp. 44–5). However, K.'s efforts to learn more about his legal situation prove fruitless. Even after engaging a lawyer, all he ever gets are unsubstantiated and contradictory rumors.

Joseph K. is allowed to continue his normal life and initially feels secure because of his own status and because of the disreputable appearance of

---

political than either the modern or the late-modern novels that will be discussed below. I refer to novels that provide access to behind-the-scenes politics and political institutions. The examples that come readily to mind are Anthony Trollope's Palliser novels, Robert Penn Warren's *All the King's Men*, Ward Just's tales of Washington D.C.'s political class, and Arthur Koestler's *Darkness at Noon*. These novels illuminate: what motivates political leaders and politicians; how they work with and compete against one another; their relationships with constituents or followers, the institutional forces and procedures that they must master and accommodate; and so forth. However, for all their virtues, precisely because they immerse themselves in the political process, in *how* power is exercised, they are neither well positioned, nor do they ordinarily aspire, to inquire into the legitimacy of the political order and/or its social, cultural and economic foundations and consequences — the principal concern of this effort to better understand the calamities of the twentieth century.

the court. As time goes by, however, he becomes obsessed with his case which absorbs so much of his time and energy that it becomes more and more difficult to attend to his affairs at the bank. He fears that these legal distractions will open the way for his rival, the bank's vice-president, to curry favor with the bank's president. Clearly, Joseph K.'s *trial* is not the court proceeding, which never takes place; his trial is the burden that he seems to *choose* to bear. In short, for much of the time until his execution in the final chapter, the process becomes the punishment.[70]

If *The Trial* is treated as a parable about the law, it can be seen as a kind of central European *Bleak House* and more broadly as a persuasive demonstration of how and why the law can go wrong. But if it is thought of in terms of modernity and late-modernity, *The Trial*, begun by Kafka in 1914, can be seen in literary terms as modern and in socio-political terms as late-modern.

THE TRIAL AS LITERARY MODERNISM

As Henry Sussman, on whom I will rely heavily in all that follows, has noted, Kafka's narrative "coincides with a far-reaching modernist experimentation concerned with basic modes of language . . . plot, narrative posture and cohesion, characterization, fictive time, space, logic and sentence structure [and] can be mapped as part of the overall reconceptualization of fictive language carried out by, among others, James Joyce, Gertrude Stein, Marcel Proust, Virginia Wolf, William Faulkner, Robert Musil and Ezra Pound." In short, Sussman, thus, has no hesitation in including Kafka in the pantheon of literary modernism.[71]

Kafka's narrative is *modern* in that the court is entirely un-court-like. Its proceedings turn the concepts of law and of courts on their heads. Early on when he is arrested, the warders who come for him eat his breakfast and then grandly offer to go out and buy a breakfast for K. In confronting the court, Joseph K. finds himself in quicksand. He is denied even the most rudimentary due process; the institutions of the court flout everything that the law is supposed to represent, and the logic that drives the institutions and its agents is incomprehensible. Nothing is as it is expected to be, and the result is the kind of destabilizing narrative which defines literary modernism. Sussman tells of Joseph K.'s "progress through a domain of deranged but compelling logic" — not unlike *Alice in Wonderland*.[72]

There are countless examples of how Kafka's narrative stands courts and law on their heads. Not only does the court conduct its business in backrooms and attics, but Joseph K. is considered guilty and is given no opportunity to prove himself innocent of a never-specified crime. When he claims to the two warders who arrest him that he is innocent while acknowledging that he knows nothing about the laws under which the court operates, they dismiss his claims with what truly is Alice-in-Wonderland logic. "You see, Willem, he admits that he doesn't know the Law, and yet he claims to be innocent" (p. 9). Thus not only the law and the courts but everyday logic and common sense are stood on their heads.

Although K. begins by assuming that this court proceeding is not all that serious given the ad hoc nature of the institution, he is warned by his uncle, who is urging him to get a lawyer, that this is by no means the case. "First of all, Uncle," said K., "it's not a trial before the normal court." "That's bad," his uncle said (p. 93). K. does hire a lawyer and the attorney assures him that this is a wise move — not because of his legal skills which are irrelevant but because he has connections inside the court. The lawyer is only one of many people who offer him counsel — based on rumors that come their way because of connections to the court and its personnel.

It therefore does not take long to discover that insofar as there are rules, just about everyone agrees that in the end K.'s situation is hopeless despite the occasional tactical success. But were there any rules? Not, it would seem in the law books, which "were old dog-eared books; one of the bindings was almost split in two at the spine, the covers barely hanging by the cords . . . K. opened the book on top, and an indecent picture was revealed" (p. 57). The court may have had no rules but it did have a track record, which was summarized by the court's official portrait painter. He explains to K. the possible outcomes that seem to differ from one another: actual acquittal, apparent acquittal and protraction (p. 152).[73] However, it turns out that *acquittal* is only temporary because the case is then sent on to the "highest court, which is completely inaccessible to you and me and everyone else" (p. 158). Much the same is true of a second acquittal and all subsequent acquittals (p. 159) as well as of the other outcomes — meaning in effect that K. is caught in a web from which he can never extricate himself. In effect, the court painter confirms K.'s belief that his innocence is irrelevant and that once charges are brought, "the court can never be swayed from it" (p. 149).

If, then, the heart of literary modernism is the fragmented and desta-bilized narrative that resonates with the indeterminate determinacy of modern life, there can be little doubt that *The Trial* is prototypically and prophetically modern.[74] At the same time, Sussman characterizes the court in terms redolent of late-modern social theory.

The Court embodies many of the potentials of repression built into twentieth-century bureaucracy and technology; but its complexities and paradoxes — and, above all, the ability to interpret them — comprise the only possible means of liberation.[75]

Joseph K. is thrust into a situation from which he cannot escape by an institution that is inexplicably and unshakably sustained by and dedicated to destroying his status, his citizenship and his life.

THE TRIAL AS LATE-MODERN SOCIAL THEORY

Simply put, from the perspective of late-modern social theory, Kafka reveals the emotional trajectory of the court's appropriation of Joseph K.'s agency. Returning once again to Sussman:

> With its anticipation of bureaucratic complexity, social isolation, and the subjective emptiness in the twentieth century, *The Trial* can be regarded as an exemplary historical work of art.[76]

What is perhaps most noteworthy is that Kafka, writing at a high point in the history of modernism, senses the late-modern critique and, therefore, the profoundly destructive contradictions of modernity.

In principle, Joseph K. is a well-established citizen in a modern society who thinks about himself and is thought of by others as respectable and secure. Thus at the outset of his trial he feels that his status at the bank is secure. "He felt confident and at ease; he was missing work at the bank this morning, of course, but in the light of the relatively high position he held there, that would be easily excused" (p. 10). But all of that is taken away from him by the pathologies that lurk beneath the surface of modern society. The court, faceless, bureaucratic and opaque, robs Joseph K. of any semblance of agency. Indeed at the outset of proceedings his status and his very identity are called into question. "You're a house painter?" queries the examining magistrate (p. 44). By the end of the book he has developed a paranoia that shakes him to the core. "Every hour away from the office troubled him; it was true he could no longer use his office time as efficiently as before . . . He pictured the vice president who was always lurking about, entering his office from to time, sitting down at his desk, rifling through his papers . . . K. felt threatened . . . from a thousand directions" (pp. 199–200).

If we ask what is so unnerving, the obvious answer is to be found in his increasingly dire position before a court which is both incomprehensible and out of reach. But why did he, a respectable citizen, not challenge this shoddy excuse for a judicial system — given his exemplary life and prominent status in civil society? To begin with, the court while not physically constraining K. immobilizes him emotionally. It becomes a continuing if sporadic presence in his life. Everywhere he turns, he is assailed by rumors that, while inflecting his circumstances in divergent ways, are convergent in communicating the bleak contingency of his prospects.

Given how quickly he crumbles, we are entitled to believe that he senses the fragility of his status. He is desperately conscious not only of his own status but of his place in the social hierarchy. While he takes considerable satisfaction in his relatively high status, he seems, perhaps unconsciously, aware that he is on a slippery slope doomed to either climbing higher or tumbling downward. He is, in short, so respectfully modern that he is complicit in his own subjugation.

The individual, viewed as *agent* in the modern project, is seen as *pawn* in the late-modern critique. One may, of course, rage against these new modes of power. However, it is also necessary to face up to the fact that this condition can be taken as an unmistakable sign of the failure of the modern project. Austin Sarat and Patricia Ewick draw upon the work of Murray Edelman to clarify the disabling impact of distinctively modern configurations of power.

> In the past four decades, scholars have corroborated Edelman's point that the forms of power exercised in local face-to-face interactions have given way to a form of power that appears impersonal, remote and intractable . . . The exercise of power is now built into the institutionalized practices of social life: government economic policy, technical requirements, far-ranging and long-term corporate expansion. [And quoting from Timothy Mitchell, 1990] "The new modes of power, by their permanence, their apparent origin outside local life, their intangibility, their impersonal nature, seem to take on an aspect of difference, to stand outside actuality, outside events, outside time, outside community, outside personhood."[77]

The novelists who provide literary access to this loss of agency may or may not be familiar with late-modern social theory, but when successful they enrich, extend, and personalize our understanding of the loss of agency, the nature of the forces arrayed against it, and the political estrangement that follows from it.

Kafka's primary focus is on bureaucratic power but he also calls attention to Joseph K. as the prototypical modern man, who senses his social vulnerability. He realizes that his social status depends on what others think of him and on the counsel they provide. He is thus the personification of what socio-legal scholar David Riesman referred to as an "other-directed" participant in a "lonely crowd."[78] In other words, *The Trial* is not only about the distinctly modernist aggregation of bureaucratic power; it also prefigures the problematic dispersal of power exposed by Foucault — namely that the erosion of agency is attributable not only to its direct suppression by a centralized state but, more insidiously, to the dispersal of power in liberal democratic states. Put in slightly different terms, Kafka anticipates Foucault's critique of power — political power but also of power per se.

5. Conclusions

The novels of political estrangement that constitute this book all reflect in their distinctively different ways the prophetic sensibilities of Kafka. These novels raise questions about political legitimacy and the social, cultural and economic foundations of the state and are of widely recognized literary merit — the literary imagination at its best. They draw on cultural narratives to capture the zeitgeist of the terrible twentieth century as it has been experienced by those robbed of agency by the institutions and ethos of a hegemonic modernism. They discredit the hopes and aspirations of the modern project and expose modernity's contradictory and ultimately self-defeating elements. In short, the late-modern novel of political estrangement reveals how and why the modern project betrays its promise of political agency — that is, the promise of "freedom made responsible for itself."[79]

In some cases, we will see how and why novels of political estrangement have been prophetic, like *The Trial*, in identifying lurking dangers — cultural canaries in the unstable modernist ethos. This is also true of some of the anti-war novels considered in Chapter 2. In other cases, the novels provide after-the-fact revisionist readings of political events like the Holocaust novels of Chapter 3 and the anti-Nazi novels of Chapter 4. For the most part, Chapter 5's novels of liberal democracy in the United Kingdom and the United States face up to contemporary events as they are unfolding. Most significantly, each of the novels reveals distinctively different adaptations to too-often terminal infirmities of democracy in the twentieth century. The book concludes with a sixth chapter that assesses the contribution of novels of political estrangement to re-imagining the past and to remembering the future.

Finally, by way of introduction, a few words are in order to clarify how and in what spirit I have chosen the novels for this volume. To begin with, I have selected novels which are widely recognized as among the most important, admired, and influential of the twentieth century. These novels focus on the events which most clearly, in my judgment, typify the myriad betrayals of the utopian promises of the modern project.

I have opted for novels of undisputed literary excellence and followed them where they led. What has emerged unbidden is the capacity of the literary imagination to provide unique emotional access to the political cultures that drive transformative change as well as resistance to it. It is in this spirit of honest inquiry that I now proceed to chapters on anti-war novels, holocaust novels, post-Nazi German novels, and to British and American novels on the contradictions of liberal democracy.

2 Anti-War Novels in the Twentieth Century: The Road to Late Modernity

> The collision was one between events and the public language used for over a century to celebrate the idea of progress.
>
> Paul Fussell, *The Great War and Modern Memory**

Beginning in the trenches of World War I, the twentieth century became, according to Raymond Aron, *The Century of Total War*. In those bloody trenches, he tells us, "technical surprise" transformed a conflict that was supposed to be settled quickly by a "few battles of annihilation," into a war of "attrition."[1]

> Defensive techniques were superior to offensive, so that by accumulating formidable firing power, it became possible to pulverize the enemy's front lines without too much difficulty but the terrain won was so broken up that it became in itself an obstacle. Enemy defenses, improvised by hastily assembled reinforcements, halted the attack, which could not be supported by an artillery paralyzed by its lack of mobility and the effects of its own fire.[2]

To fight this war of attrition, it was necessary to engage in *total mobilization* of home-front resources.[3] Moreover, because elements of this European war and its repercussions spread to the Middle East, the United States and Africa, everyone seemed to agree, despite the obvious Euro-centric exaggeration, that this was a *world* war.

Of course, World War I was, we now know, only a prelude to the more truly worldwide conflagration of the 1930s and 1940s. This time technical surprise mostly favored the offense — from the German blitzkrieg of 1939 to the atomic bomb of 1945. While the century was without any additional world wars, those wars that were fought often amounted to smaller-scale versions of total war. They were achingly destructive, depersonalized and enveloping in ways that largely obliterated the distinction between combatants and noncombatants.[4] Twentieth century warfare generated

---

* New York: Oxford University Press, 1977, p. 169.

not only epic destruction but epic futility as well. The purposes that the wars of the twentieth century were intended to serve often proved illusory, while their appalling costs were all too real. Indeed, one war all too often provided the breeding grounds for the next one. In short, the years since Aron was writing have done nothing to soften his characterization of *the century of total war*.

Novelists responded to this combination of ever-increasing devastation and futility by revealing and, in some cases anticipating, changes in political sensibility. If the romantic war novels of the *late nineteenth century* often emphasized the heroic and the honorable,* the novels of *the early twentieth century*, with which this chapter begins, put the emphasis on tragedy and irony. They repudiate war and call attention to its association with modern technology and professional knowledge. Thus, they raise doubts about the modern project. On the other hand, they retain some vestigial belief that the modern project can be redeemed. This redemptive possibility emerges in a rudimentary anti-capitalist and populist politics which suggest that modernity and democracy are, at least, not mutually exclusive.[5]

In contrast, the *post-World War II* era anti-war novels are often driven by the most elemental theme of *late-modern* social theory — that is, the *dialectic of the modern project*, in which its achievements, most notably science, rationality, and knowledge, produce the seeds of its own destruction.[6] There is a notable tendency to treat war as a dilemma — perhaps inescapable, perhaps not — but as modernity gone terribly and irredeemably wrong. As Margot Norris puts it: "Among our various constructions of the modernity of the twentieth century, we must list as its premier legacy the combined will and technology that made it the *bloodiest* in the history of the world."[7] To convey this bleak vision, novelists resort to paradox, contradiction and parody. Their goal is to illuminate the alienating impact of ever more "impersonal, remote and intractable" power put at the service of the ever more destructive and self-defeating modes of total war.[8]

---

* To look solely at the war novels of the twentieth century — or, to be more precise at its anti-war novels — is not to affirm the superior value of this relatively recent literature. Surely, as many have suggested to me, a true history of the anti-war novel could hardly exclude *The Red Badge of Courage* — or, for that matter, *The Odyssey* and *The Iliad*, not to mention many other forebearers of the twentieth century's literary responses to war. Among World War I novels not included, Jaroslav Hasek's *The Good Soldier Svejk* comes immediately to mind. But then my purpose is not to write a critique of anti-war literature. Rather I consider the evolution of the anti-war novel during the twentieth century as one element in the emergence of a late-modern political literature in response to the bitter fruits of the modern project.

In sum, I will argue in this chapter that over the course of the twentieth century distinctively different sensibilities came to the fore in anti-war novels — each representing ever more disillusionment not only with war but with the utopian promises of the modern project.

1. Between the Wars: The Pacifist-Populist, Anti-War Novel

> "We are the Dead. Short days ago
> We lived, felt dawn, saw sunset glow,
> Love and were loved, and we lie
> In Flanders Field"
>
> John McCrae, "In Flanders Fields"*

Paul Fussell's survey of the British literary heritage of World War I, *The Great War and Modern Memory*, provides illuminating but only partial access to what the anti-war novels of the years between the wars have to tell us. Following his lead I will argue that the irony expressed in literature and art in the wake of World War I represented a first rather cautious questioning of modernity. Irony, as I see it, prepared the way for a subsequent and definitive break with modernity and a subsequent embrace of late-modern sensibilities. Literature and art were both reflecting and prefiguring the sea change in the political ethos.

In the three celebrated World War I novels we will consider, irony is an important theme, as is the retreat from pre-World War I romanticism about war — just as Fussell suggests. An idealist version of populist politics emerges in reaction to the wanton destruction of trench warfare — prefiguring the late-modern anti-war novels that emerged in the wake of World War II and which are taken up in the next section of the chapter.

A Farewell to Arms

Ernest Hemingway's account of World War I, after all is said and done, is hardly a war novel at all — much less an anti-war novel. True, it is set entirely during the war, it involves battles and it echoes familiar themes of comrades in life-threatening and appalling circumstances. But the dominant theme is *love* in a time of war.[9] In addition, Hemingway's setting is the quirky Italian front and his focus is on an expatriate American officer serving in a medical unit of the Italian army. Accordingly, the circumstances of the novel are much less dire and degrading — officers living mostly as gentlemen — than those in the trenches on the Western Front. *A Farewell to Arms* is, then, something of an anachronism in that it

---

* Quoted in Paul Fussell, *The Great War and Modern Memory*, p. 249.

represents war in terms very close to the romanticism that Fussell detects in the run up to, and the early days of, World War I.

As Lt. Frederic Henry's English girlfriend, Catherine, points out, Italy is a "silly front" (p. 20). The war takes the winter off because of mountain snows, and that respite becomes the occasion for a love affair between Henry and Catherine, which is the main business of the book. The war intrudes most insistently through Henry's serious wound and in the grim and chaotic retreat from Caporetto. In each instance, however, the war clouds are lined with silver. The wound results in an extended hospital stay and "a lovely summer" (p. 112) of horse racing, love, drinking and other diversions. This interlude takes up almost 80 pages, or roughly one-quarter of the book. As for the retreat from Caporetto, it becomes mostly a tale of increasing disillusionment, detachment and ultimately desertion from the Italian army and a perilous but romantic flight with Catherine from Italy to Switzerland and from war to a cozy chalet in the mountains where they wait out Catherine's ultimately tragic pregnancy. As Henry puts it: "I made a separate peace" (p. 243).[10]

More broadly, Hemingway reveals that he is drawn to war as a site of adventure, honor and agency. These manly virtues trump dehumanization, degradation and death — the dominant notes struck in the novels of Erich Remarque and Dalton Trumbo that we look at next. Lt. Henry finds war appealing in part because of the way in which all the normal conventions of life are suspended and one can function with impunity in any number of milieus. Indeed, he sees Catherine as "probably a little crazy" (p. 30) and war providing a "strange excitement" (p. 13).[11] Outside the hospital the soldiers live wild and dissolute lives and are treated with kid gloves by the civilians with whom they interact. In the hospital, he and Catherine (and she a nurse!) flout the rules, and each of them sees all of this as an adventure made more poignant and more exciting for being played out against a background of possible death and injury.[12]

The two expatriates come off as being *in* the war (at least some of the time) but never truly *of* the war. Henry maintains his psychic distance from the war, which has "nothing to do with him" (p. 30). He and Catherine are throughout agents of their own fates — having chosen to participate and then choosing to opt out. True, Henry feels bound to his comrades by a sense of loyalty[13] and feels he and the others share a bond of mutual danger and, indeed, brotherhood. Accordingly, when he leaves the front and comes for Catherine, he tells her: "I feel like a criminal. I've deserted the army" (p. 251).

However, this is clearly a fleeting second thought. Having decided that the Italian army is more of a danger to him and his small coterie of men, desertion becomes not a problem but a (the) solution. His "anger was washed away along with any obligation" (p. 232). And here we have the final triumph of agency, because both his flight from the army and his subsequent flight to Switzerland with Catherine are fraught with danger which Henry meets with resolve, resourcefulness and heroism.

All Quiet on the Western Front

Erich Maria Remarque's soldier's-eye view of World War I contrasts dramatically with Hemingway's *A Farewell to Arms*. The bulk of the novel details the many horrors of the foot soldiers' war in the trenches on the Western Front. Remarque's dominant message is simply that war is hell — almost literally so. But there are also two accompanying messages of betrayal, which identify the self-serving war-mongering of the economic and military elites and the false promises of the modern project. Taken together, these latter messages strike populist and anti-modernist notes, in which progress and war emerge as a conspiracy against rank and file workers and soldiers.

Insofar as the experience of war has any redemptive benefit, it would seem to be in the salt-of-the-earth solidarity among comrades and, to an extent, between combatants and the enemy. "Comradeship" and "*esprit de corps*" are, according to the narrator Paul Baumer, "in the field developed into the finest thing that arose from the war" (pp. 26–7).

> We sit opposite one another, Kat and I, two soldiers in shabby coats, cooking a goose in the middle of the night. We don't talk much, but I believe we have a more complete community with one another than even lovers have (p. 94).

Paul takes solace from his comrades' voices, which are "the strongest, most comforting thing there is anywhere" (p. 212).[14]

Because this is the solidarity of collective dehumanization it provides cold comfort. The dehumanization begins with military training which, as Paul puts it, makes them "hard, suspicious, pitiless, vicious, tough — and that was good; for these attributes were just what we lacked" (p. 26). Then, there are the squalid living conditions in the trenches where the "repulsive" rats are "so fat — the kind we call corpse rats" (p. 102). The soldiers are in constant fear for their lives while witnessing the pain, the suffering and the death of their comrades. "We have become wild beasts. We do not fight, we defend ourselves against annihilation" (p. 113). However, in becoming wild beasts so as to avoid physical annihilation, they are, Remarque reveals, spiritually and emotionally annihilated — resulting in an alienation from society and from self.[15]

The annihilation is particularly devastating for "the young men of twenty" who have been robbed of their youth and their futures. They are without the older men's insulation of the everyday: "wives, children, occupations, and interests . . . that the war can not obliterate . . . We young men of twenty . . . have only our parents, and some, perhaps, a girl — that is not much, for at our age the influence of parents is at its weakest and girls have not yet got a hold over us" (p. 20). When he returns home on leave, he finds himself completely at odds with civilians, including a home-front major who chastises him for not saluting: "You think you can bring your front-line manners here, what? . . . Thank God, we still have discipline here!" (p. 163). But he also finds himself estranged from the family and friends for whom he is fighting. "They talk too much for me. They have worries, aims, desires, that I cannot comprehend" (p. 168).

> [T]he things and events of our existence . . . cut us off and made the world of our parents incomprehensible to us — for then we surrendered ourselves to events and were lost in them, and the least little thing was enough to carry us down the stream of eternity (p. 122).

Paul's estrangement radiates inward to his own life. "All I do know is that this business about professions and studies and salaries and so on — it makes me sick, it is and always was disgusting. I don't see anything at all" (p. 87).

Being at home is revealing but dreadfully so. "I ought never to have come here. Out there I was indifferent and often hopeless — I will never be able to be so again. I was a soldier, and now I am nothing but an agony for myself, for my mother, for everything that is so comfortless and without end" (p. 185). "But now I see that I have been crushed without knowing it, I find I do not belong here any more, it is a foreign world" (p. 168).

While the novel is, then, dominated by a searing and straightforward account of the dehumanization of trench warfare,[16] there is also an unmistakable awareness of the contradictions of the modern project. War is seen as bending technological achievements to its own destructive purposes — with flamethrowers, improved tanks and airplanes offered as cases in point. Attention is called to the way that airplanes serve as artillery spotters and thus become agents of sudden death from distant and unseen big guns. Paul observes bitterly that for war, "the keenest brains of the world invent weapons and words to make it yet more refined and enduring" (p. 49).

Medical knowledge and the medical profession are similarly disparaged. Early on, mention is made of "splendid artificial limbs" (p. 28), which as everyone knows are not splendid (see p. 260). And the hospital is both a testimonial to the ravages of war and a laboratory for mobilizing medical support of war making.

> A man can stop a bullet and be killed; he can get wounded, and the hospital is the next stop. There, if they do not amputate him, he sooner or later falls into the hands of one of those staff surgeons who, with the War Service Cross in his button-hole, says to him: "What, one leg a bit short? If you have any pluck you don't need to run at the front. The man is A1. Dismiss!" (p. 281).

The surgeon serves both his military masters and himself because: "What he wants is little dogs to experiment with, so the war is a glorious time for him, as it is for all surgeons" (p. 259). What then of so-called civilization? "It must all be lies and of no account when the culture of a thousand years could not prevent this stream of blood being poured out, these torture-chambers in their hundreds of thousands. A hospital alone shows what war is" (p. 263).

Towards the end of the book the overtly political themes are introduced, again prompted by Paul's home leave. He becomes aware of the contrast between the squandering of resources through war profiteering and military incompetence and the ever more desperate lot of the soldiers in the trenches and the poor at home. "The factory owners in Germany have grown wealthy; — dysentery dissolves our bowels" (p. 280). With respect to his mother's cancer operation, he observes that poor people need operations that they fear they cannot afford. Yet they "don't dare to ask the price," because they also fear that "the surgeon might take it amiss" (p. 197). "And generals too," adds [Paul's comrade] Detering, "they become famous through war . . . There are other people behind there who profit by the war, that's certain" (p. 206).

Johnny Got His Gun

Dalton Trumbo's account of World War I, written just prior to the beginning of World War II, purges the last vestiges of the romantic "band of brothers" vision of warfare. Instead, *Johnny Got His Gun* offers a bitter and unequivocal denunciation of the unforgivable, but, paradoxically, not unredeemable, costs of World War I. It is unthinkable to forgive those responsible for what befell Joe, Trumbo's ravaged victim of trench warfare, who lies in a hospital without sight, hearing, speech or limbs. As Joe's story, told by Joe, unfolds, the injustice of it all overwhelms everything except Joe's determination to recapture at least a semblance of his identity and in so doing to redeem his sacrifice by bearing witness to that injustice.

Ever so gradually, Joe, and hence the reader, become more grimly aware of Joe's hopeless predicament. He and we learn that he is not *only* "wallowing in blackness" (p. 14). He is in effect *incommunicado* — utterly cut off from the world and even from the nurses and doctors who care for him. He does not know whether he is in an American, a French or a British hospital. He lays inert in bed, a fully sentient being — treated as if he were in what we now refer to as a persistent vegetative state. He seethes with frustration and with a sense of injustice. He tells himself: "It wasn't your fight, Joe" (p. 24). It was not his fight, because he was dragooned into the army when, as a post-adolescent, he was picked up as a vagrant and given the "Hobson's choice" of going to jail or joining the army (p. 189).[17]

As he lies in bed musing over his youth and the simple pleasures of a normal life, Joe recalls the barnstorming pilot who brought the first airplane to his hometown. He reflects on the welcome given to the pilot as the dashing embodiment of "the greatest step forward man had made in a hundred years" (p. 19) — and yet only one element of the technological progress that promised a new era of "peace and prosperity" (p. 20). Joe then recalls that shortly thereafter the pilot completed his cross-country barnstorming tour in San Francisco where he "fell into San Francisco Bay and died" (p. 20). Thus, an initial shadow of death is cast over the technological wonders of the modern age. There is no further mention of the airplane or air warfare in World War I, but the implication is clear enough.

More central to the narrative and to Joe are the bitter ironies of medical science. His doctors, Joe presumes, are taking great pride in the very dubious achievement of keeping him alive. He speculates about their self-congratulatory sense of achievement. "[O]ur triumph here is the greatest thing we ever did" (p. 85). His own view is that medical science can neither make him physically whole nor can it make those who are shell-shocked emotionally whole (p. 153). Drugs are the treatment of choice for both forms of incapacitation. In Joe's case, the drugs used ostensibly to make him more comfortable obliterate his consciousness — just about the only remaining vestige of his humanity. Under their influence, he "couldn't tell whether he was awake or asleep" (p. 97).

As the book proceeds, the focus shifts from Joe's boyhood and hometown to the war itself and from a rather incidental indictment of technology into a concentrated assault on the war and those responsible for it. What emerges is an unequivocal denunciation of the rich, who use the poor as cannon fodder for their own ill-conceived and self-interested purposes. In short, *Johnny Got His Gun* becomes fully engaged in populist politics (see pp. 110, 114, 30, 34 and 44). If the narrative were to have stopped here, Trumbo's and Remarque's bleak outlooks would be essentially indistinguishable from one another — although politics is much more at the core of Trumbo's novel.

Yet when all is said and done, *Johnny Got His Gun* also offers a hopeful, if far from optimistic, tribute to the indomitable human spirit. The narrative glue that holds the novel together is not the horror of war, the irony of modernity or even the exploitative politics of war, but Joe's ultimately successful struggle against overwhelming odds to reclaim his humanity. At the outset, as he becomes increasingly aware of his utter helplessness, Joe says to himself that "it would be a lot better if you were dead" (p. 24), and the reader cannot help but agree.

However, as Joe pursues his heroic journey towards agency, both he and the reader experience moments of tremendous exhilaration. Through a painful series of ups and downs, he manages to teach himself to keep track of time and, thus, to gain awareness of the days and the seasons. "What the hell did it matter if you don't have a nose left so long as you could smell the dawn" (p. 138). He felt as if "he had made a new universe" (p. 143). Finally, he experiences "hysterical happiness" (p. 199) as he finally succeeds in communicating with his caregivers by tapping out Morse code with his head on his pillow. "But this happiness, this new wild frantic happiness was greater than anything he could contain" (p. 215).[18]

The denouement of the novel seems, initially, to return us to its bleak political context. Joe seeks to put his newly found agency at the service of democratic pacifism. He comes to see that if he is released from the hospital and allowed to go forth, he, who comes the closest imaginable to knowing death, also can see through, and bear witness to, the ultimate fraud of the clichés of war. "[D]eath before dishonor is pure bull" (p. 116), because there is "nothing noble about dying" (p. 118). Predictably, the authorities deny his request as against regulations.[19] Joe insists that he be released.

> Then against the stump of his left arm he felt a sudden wet coolness. The man who tapped his answer was applying an alcoholic swab. Oh god he thought I know what that means don't do it please don't. Then he felt the sharp deadly prick of the needle . . . In his last moment of consciousness in his last moment of life he would still fight he would still tap . . . His taps became slower and slower and the vision swam toward him . . . (pp. 238–9).

But note that the book ends not with the needle of oblivion but with Joe's messianic vision that his silencing is a perverse tribute to the power of the democratic pacifist message. So that the next time: "If you tell us to make the world safe for democracy we will take you seriously and by God and by Christ we will make it so" (p. 242).

The contrast between Hemingway, on the one hand, and Remarque and Trumbo, on the other, is first and foremost a contrast between Hemingway clinging to a predominantly romantic vision of war despite the total war experience of World War I* and Remarque and Trumbo seeing total war as physical, emotional and spiritual mayhem that extinguishes agency and humanity. But in addition, Remarque and Trumbo anticipate the late-modern, anti-war novel by identifying the destructive contradictions of modernity. Note, however, that these contradictions are not the raison d'être that they become in Pat Barker's World War I trilogy, which will be considered in the next section of the chapter. Similarly, we get no taste of the pervasive sense of paradox that is intrinsic to Kurt Vonnegut's *Slaughterhouse 5* and Joseph Heller's *Catch 22*,† both of which will also be considered in the next section. Finally, the politics of Remarque are straightforward and populist — with readily identifiable victims and villains and thus with an unspoken but unmistakably revolutionary message.

2. The Late-modern Anti-War Novel of the Late 20th Century

We are the unwilling, led by the unqualified, doing the unnecessary, for the ungrateful.‡

---

* Put another way, Hemingway associates war with the opportunity to pursue and protect honor while at the same time trying to preserve as much civility as is possible. It might seem that Lt. Henry's desertion from the Italian army and his flight to the petit bourgeois pleasures of Switzerland demonstrate the triumph of civility over honor. A different and a more accurate interpretation of Henry's action is that he finally concludes that the quality he finds most appealing in the Italian people, their good-natured civility, precludes them from waging war with honor. In short, it is the Italian army, not Lt. Henry, who chooses civility over honor — leaving Henry with no option but to flee.

† One cannot imagine Remarque normalizing death as does Vonnegut's invocation "and so it goes" with each loss of life. Similarly, while Remarque honors Kaz as an accomplished scrounger with a "sixth sense" (p. 37), he scrounges opportunistically for the basics of life and is thus literally in a different class from Milo Minderbinder, the predatory capitalist of *Catch 22*.

‡ Engraving on a Vietnam-Era Zippo lighter. "'Zippo Songs Lit by Vietnam'" National Public Radio, *Weekend Edition*, July 10, 2004. For two reasons I have not included any Vietnam War novels although there are several that were well received and deservedly so. To name just two: Robert Olen Butler, *The Alleys of Eden* (New York: Henry Holt, 1994) and Tim O'Brien, *Going After Cacciato* (New York: Broadway Books, 1999). Each of them in its own way illuminates the emotional and physical

The late-modern anti-war novel is both an outgrowth of, and distinguishable from, the populist anti-war novel of the previous section. The hallmarks of the late-modern anti-war novel are *paradox* and *negation*. Neither reveals any light at the end of the tunnel nor anywhere to point the finger of blame.

- The former, exemplified by Pat Barker's World War I trilogy, probes the multiple, inevitable and irresolvable contradictions of total war. The logics of modernity, personified by psychoanalyst and neurologist, Dr. William Rivers, are deployed to make sense of the circumstances of total war but found hopelessly wanting by both Dr. Rivers and his patients — yielding paradox and betrayal rather than understanding.
- The latter is to be found in the anti-war novels of Kurt Vonnegut and Joseph Heller who, in effect, throw up their hands in the face of total war, which is both inescapable and irrational. Accordingly, Vonnegut and Heller turn to black humor, which is mostly abrasive in the mode of Groucho Marx and sometimes poignant in the mode of Harpo. In effect, they use literary nonsense to make sense out of the nonsensical consequences of the modern project.

There is an additional distinction between novels of paradox and the novels of negation, with cynicism looming in the latter but found only at the margins of the former, which are infinitely respectful of the futile search for agency.

Regeneration

The first book of Barker's trilogy of World War I amply illustrates the suasive power, and the late-modern tendencies, of the anti-war novel of paradox. The novel is a fictionalized version of the wartime experiences of neurologist and pioneering psychoanalyst William Rivers. He treats

---

costs of combat as well as the cultural alienation of waging asymmetrical warfare against a literally underground enemy who above ground can melt into the civilian population. The costs of combat are well-chronicled in the WWI and WWII novels that are included. None of these novels, including those of the Vietnam War, opens the Pandora's Box of the post-war PTSD-misfortunes of survivors who came home profoundly compromised by physical and emotional scars. Remarque, as we have just seen, does make an evocative, but passing and ancillary reference to contradictory forces in play on the home front and the battlefield, and Kurt Vonnegut's *Slaughterhouse 5* confronts the issue more directly but in a fashion that calls out for further elaboration. It was surprising not to find a Vietnam war novel that explored the long term emotional and physical costs of the war, given its centrality to the decades-long public discourse and to the dramatic impact of the 1978 film *The Deer Hunter* which was, in effect, all about PTSD.

the "war neuroses" of British officers who have been traumatized by the carnage of trench warfare on the Western Front. Barker moves back and forth between her own characters, most notably William Prior, and well-known literary figures actually treated by Rivers at Craiglockhart War Hospital, most notably the poet Siegfried Sassoon.

The appalling conditions faced by the soldiers in the British trenches, as portrayed by Barker, are indistinguishable from those of Remarque's German soldiers on the Western Front. Remarque's first-person soldier's narrative is, however, transformed by Barker into a doctor-patient struggle over memory, which the doctor is trying to help the soldiers recover but which the traumas of the trenches have driven from their consciousness. This struggle in itself represents something of a contradiction, of course. But the deeper contradictions are, as we shall see presently, within Rivers himself. The result is a novel of ambiguity, paradox, idealism, irony and multilateral victimhood — characters trapped in no-win situations and thus without any meaningful capacity to control their own destinies. Barker's triumph is in her use of psychoanalytic insights to make this universal loss of agency intellectually convincing and emotionally absorbing.[20]

Dr. Rivers draws on his therapeutic experience as well as his familiarity with early psychoanalytic theory to identify paradoxes of warfare. In so doing he invalidates much conventional wisdom concerning the combat experience.

> One of the paradoxes of the war — one of many — was that the most brutal conflicts should set up a relationship between officers and men that was . . . domestic. Caring . . . And the Great Adventure — the real-life equivalent of all the adventure stories they'd devoured as boys — consisted of crouching in a dugout, waiting to be killed. The war that promised so much in the way of 'manly' activity had actually delivered 'feminine' passivity, and on a scale that their mothers and sisters had scarcely known" (pp. 107–8).

Men, and particularly soldiers, are supposed to be tough, aggressive and brave, but are put into situations where they experience *fear* of the enemy, *tenderness* towards their comrades, and the overall *passivity* of being "*mobilized* into holes" (p. 107). Accordingly, Rivers concludes that: "Any explanation of war neurosis must account for the fact that this intensely masculine life of war and danger and hardship produced in men the same disorders that women suffer in peace" (p. 222).[21]

The combination of trauma and imposed passivity generated a devastating emotional dissonance among the officers treated by Rivers: both war neuroses and an especially potent resistance to therapy. Rivers was convinced that the neurotic symptoms of his patients — muteness and paralysis, for example — were the result of repressing horrible experiences that were "so vile, so disgusting" that the soldiers were all too understandably determined to put behind them.

> [Captain Burns had] been thrown into the air by the explosion of a shell and had landed, head-first, on a German corpse, whose gasfilled belly had ruptured on impact. Before Burns lost consciousness, he'd had time to realize that what filled his nose and mouth was decomposing human flesh. Now, whenever he tried to eat, that taste and smell recurred (p. 19).

Despite their reflexive resistance to his therapeutic ministrations, Rivers remained convinced that only by remembering what they wished to forget would the symptoms be relieved.[22]

We also come to understand how much more difficult this becomes insofar as the soldiers feel shame at their failure to respond to danger as soldiers should. "Fear, tenderness — these emotions were so despised that they could be admitted into consciousness only at the cost of redefining what it meant to be a man" (p. 48). The officers are, in addition, so trapped in the sense of honor and camaraderie that they can neither allow themselves to acknowledge the emotional costs that the war has imposed on them nor can they see any *conscious* alternative to returning to the trenches. Rivers is, then, hardly surprised by Lieutenant Prior's furious anger when he learns that Rivers has succeeded in getting a medical board to agree that Prior is unfit to return to combat. "At the moment you hate me," Rivers tells Prior, "because I have been instrumental in getting you something you're ashamed of wanting" (p. 209).

But this book is at least as much about Rivers as about his patients, and the underlying message is that he too is trapped. To begin with, he is both empowered and neutralized by his professional role. As a therapist he has the professional knowledge to alleviate his patients' suffering and the professional responsibility to do so to the full extent of his ability. However, insofar as he is successful, these officers are returned to combat. This means sending them off to be killed and/or to suffer a recurrence of their war neuroses. Do no harm?

The result is that Rivers undergoes a terrible crisis of confidence in himself and in his vocation. *Captain* Rivers, probably unconsciously, tries to shield *Doctor* Rivers from this impasse by taking refuge in the same sense of military and patriotic duty that drives his patients. However, his patients also teach him the true hell of war and thus the emptiness of his belief that, "when you put the uniform on, in effect, you sign a contract.

And you don't back out of a contract merely because you changed your mind" (p. 23). Predictably, Rivers becomes aware that, not unlike his patients, he is suffering neurotic symptoms.[23]

All of these elements come together in Rivers' efforts to treat the poet Siegfried Sassoon, a decorated hero of the trenches, who has publicly declared his unwillingness to serve further in a war which he deems ill-fought and hence futile. Sassoon wants to be court-martialed in order to call attention to incompetence of the military and government authorities. "[T]he only way that I can get publicity is to make them court-martial me" (p. 6). However, his influential friend and fellow poet Robert Graves goes behind Sassoon's back and prevails on the authorities to send him to Rivers to be treated for a war neurosis. In Graves' view, Rivers' treatment center represents the less objectionable alternative to a decision by the authorities to suppress Sassoon's protest by simply locking him away in an asylum.

Eventually, his work with Sassoon and the others leads Rivers to epiphanies that illuminate but do not liberate him from either his professional double bind or his sense of duty as an officer. Specifically, he learns that his work at Craiglockhart must be about the war rather than simply about the therapeutic experience. Much to his chagrin he quickly discovers that Sassoon's opposition to the war does not stem from cowardice or a lack of patriotism. Even more problematic is Rivers' realization that Sassoon is not suffering from a war neurosis but from "a very powerful *anti*-war neurosis" (p. 15). "He *wanted* Sassoon to be ill," because "he'd be a lot less trouble if he were ill" (p. 8).

If Rivers could treat Sassoon for war neurosis, then it would be possible to stay clear of the politics of war, and he could continue to function purely as a psychotherapist. Once, however, Rivers determined that there is no "war neurosis" to treat, things became more delicate and confounding — due in no small part to what he learns from Sassoon and the others about the toxic idiocies of warfare on the Western Front. In short, he realizes that Sassoon is neither a knave nor a dupe of pacifists but an unimpeachable voice of all that is wrong with the way the war is being waged and in which he, Rivers, is perforce complicit.

Even when Rivers is faced with authentic war neuroses, he cannot escape the war by taking refuge in his therapeutic responsibilities. Indeed, as the outrages inflicted on his patients become ever more agonizingly apparent to Rivers, he cannot escape concluding that their disabling symptoms stem from these outrages and not from any "innate weakness" — thus making the war and his role in it "the issue" (p. 115). This leads him to an even more devastating element of his own complicity. In getting men to verbalize their gruesome encounters with the unspeakable, he is really silencing them — depriving them of their only way of bearing witness to the awful truths of warfare on the Western Front. After all, they are emotionally unable to put their masculinity, their loyalty to comrades, or their patriotism at risk by acknowledging their terror or their degradation.[24] They cannot overtly voice their opposition to the war but have done so *covertly* through their neurotic symptoms.

In the end, Rivers comes to understand his professional knowledge as a double-edged sword that empowers both him and his patients and at the same time robs them of political agency. In musing about his relationship with Sassoon, Rivers notes "the irony . . . that he, who was in the business of changing people, should himself have been changed by somebody who was clearly unaware of having done it" (pp. 248–9).

> Now in middle age, the sheer extent of the *mess* seemed to be forcing him into conflict with the authorities over a wide range of issues . . . medical, military. Whatever. A society that devours its own young deserves no unquestioning allegiance (p. 249).

From the stubbornness of their resistance to therapy, Rivers comes to fully appreciate "the sheer extremity of the suffering" (p. 19) and its destructive impact on personality — leading in some cases to its "complete disintegration" (p. 184). He could find in Captain Burns, "no trace of the qualities he must have possessed in order to be given that exceptionally early command" (p. 184).

Despite this realization, Rivers remains trapped in his professional role just as his patients remained trapped in their thwarted masculinity. Neither he nor they transcend their sense of patriotic duty. On the one hand, Rivers is convinced that "[n]othing justifies this. Nothing, nothing, nothing" (p. 180). Yet it is Rivers who counsels Sassoon not to continue publicizing his opposition to the war and instead to appear before the medical board as cured of his nonexistent war neurosis and thus fit for duty.

> [Sassoon had] given up hope of influencing events. Or perhaps he'd just given up hope. At the back of Rivers's mind was the fear that Craiglockhart had done to Sassoon what the Somme and Arras had failed to do. And if that were so, he couldn't escape responsibility (p. 221).

The officers are, of course, similarly trapped. Sassoon returns all too willingly to the troops that he has left behind — convinced by Rivers and Graves that political opposition is fruitless and that his only choice is to share the peril of his troops. Similarly, Prior has no choice but to resist the "shame of home service" (p. 206) and to persist in his ultimately successful and ultimately fatal determination to return to the trenches.[25] For Prior, returning to combat is his way of defending his identity — of avoiding, one might say, the destruction of his personality. "I don't think about myself as a person who breaks down" (p. 105). In the end, then, Rivers is unable to turn his back on either his professional or his patriotic responsibilities — nor can he escape a profound sense of shame for not behaving differently.

Slaughterhouse-Five: The Children's Crusade, A Duty Dance with Death

Kurt Vonnegut's 1969 novel of the firebombing of Dresden in World War II shares with Barker's *Regeneration* a core, late-modern understanding of total war. In both books, total war generates inertial forces of its own making — a momentum that is beyond the control of those who launch it and those who fight it. As Vonnegut puts it: "There are almost no characters in this story, and almost no dramatic confrontations, *because most of the people in it are so sick and so much the listless playthings of enormous forces*" (p. 164, italics added).[26] For Vonnegut as well as for Barker, to truly comprehend total war it is necessary to abandon the implied agency of identifying and distinguishing between victims and villains — looking instead to forces that are embedded in the fabric of society.[27] Moreover, each novelist chooses to view total war through the prism of mental illness. They do so, however, in dramatically different ways — thus revealing competing conceptions of the late-modern predicament.

Slaughterhouse is the story of Billy Pilgrim who, following many years of conforming unexceptionally to what is expected of a prosperous optometrist and devoted family man, suddenly exhibits readily recognizable signs of mental instability. He claims that aliens regularly visit and transport him to their planet, Tralfamadoria, on a Barca lounger stolen from Sears (p. 77). He also experiences frequent mental lapses. As a result, there is general agreement that Billy is mentally ill. To those around him, Billy's military service is a thing of the past. They have, it seems, forgotten his breakdown while in optometry school immediately after the war and, accordingly, they locate the source of mental illness elsewhere in his life. Psychologists attribute Billy's delusions to childhood trauma (p. 100). His daughter traces the delusions to an airplane crash from which Billy emerged as the sole survivor (p. 25).

The real heart of the problem, however, is his outwardly seamless transition from prisoner of war in Dresden to a comfortable and largely uneventful middle-class, middle-western existence — a fraud which Billy unconsciously perpetrates on himself. He does so as protection against the terrible trauma he experienced during his imprisonment in Dresden. Billy, it turns out, arrived in Dresden before the bombs fell. Ominously, he and the other prisoners were housed in slaughter-house-five — available only because "all the hooved animals in Germany had been killed and eaten and excreted by human beings, mostly soldiers. So it goes" (p. 152). After the firestorm Billy emerged from the slaughterhouse into a wasteland. "Dresden was like the moon now, nothing but minerals. The stones were hot. Everybody else in the neighborhood was dead" (p. 178). He also witnessed post-firestorm killing. "American fighter planes came in under the smoke to see if anything was moving . . . Then they saw some people moving down by the riverside and they shot at them. They hit some of them. So it goes" (p. 180).[28]

Once the carnage finally ended, there were "hundreds of corpse mines" (p. 214). However, going into the mines to recover the bodies proved too dangerous to the body and spirit. "So a new technique was devised. Bodies weren't brought up any more. They were cremated by soldiers with flamethrowers right where they were" (p. 214).

At first glance, Billy's decades-long repression of battlefield trauma and the inevitable emergence of post-traumatic reactions seem indistinguishable from the wartime neuroses which Rivers treats in *Regeneration*. Vonnegut, however, wants us to view the Tralfamadorian visitations not as symptoms of war neurosis, but as sources of enlightenment. It matters not to Vonnegut, and is not meant to matter to readers, whether Billy has been transported to Tralfamadoria. Either way, he emerges as a voice from outer space seeing everything on earth with fresh eyes. Total war is madness masquerading as rationality. It follows that total war can induce madness in those who fight it. Yet only those thus afflicted are capable of seeing the madness of warfare for what it is. Only the supposedly delusional Billy is truly sane. In *Slaughterhouse* there is not, nor can there be, a Dr. Rivers or, for that matter, anyone on the home front, with one notable exception, who is able to comprehend both the madness of warfare and the madness it inflicts on its victims. Tellingly, the exception is madcap science fiction writer, Kilgore Trout, who is also something of a space traveler. Trout is a soul mate who is able to mediate between the two worlds of the emotionally scarred but newly enlightened Billy Pilgrim (e.g. pp. 166 ff.).

Vonnegut's black humor further distances his conception of total war from Barker's. For Vonnegut, black humor is not simply counterpoint to the tragedy of total war, but tragedy's voice — conveying the endless perversities perpetrated in the name of God and country. In punctuating each mention of death with the phrase "so it goes," Vonnegut underscores the normalization of death within the context of total war. Further illuminating the normalization of death is Kilgore Trout's robot with halitosis, which has "dropped jellied gasoline on people" (p. 168). The robot was initially shunned by people — not because of war crimes but because it had halitosis, which "they found . . . unforgivable. But then he cleared that up, and he was welcomed to the human race" (p. 168). Just as insanity serves sanity, so too the jarring perversities of black humor serve to drive Vonnegut's non-linear narrative as it lurches back and forth through time and through space — making a shambles of common sense and conventional sensibilities.

Catch 22

Joseph Heller's highly esteemed novel of World War II seems at first glance to be no more than a depiction of the staggering, topsy-turvy incompetence of the American military — or at least of one particular bombing squadron stationed on the fictitious island of Pianosa in the Mediterranean. While the novel is certainly more than that, multiple dimensions of military ineptness are front and center. Consider, for example, ex-P.F.C. Wintergreen's intervention.

> General Dreedle . . . was incensed by General Peckham's recent directive requiring all tents in the Mediterranean theatre of operations to be pitched along parallel lines with entrances facing back proudly toward the Washington Monument. To General Dreedle, who ran a fighting outfit, it seemed a lot of crap . . . There then followed a hectic jurisdictional dispute between these overlords that was decided in General Dreedle's favor by ex-P.F.C. Wintergreen, mail clerk at Twenty-seventh Air Force Headquarters. Wintergreen determined the outcome by throwing all communications from General Peckham into the wastebasket (p. 35).

There is also profound ignorance on display. Captain Black distrusted Captain Yossarian, knowing he was "subversive because he wore eyeglasses and used words like *panacea* and *utopia*, and because he disapproved of Adolf Hitler, who had done such a great job of combating un-American activities in Germany" (p. 43).

The bungling that pervades this saga of patriotic claptrap and martial blather is not haphazard but strategic. Virtually all of the characters are obsessively engaged in the pursuit of self-interest and supremely uninterested in military success — except insofar as its by-product is personal upward mobility. Doc Daneeka's fledgling civilian medical practice was foundering:

Fortunately, just when things were blackest, the war broke out. It was a godsend, Doc Daneeka confessed solemnly. "Most of the other doctors were soon in the service, and things picked up overnight" (p. 49).

The doc's run of good luck came to an abrupt halt when he was drafted. While Daneeka brooded aimlessly about his lost opportunities, the higher ups saw the war as an opportunity for career advancement.

To demonstrate to his superiors that he is worthy of promotion to general, Colonel Cathcart keeps raising the number of missions that his flyers must complete before being rotated back to the United States — thus keeping the rotation home excruciatingly out of reach. Cathcart also is determined to get an article about his squadron into *The Saturday Evening Post* and therefore orders his bombers on an especially dangerous mission. As he explains to the chaplain, "That's right . . . [t]he sooner we get some casualties, the sooner we can make progress on this. I'd like to get in the Christmas issue if we can. I imagine the circulation is higher then" (pp. 292–3).

Note also Lt. Colonel Korn's patronizing explanation to a puzzled Yossarian as to why it is that Colonel Cathcart wants to be made a general.

Why? For the same reason that I want to be a colonel. What else have we got to do? Everyone teaches us to aspire to higher things. A general is higher that a colonel, and a colonel is higher than a lieutenant colonel. So we are both aspiring (pp. 435–6).

Korn, Cathcart and many of the other characters have woven self-interest into the fabric of their military lives and elevated it to a moral principle — into, that is, something to believe in. For them, the war has simply become an occasion for the pursuit of their all-too-American dreams.

Only Yossarian resists this higher calling, and in so doing generates moral tension between himself and virtually all of the other characters — particularly Lt. Milo Minderbinder, who is the supreme practitioner of the art of expedient self-interest. Indeed, Milo inflates self-interest beyond moral principle — transforming it into an autonomous hierarchy of power and authority within the military with Milo at the top. Paradoxically, Heller initially represents both Yossarian and Milo as masters of expedient self-interest and thus as guys who seem to speak the same language. As it turns out, their commitments to expedient action could hardly be more dramatically different — thus prefiguring Yossarian's abandonment of expediency at the end of the novel.

The expediency of Milo Minderbinder — formerly a pilot and currently a supremely enterprising mess officer — is 100 per cent *predatory* and Milo's unswerving allegiance is to possessive individualism.[29]

> Milo had a long, thin nose with sniffing, damp nostrils heading off to right, always pointing away from where the rest of him was looking. It was the face of a man of hardened integrity who could no more consciously violate moral principles on which his virtue rested than he could transform himself into a despicable toad. One of these moral principles was that it was never a sin to charge as much as the traffic would bear (p. 73).

Au contraire, one is tempted to add. The sin would be not to do so.

Milo's transgressions, all in pursuit of profit, range from the trivial to the grandiose and from relatively harmless to decisively lethal. He begins small, and arguably harmlessly, by using military aircraft to gather produce and other comestibles from around the Mediterranean to improve the fare he serves in his mess halls. From this humble beginning, he proceeds to build a massive syndicate that not only buys and sells commodities but even contracts for military action. Along the way, he purloins medical morphine and CO_2 canisters from life vests and puts them to more profitable use. Moreover, the syndicate's buying and selling includes both the Allies and the Axis.

When the syndicate runs into financial problems, Milo contracts with the Germans to use American airplanes to bomb his own base.

> Milo's planes separated in a well-coordinated attack and bombed the fuel stocks and the ordinance dump, the repair hangars and the B-25 bombers resting on the lollipop-shaped hardstands at the field. His crews spared the landing strip and the mess halls so they could land safely when their work was done and enjoy a hot snack before retiring (p. 267).

This is *almost* Milo's undoing.

> Decent people everywhere were affronted, and Milo was all washed up until he opened his books to the public and disclosed the tremendous profit he had made. He could reimburse the government for the people and property he had destroyed and still have enough money left over to continue buying Egyptian cotton. Everybody, of course, owned a share (p. 269).

As Milo never tired of reminding anyone who questioned his practices, "What's good for M & M Enterprises is good for the country" (p. 446).[30] To Milo, who would like nothing better than to "see the government get out of war altogether and leave the whole field to private industry" (p. 269), the syndicate is market democracy at its very best.

Yossarian is also committed to expedient self-interest. He wants out of the war and does everything he can to get himself returned to the United States as soon as possible — without any detouring through the Pacific theatre of operations. His obsession with survival leads Yossarian to engage in all manner of transparent subterfuge to be declared unfit for combat — all to no avail. The novel opens with Yossarian in the hospital feigning a liver ailment. Subsequently, he exhibits various kinds of bizarre behavior in an effort to be declared certifiably insane. When he finally refuses to fly any more bombing missions, Major Danby accuses him of putting squadron morale in jeopardy.

> "The country's not in danger anymore, but I am . . .
> Major Danby replied indulgently with a superior smile, "But Yossarian, suppose everyone felt that way."
> "Then I'd certainly be a damned fool to feel any other way, wouldn't I?" (p. 456).

Yossarian is self-interested, but whereas Milo seeks wealth and power, Yossarian wants only to survive.[31]

In addition, Yossarian, virtually alone among the characters in this book, is aghast at the destructiveness of war and is appalled by the suffering and death of his fellow flyers and even of those upon whom his bombs fall. One of the few truly tragic scenes of suffering in this novel occurs when Yossarian witnesses and, indeed, unwittingly contributes to, the death of Snowden during a bombing mission (pp. 449–50). This experience continues to haunt Yossarian throughout the novel.

Eventually, Yossarian comes to understand a deeper and distinctly late-modern lesson of the war.

> Every victim was a culprit, every culprit a victim, and somebody had to stand up sometime to try to break the lousy chain of inherited habit that was imperiling them all (pp. 415–16).

It is this understanding that gives Yossarian the strength to turn away from his own self-interest. His refusal to fly finally gets the attention of his superiors who, fearing that others will take their cues from Yossarian, offer to send him home a hero. "We're going to promote you to major and even give you another medal . . . You'll live like a millionaire. Everyone will lionize you" (p. 437).

But the offer has a catch, catch 22. Yossarian must promise to like Colonel Cathcart and Lt. Colonel Korn (who devised the scheme) and not to denounce them when he is back in the United States. Yossarian realizes that to do so is, in effect, to betray his fellow flyers.

> "That's a pretty scummy trick I'd be playing on the men in the squadron, isn't it?"
>
> "Odious," Colonel Korn agreed amiably . . .
>
> "But what the hell!" Yossarian exclaimed. "If they don't want to fly more missions, let them stand up and do something about it the way I did. Right?"
>
> "Of course," said Colonel Korn.
>
> "There's no reason I have to risk my life for them is there?"
>
> "Of course, not."
>
> Yossarian arrived at his decision with a swift grin. "It's a deal!" he announced jubilantly (p. 418).

When all is said and done, however, Yossarian cannot go through with it, as he tells the Chaplain. "Christ, Chaplain! Can you imagine that for a sin? Saving Colonel Cathcart's life! That's the one crime, I don't want on my record" (p. 445). The novel ends with Yossarian striking out on his own for Sweden from the Mediterranean island where the squadron is based.

Note that Heller, like Vonnegut, contributes black humor, the problematizing of mental illness and a non-linear narrative to the late-modern anti-war novel. What then, if anything, is distinctive about *Catch 22*?[32] *Catch 22* is not strictly speaking an anti-war novel. True, it is anti-war and its setting is a dysfunctional bomber unit in the closing days of the Second World War. However, the anti-war message is ancillary to a critique of America's obsessive materialism. In choosing war as the lens through which to view this obsession, *Catch 22* reveals as much about America as about war.

The book stands as a warning that the wartime military is almost entirely untethered to the constraints associated with the ideals of civil society. Possessive individualism unchained. An Hobbesian state of nature. Civil society without a social contract. From this perspective the wartime military serves as a kind of hyper-microcosm, which reveals Americans at their worst who are under the all too plausible delusion that they represent America at its best. Total war thus becomes rather like the canary in the mine, an indicator of where the country is headed if its self-centered obsession with material acquisition and upward social mobility is not reined in.

Of course, each of the novels in this chapter is critical of life on the home front to a greater or lesser degree. But not even Vonnegut goes so far as Heller, who completes a turn of 180 degrees from the predominant anti-war vision of civil society as a refuge from the madness of war, to total war as a metaphor for America's fragmented and unstable version of civil society.

3. Conclusions

This chapter traces the transformation of the anti-war novel over the course of the twentieth century from a primarily pacifist critique of total war to a broad assault on the pathologies of modernity. In the early part of the century, anti-war novels focused almost exclusively on the human costs of total war, with only incidental attention to the politics that make total war possible and to the irony of modern technology being diverted from peaceful progress to destructive warfare. Insofar as politics does intrude, the message is unequivocally populist, a tale of the rich and the powerful using war to feather their own nests and doing so at the expense of soldiers, workers and society's dispossessed.

During the latter part of the century, politics intrudes ever more insistently into, and finally eclipses, war in these anti-war novels. Nor are their politics populist. What emerges instead are late-modern politics defined by a blurring of the lines between victims and victimizers, war and peace and, most tellingly, between reason and madness. As this happens, assessing blame becomes much more problematic, and the home front is transformed bit by bit from a secure refuge from the insanity of total war into the source of that insanity. Among the novelists considered in this chapter, while only Heller identifies civil society (rather than total war) with madness, Barker certainly moves us in that direction.

Madness is the essential metaphor for infusing the late-modern paradox into the fabric of the post-World War II novels. On the one hand, madness and political agency are intrinsically at odds with one another. On the other hand, the madness that constitutes total war is attributed to the perverse rationality and treacherous technology of modernity.

The populist paradigm

The pacifist narrative of populist anti-war novels is rather simple and straightforward. These novels are overwhelmingly about the hell of war with the home front providing counterpoint. Remarque is acutely attuned to the sense of alienation that separates combatants from those on the home front who do not and cannot fully appreciate the hell of war. But the overwhelming yearning of his alienated combatants is to return to the normalcy of a peacetime existence. They hope that this will somehow be possible, despite the afflictions visited upon them by their descent into the hell of war.

The populist political narrative found at the margins of these novels is equally direct and uncomplicated. The rich and the powerful are portrayed as villains who are responsible for, and profit from, the war while its costs are borne by soldiers in the trenches and the working class on the home front. Indeed, Dalton Trumbo's *Johnny Got His Gun* concludes with the message that peace is a corollary of democracy and, therefore, that war thrives when democracy is allowed to deteriorate. With the possible exception of Joe in *Johnny Got His Gun*, none of the characters in these novels see themselves as political actors in a populist drama. They are instead hapless victims of a war that has enveloped and disempowered them. In short, while political agency is implied by political populism, these novels are not really about politics or agency but about war.

The late-modern paradigm

Barker's *Regeneration* may seem, at first glance, largely indistinguishable from pacifist novels of the earlier era. Surely, all of her characters find their wartime experiences abhorrent and yearn for the normalcy of a peacetime life. However, Barker takes us well beyond an anecdotal critique of the modern project gone wrong into a penetrating inquiry that is a first step towards using a tale of total war to destabilize the boundary between sanity and insanity. The real insanity, she reveals, is to be found among those who precipitate war and fight it so stupidly and wastefully, not among those who are unable to bear the unbearable afflictions visited upon them. In addition, Barker reveals that professional knowledge, a cornerstone of the modern project, does at least as much to suppress agency as to liberate it. In effect, all of the characters, whatever their level of insight, are victims of their circumstances, not masters of their fates.

Like Barker, Vonnegut exposes knowledge as betrayal in the context of total war. The mission to eradicate Dresden, a city that encapsulated the best of Enlightenment beauty and whose residents were no threat whatsoever, is modern technology run amok — running roughshod over common sense and over the received beauty of Western culture.[33] Then the Allied authorities added insult to injury by their self-righteous efforts to justify the unjustifiable. "I deeply regret that British and U.S. bombers killed 135,000 people in the attack on Dresden, but I remember who started the last war and I regret even more the loss of more than 5,000,000 Allied lives in the necessary effort to completely defeat and utterly destroy Nazism" (pp. 186–7).[34] Consider also the use of flamethrowers in an effort to *purify* the desecration of the "corpse mines" (p. 214). This is not simply fighting fire with fire but literally weapons technology consuming itself.

Vonnegut thus replicates and parodies the more straightforward anti-war themes of Remarque, Trumbo and Barker. *Slaughterhouse* invokes the horrors of Dresden, not simply to drive home the costs of total war or to shake the reader's complacency, as did Remarque and Trumbo. Unlike Barker, Vonnegut does not only convey the unspeakable experiences which were repressed by combatants. He also associates the carnage of the firebombing with the irrationality of the hyper-rational underpinnings of total war and with the conventional pieties of the home front. If Barker destabilizes the boundary between sanity and insanity, Vonnegut obliterates it and does similar violence to the boundary between war and peace. Barker believes that the madness engendered by total war is redolent of contradiction and ambiguity, which Rivers clarifies only through a mighty effort of intellect and empathy. Vonnegut, in contrast, exposes total war itself as unambiguously mad and so intrinsically contradictory that it is comprehensible only through parody.

Vonnegut is, therefore, much more subversive — but not as subversive as Heller, who also locates the roots of total war's madness in the fabric of everyday life in the United States. For Vonnegut the madness of civil society is bound up in its failure to comprehend the horrors of total war. His beef is with a civil society which is cocooned, self-absorbed and incapable of taking stock of itself. Still, total war is the target for him, as for Barker. They both associate madness with the inescapable tyrannies of total war.

Heller's critique of America cuts more deeply and is developed more systematically, and its message is that American society is mad in the sense that it is pathologically depraved. It is not, in other words, the madness of total war that drives Heller's narrative, but America's own intrinsic idiocies. All of Heller's characters may be seen as certifiably mad and/or absolutely sane.

- They are certifiably mad if the reader chooses to understand the tyranny of total war as the novel's center of gravity. Over and over again, Heller reveals officers and enlisted personnel, combatants and noncombatants, commanders and subordinates acting in ways that are self-defeating in military terms. And when, every once and a while, a militarily successful effort does occur, it is more by accident than by intent.
- On the other hand, everyone's behavior is readily explicable and altogether constructive if total war is transformed from an unmitigated disaster punctuated by occasional moments of honor

into a terrain of unlimited material opportunity unfortunately dogged by the messy and the destructive.

Clearly, Heller's characters are not corrupted by war, but bring their corruption with them. To make matters worse, they identify their corruption with the moral imperative of material acquisition and upward mobility which is enshrined in American culture. In this sense, *Catch 22* is best seen as an anti-war novel in which the war, as such, is incidental.

It is important to understand that the construction of the late-modern, anti-war novel is an evolutionary process that proceeds unevenly and episodically through the course of the twentieth century. The progression from the heroic to the populist and the late-modern is comprised of tendencies that bleed into and draw sustenance from one another. Novelists both anticipate sea changes in anti-war sensibilities and cling to the vestiges of earlier understandings. What stands out in this otherwise amorphous process is an ever-increasing disillusionment with the promises and the values of modernity, which begin as ironic counterpoint to the destructive follies of total war and end as their cause. Either way, total war is identified with the progressive destruction of political agency, thus giving rise to political novels which bear witness to political estrangement.

3   The Alchemy of Catastrophe: Seeking Spiritual Solace in the Ashes of the Holocaust

> Redemption through cataclysm: what had once been transformed might be transformed again.
>
> Anne Michaels[1]

The tragedy of the Holocaust could easily have led Jews to renounce their faith and the God that had chosen and then abandoned them. As the narrator of Primo Levi's *If Not Now, When?* puts it:

> And the Holy One, blessed be He, why is he hiding behind the gray clouds of Polessia instead of succoring His people? 'You have chosen us among the nations': why us, exactly? Why do the wicked prosper, why are the helpless slaughtered, why are there hunger, mass graves, typhus, and SS flamethrowers into holes crammed with terrified children? And why must Hungarians, Poles, Ukrainians, Lithuanians, Tartars rob and murder the Jews, tear the last weapons from their hands, instead of joining with them against the common enemy? (p. 92).

In retrospect, however, the post-Holocaust twentieth century was not about renunciation, but about revival. Jews returned, and continue to return, to their religious roots. Has this revival occurred despite, or because of, the Holocaust? Whatever historians and social theorists may say, novelists, frequently victims themselves, reveal the Holocaust as a spiritual catalyst by penetrating the emotional core of this transformation of consciousness.

To do so, they focus on the hazards of assimilation* and on the

---

* The hazards of assimilation are portrayed over and over again in these novels and in much the same terms. Critics of this perspective, and there are many, argue that to focus on assimilated Jews led astray by the worldly rewards of assimilation is to blame and stigmatize the victim. Perhaps so. But to portray the hazards of

nullification of Jewish citizenship in Germany — a Germany that had been widely viewed as the beacon of Enlightenment values and cultural achievement. Germany had taken the lead in granting full citizenship to Jews and had incorporated them into virtually all facets of German life. Well after the fact, social theorists discerned that assimilation was the problem, not the solution. Germans felt endangered by Jews who were insinuating themselves into German life and threatening to undermine it from the inside.[2] Paradoxically, the unassimilated Jews, mostly from Eastern Europe, who maintained their traditions, were not the primary targets of the most rabid of German anti-Semites. They were unwelcome because they were different and were, therefore, the victims of discrimination and humiliation. But precisely because they were readily distinguishable, they were deemed much less subversive of German values.

Novelists were a little faster off the mark, with Aharon Appelfeld's *Badenheim 1939* laying bare the compelling allure of self-deluding and divisive misperceptions of the assimilated Jews. He portrays assimilated Jews thinking of their non-assimilated fellow Jews as reminders of Jewish difference and, thus, as a cause of lingering anti-Semitism. In addition, assimilated Jews are portrayed as thinking of their ascribed citizenship as reliable protection against the rising tide of anti-Semitism fomented and exploited by the Nazis. Both Appelfeld and Imre Kertesz offer poignant and exasperating depictions of assimilated victims of the Holocaust who, even after being caught in its tentacles, failed to appreciate what was happening to them

The novels also portray and validate the gravitational force of *the spiritual* as a life-affirming alternative to the toxic nihilism and wretched sense of betrayal and deprivation that were hallmarks of the Holocaust. In constructing narratives of life from the detritus of death, these novels both anticipate and make expressive sense out of the revival of Jewish faith in the post-Holocaust world — but secular, as well as religious spirituality, are represented as sources of solace, even of redemption. Either way, these novels turn their backs on political engagement, which is not deemed relevant to the search for peace of mind in the aftermath of the Holocaust — nor for that matter to preventing a reemergence of the climate of fear and hatred on which it preyed.

With all that said, a disclaimer is in order before going on. My inquiry is confined to eight novels — works by Imre Kertesz, Elie Wiesel, Anne Michaels, Jurek Becker, Thane Rosenbaum, Ian MacMillan and (two by)

---

assimilation need not be invidious or judgmental but rather a window into its existential dilemmas.

Aharon Appelfeld. This is, of course, only a tiny fraction of the veritable tidal wave of Holocaust novels.[3] I make no claims about the applicability of my interpretations to the Holocaust literature as a whole, nor about the literary superiority of the novels that I have selected.[4] They are, however, written by widely acknowledged masters of Holocaust literature. It is, therefore, reasonable to infer that their rejection of democratic politics and embrace of a spiritual awakening are within the mainstream rather than at the margins of Holocaust literature.

We will now turn to a three-stage account of the Holocaust: its degrading prelude, its dehumanizing core, and its doleful and relentless aftermath and spiritual legacy. Woven through the literary accounts of these three stages are themes that arise and are pursued, albeit unevenly, in each of the novels. Rather surprisingly, these novels do not look beneath the surface for the causes of the Holocaust. They settle for attributing it to anti-Semitism without providing any insight into the transformation of anti-Semitism in 1930s and 1940s Germany from its traditional crusades to convert, expel or assault Jews, into genocide. Post-World War II German literature does tackle these issues, which will be taken up in Chapter 4.

1. At the Threshold: the Eradication of Jewish Citizenship

Novelists certainly were not the first to call attention to the incremental expropriation of Jewish citizenship by the Nazis. Novelists have, however, provided access to the *emotional subjection of Jewish consciousness* as rights were transformed into privileges, as these privileges were withdrawn, and as ultimately Jewish civil existence was extinguished. Aharon Appelfeld's haunted and biting allegory, *Badenheim 1939*, indelibly captures the painful and poignant disempowerment of confidently assimilated Jewish citizens.[5] In contrast, Jurek Becker's *Jacob the Liar* reveals with affection and mordant humor the spiritual resources available to Jews who are in emotional touch with the ancient injuries of anti-Semitism: ghettoes, expulsions, pogroms and countless other indignities.

Badenheim 1939

> *And the people were sucked in . . . Nevertheless Dr. Pappenheim found time to make the following remark: 'If the coaches are so dirty it must mean that we have not far to go.'*[6]

Aharon Appelfeld provides an allegorical evocation of the plight of the assimilated Jewish bourgeoisie — most of them with effete cultural pretensions. They have gathered at the Badenheim spa in the spring of 1939 for the annual music festival produced by the self-important impresario, Dr. Pappenheim. The reader, fully aware of what is about to befall Jews, understands from the outset that 1939 is going to be different from all other years. The characters, on the other hand, are oblivious to their fate and also, as things begin to go awry, blind to what is happening to them.

OMENS

The early portion of the novel is imbued with the hopes and expectations of spring. We are treated with more than a modicum of irony to an excursion through the discreet charms and petty concerns of the bourgeoisie. "Hammocks went up in the gardens and nets in the tennis courts. People took off their winter clothes and put on sport shirts" (p. 24). The pastry shop with its irresistible delicacies, the transitory comforts of alcohol, and the intoxications of springtime in Badenheim all conspire to provide the visitors welcome respite from the rigors of the urban, work-ridden, winter world.

> Such was the spring in Badenheim. There was a secret intoxication in the air. Respectable businessmen did not bring their wives here, but anyone who had breathed the air and been infected could not keep away (p. 21).

Thus, the attractions of Badenheim are not simply liberating but intoxicating, disreputable and, more ominously, *infected*.

At the same time, for those who provide for the visitors — whether with cultural diversion, as does Dr. Pappenheim, or with temptations served up in the pastry shops and cafes — Badenheim is about striving for status, about making a living, and the like. There is labor strife between the impresario, Pappenheim, and his musicians as well as the owner of the pastry shop and his baker. Pappenheim is haunted by worries that his distinguished musical artists and literary figures will not show up — thus jeopardizing his career ambitions to put the Badenheim festival on the cultural map of Europe. The matter of overindulgence — financial, nutritional and even sexual — becomes an ever-growing problem (p. 35).

More portentously, we are made increasingly aware of two fundamentally discordant developments looming behind the pleasures and anxieties of the bourgeoisie. Most threatening is the increasingly intrusive role of the Sanitation Department, which takes on ever more anti-Semitic overtones. At the outset, its responsibility is to make certain that the "sewage" system is ready for the influx of visitors. But then comes the order that all Jews must register (p. 32). Still more definitively, the Sanitation

Department office takes on the trappings of a travel agency with posters extolling the attractions of Poland and of work:

> Labor Is Our Life . . . The Air In Poland is Fresher . . . Sail on the Vistula . . . The Development Areas Need You . . . Get to Know the Slavic Culture (p. 43).

These developments follow an altogether predictable path: closing off entry and exit from the city; confining life "to the hotel, the pastry shop and the swimming pool" (p. 55); shutting off the water and thus depriving hotel guests of the swimming pool; and so on through the arrival of dispossessed Jews (pp. 121–2) — all eventuating in the final deportation.

NARRATIVES OF DENIAL AND CLASS

These developments are not, however, comprehensible to the Jews of Badenheim, whose sense of their own trajectory is obscured by a mélange of competing, contradictory and ultimately irrelevant misconceptions. These misconceptions are rooted in the widely acknowledged and entirely uncontested social hierarchy of Badenheim. The so-called *Ostjuden* have not yet been able to shed the stigma of their Polish-Jewish origins, albeit not for want of trying. They are painfully aware of their déclassé status and strive for acceptance among their social betters. The assimilated Jews, and especially those with aristocratic connections and pretensions, feel secure in their status and therefore can afford to be unobtrusively, rather than overtly, contemptuous of the *Ostjuden* among them. As the summer wears on, however, things begin to go terribly and unmistakably wrong. As problems multiply, the Badenheimers and their vacationing visitors cling ever more desperately to the false promise of assimilation.

The assimilated Germans become increasingly determined to underscore the social distance separating them from *Ostjuden*. They reassure themselves of their status by disassociating publicly from the *Ostjuden* "riffraff" (p. 61). But they are also reminded of their own precarious position. We learn, for example, that Frau Zauberblit is the former Frau General von Schmidt and that the separation from her husband was occasioned in part by his distaste for Badenheim: its people and its diversions. Now in the spring of 1939 their daughter, resplendent in the Aryan features inherited from her father, comes to get Frau Zauberblit to sign a document renouncing her maternal rights (p. 48).

Still, the assimilated doggedly cling to their hollowed-out civil and social identities. They balk at registering for the impending journey to Poland with assertive proclamations of their own unimpeachable credentials. Thus, when Frau Milbaum queries Dr. Langmann about registering, he declares that he is getting out of Badenheim *on his own*.

"I still regard myself as a free Austrian citizen. Let them send the Polish Jews to Poland; they deserve their country. I landed in this mess by mistake. Can't a man make an occasional mistake?" (p. 61).

The answer to that question is clearly no and, more to the point, that there has not been a mistake.

The unassimilated *Ostjuden* are more sensitive to the implications of their shrinking civil status. Consider the pharmacist's wife, Trude, who senses peril well before it becomes even vaguely apparent to the others. Her husband Martin believes she is emotionally distressed because of their daughter Helena's ill-advised marriage and subsequent departure from Badenheim. But he also is dismissive of her angst which he attributes to her outmoded upbringing in the "mountains among the Jews . . . She was haunted by a hidden fear, not her own, and Martin felt that he was becoming infected by her hallucinations" (p. 17). Of course, Martin's fear of infection indicates just how thin is the veneer protecting the assimilated bourgeoisie and foretells how quickly it will break down.

INVERSION OF THE SOCIAL ORDER

This brings us to the heart of Appelfeld's allegory: the social convulsion wrought by the increasingly heavy hand of the Sanitation Department — a convulsion which turns the social hierarchy on its head while at the same time leading to a desperate and *unconvincing* revival of Judaism. While the unassimilated *Ostjuden* are the first to sense danger, they quickly proceed to develop their own narrative of denial. They romanticize the lives that they left behind in search of the fruits of assimilation and a civil existence. Consider the reflections of one of the band members, Leon Samitzsky.

Fifty years ago, when he was a child, his parents had emigrated from Poland. He remembered the scenes of his childhood with a surreptitious affection (p. 19).

As Samitzsky and other *Ostjuden* become increasingly and self-consciously Jewish, they begin to rationalize Poland more as an opportunity than as a threat.* They wax poetic about their Polish roots and paint idealized

---

* This conceit is both echoed and reinflected in Kertesz's *Fateless*, in which the teenage narrator, Georg, gullibly volunteers for transport to the east in return for the promise

pictures of life in the self-same Poland from which their parents fled in search of citizenship and to escape pogroms.

As they begin to make a virtue out of the impending necessity of a return to Poland, the indicia of social status are scrambled. The assimilated, to all intents and purposes "goyim," risk being left behind. And for those "goyim" who might somehow wangle a passage to Poland, there is the fear of not fitting into the newly enticing milieu of Jewish Poland. Accordingly, there is a rush to learn more about, and to embrace, Judaic culture, the Jewish religion and the Yiddish language. They even go so far as to reclaim a long-forgotten rabbi who has been languishing in poverty without a congregation. They celebrate his wisdom and his inspiring spirituality. In short, by the end of the novel, things have come full circle. The Jews of Badenheim, especially the scorned *Ostjuden*, come to embrace Judaism and Judaica as the only available source of solace and perhaps of salvation. Eventually, many of the assimilated begin to come around — thus, in effect, inverting the social order.

These death-bed conversions are portrayed as opportunistic, shallow and amounting to no more than a reformulated discourse of denial.[7] This is particularly true among the assimilated Jews. The distracted intellectual, Professor Fussholdt, who had scorned Herzl and Buber while praising the satiric and thinly veiled anti-Semitic writing of Karl Krauss (pp. 80–1), works obsessively through the night prior to deportation to complete his magnum opus in which he details "his hostility to everything considered Jewish culture, Jewish art . . ." (pp. 168–9). Professor Fussholdt's wife, Mitzi, prepares for the journey by applying makeup. At the railway station, Dr. Langmann buys the financial weekly and the traveling salesman Salo advises the musicians that, like him, they should submit "form 101," claiming travel expenses from their employer. Others chat about invoking their pension rights in Poland or look forward to their arrival in Warsaw where they can get the morning coffee that their early departure has meant foregoing (pp. 158, 159 and 169–73).

But the novel also celebrates the spiritual resources of Judaism and contrasts this spirituality with the material gratifications, the empty promises, and precarious status of citizenship in the modern, secular state. Beyond all the rationalizing and the denial, there are glimpses of the solace offered by a return to the religious and cultural traditions of Judaism. The mere act of registering as a Jew brings an end to Trudy's hallucinations. When Martin returns from registering them both as Jews, Trudy "looked at him

---

of good work provided by, and under the efficient and industrious supervision of, Germans.

with eyes full of affection, as if he had brought a message from a different world" (p. 79).[8]

It seems reasonable, therefore, to infer that *Badenheim 1939* provides a glimpse of a paradox which runs through the Holocaust novels — namely, that Nazi oppression brings Jews together as Jews. Insofar as that is the case, it would seem to lend credence to Sartre's controversial proposition that in the modern world there would be no Jews without anti-Semites.[9] Still, the emotional landscape of Badenheim is dominated by the reflexive resistance of assimilated Jews to the spiritual rewards of Judaism. The allure and staying power of assimilation becomes so deeply engrained that an authentic reengagement with religion is at best contingent. In Sicher's words: "Assimilation has brought loss of cultural identity, apostasy, exogamy, and self-hatred."[10]

Thus, *Badenheim 1939* becomes a cautionary tale. Belief in the safety of citizenship leads inexorably to a poisonous and resistant denial that neutralizes even the most unequivocal omens of civic dispossession. Nothing makes this clearer than the novel's concluding comment by the narcissistic impresario Pappenheim. Upon observing the appalling conditions in the railway car they are about to board, he declares: "If the coaches are so dirty it must mean that we have not far to go" (p. 175).

Jacob the Liar

We are heading for wherever we are heading.[11]

Consider, to begin with, the opening episode of Jurek Becker's novel that turns Jacob into a liar. For reasons almost entirely beyond Jacob's control, he finds himself caught up in a potentially disastrous prank devised by a watchtower guard. The Nazis have imposed an 8 p.m. curfew on ghetto dwellers. Jacob certainly has no intention of breaking the curfew. Indeed, has he broken the curfew? Jacob cannot know, because ghetto residents are denied access to any kind of timepiece. According to the tower guard who freezes Jacob in a spotlight, he has indeed violated the curfew. The guard orders a terrified Jacob to report to the military office.

What you do now is go in there and report to the duty officer. You tell him that you were out on the street after eight o'clock, and you ask him for a well-deserved punishment (p. 4).

Once inside the military office Jacob discovers among other things that it is only 7:36. The duty officer, who is napping when Jacob arrives, is not about to be further inconvenienced by cooking up a punishment for a non-existent crime.

Jacob sees his vindication, if that's what it is, as something of a miracle, because "above all he knows that the chances of a Jew leaving this building alive are very poor. To this day, no such case has ever been heard of" (p. 5). Not only does he depart with impunity, he overhears a radio broadcast which provides remarkably good news — namely that the Russian forces have advanced to within 250 miles of the ghetto. But these ostensible blessings are transmuted into, so to speak, the cross that Jacob bears throughout the remainder of the novel.

Jacob is eager to share the good news of the approaching Russian army and immediately does so — but only with his two deceased and long absent roommates. Jacob knows better than to let the cat any further out of the bag at his workplace.

> It would be wonderful if they already knew about it without him, if they had met him with the news . . . He would have rejoiced with them . . . But as soon as Jacob arrived at the freight yard he realized that . . . [t]he lucky break hadn't happened; . . . two lucky breaks in such a short time can only happen to Rockefeller on a Sunday (p. 18).

Circumstances, however, "force" Jacob to reveal the Russian advance to his fellow slave-laborer, Mischa — and to do so with a lie — *the lie*: "I have a radio" (p. 23).

Why does Jacob tell about the Russian advance and, above all, why does he do so with a lie? It's all because of potatoes. Mischa decides to steal potatoes from a freight car even though he is virtually certain to be caught out by the guards. In his desperate effort to distract Mischa, Jacob blurts out the whole story of the guard and the military office — a tale so unlikely that Mischa ignores what Jacob has to say and continues to be fixated by the potatoes.

> Here you overcome all your scruples, ignore all the rules of caution and all your misgivings, for which there are reasons enough, you carefully choose a blue-eyed young idiot to confide in, and what does that snot-nose do? He doesn't believe you (p. 21).

Only when Jacob invents a secret radio does the story become sufficiently plausible to capture Mischa's attention, divert him from the potatoes and focus him on the impending liberation.

Jacob has resolved one problem but, as he quickly realizes, at the cost of mortgaging whatever future he may have.

> He is angrier than ever. He has been forced to launch irresponsible claims, and it's that ignorant idiot who forced him, just because he didn't believe him, because he suddenly had a craving for potatoes . . . "Pull yourself together and get up. And above all, keep your trap shut. You know what that means, a radio in the ghetto. Not a soul must find out about it" (p. 23–4).

So Jacob's lie succeeds where the truth fails him. This same sequence of truth being overwhelmed by invention plays out over and over again. An ever-expanding web of lies is incorporated into the culture of the ghetto with unpredictable and lethal consequences. As Sanders Gilman puts it: "The world of whole-ness, of the normal, is recreated in the lies of Jacob, but they are lies that he consciously knows will ameliorate the world in which he and the child find themselves."[12]

Jacob is driven to distraction as he is constantly besieged for news which he does not have and that he finds himself ever less able to invent.[*] He tries to extricate himself from his newsless predicament. However, when he declares that "the radio is dead" (p. 96), Kowalski scours the ghetto and comes up with a radio repairman.

> An insane rage toward Kowalski almost chokes Jacob. Trying to play God, this cretin of a friend arranges for repairs without the vaguest idea of their extent and . . . expects you to feel grateful to him for his enterprising efforts (p. 130).[†]

---

[*] In search of news he enters an outhouse reserved for Germans, because a soldier has gone in with a newspaper and left without it. Unhappily, the newspaper has been torn into squares for obvious outhouse-related purposes and there are no pages left intact or any news about the Eastern Front. If not for a diversion created by Kowalski, who is beaten by one of the guards, Jacob's trespass would have been discovered. Kowalski's seemingly selfless act is not about friendship, nor is it selfless. Indeed, he is angry because he is convinced that Jacob's only goal was "a high class shit" (p. 90). Kowalski's intervention is all about the hidden radio.

[†] But of course Jacob himself is playing God, albeit with ever-flagging enthusiasm. When Lina, a young orphan that Jacob has taken under his wing, accidentally finds out about the radio, Jacob creates an elaborate charade in the cellar in which he becomes the radio — concealed from Lina behind a partition. His "broadcasts" include a fairy tale, a brass band and of course the news. Among the choice reports that he airs (in "a high voice") is Churchill reassuring the radio audience that: "I am firmly convinced that the whole shlimazl will soon be over, in another few weeks at most" (p. 140).

To head off the repairman Jacob is forced to bring the radio back to life, with the result that he is once again besieged by queries.

Jacob's predicament and his reportage underscore the resilience of the ghetto. Even the disembodied imminence of liberation by the Red Army revives ghetto morale — imparting a future to those who had despaired of having one. The narrator, who seldom intervenes, allows himself to celebrate the irresistible allure of the future's bittersweet promise. "I am already wild with joy and can think of nothing else. Everything I once owned will belong to me again except Hannah [his wife], who was executed" (p. 54). Even Jacob, who invents the front, begins to imagine the postwar years when he will be able to adopt Lina, the eight-year-old orphan for whom he has cared and with whom a deep bond has developed. "He can see difficult times ahead. As a child she is already eight years old, and as a father I am barely two" (p. 66).

Others are similarly moved. Consider, for example, the eminent Dr. Kirschbaum who fears that the Germans will get wind of Jacob's radio and take it out on everyone. He drops in on Jacob to convince him to abandon the radio, but leaves persuaded by Jacob that the radio reports have breathed new life into the ghetto.

> "And even if I tell people a thousand times, the Russians won't alter their route. But I would like to draw your attention to one further detail. Since the news has been passed around the ghetto, I have not heard of a single suicide. Have you?"
>
> At that Kirschbaum looks astonished and says: "You're right!"
>
> "And before that there were many, nobody knows that better than you. I can remember your being called on many occasions, and usually it was too late."
>
> "Why didn't I notice that?" Kirschbaum asks (p. 166) and then departs.*

---

* The "assimilinski" (p. 110) are ancillary to *Jacob the Liar* although the narrator muses about the assimilated Dr. Kirschbaum, who asks: "What does it mean, of Jewish origin? They force you to be a Jew while you yourself have no idea what it really is. Now he is surrounded only by Jews, for the first time in his life nothing but Jews. He has wracked his brains about them. Wanting to find out what it is that they all have in common in vain. They have nothing recognizably in common, and he most certainly nothing with them" (pp. 64–5). However, when Dr. Kirschbaum is called in to treat the infamous camp commandant, he arguably goes, not as a doctor, but as a Jew — or at least as anti-Nazi. Escorted by two German S.S. officials to the commandant's home, his "exit from the car proceeds in a surprising manner: sliding unhurriedly toward Preuss [one of the S.S. officers], he falls out of the car onto the neglected ground" (p. 176) — having taken a lethal dose of "heartburn" medication from his black bag during the drive.

However, a variety of unintended and dire consequences also flow from Jacob's news bulletins. Herschel Schtamm is so determined to share the news with a sealed transport of Jews headed for the camps that he ignores the warning of guards to stay away from the boxcars. He is shot and Jacob's head fills with self-reproach — in part because he alone sees the rifle being aimed at Herschel and fails to sound an alarm, but mostly because it was his lie. But if lies can kill, so too can the truth, as Jacob discovers when he finally levels with Kowalski. Kowalski seems to take the news in stride, but on his way to work the next morning Jacob discovers that Kowalski has hanged himself during the night (p. 222).

At the conclusion of the novel, the narrator intervenes one last time to offer two endings, one ironically fulfilling and one indeterminate and tragic. In the former, we come full circle to another, this time fatal, encounter between Jacob and a tower guard. Jacob is riddled by machine gun bullets and dies at the wire which surrounds the ghetto — just an instant before the arrival of the Russian liberators. Of course, this *not*-in-the-nick-of-time liberation is entirely consistent with the law of unintended consequences that dogs Jacob throughout the novel. More to the point, Jacob ends this version of the novel by, in effect, *choosing* to escape or die. He has not blundered into curfew, not allowed himself to be subjected to the guard's torment, and not put himself in the hands of the duty officer. He has made a choice — chosen, that is, to break the curfew and to remove his yellow star before attempting to escape.

The narrator, however, takes away with the left hand what he has given with right. He makes it clear that this is an imagined ending. What really happens is that the narrator, Jacob and Lina, along with all of the others, board the train and allow themselves to "head for wherever we are heading" (p. 243).

While *Jacob the Liar* ends precisely as does *Badenheim 1939*, the two books contrast sharply with one another. Appelfeld tells a parable of the incremental nullification of a privileged citizenship — a tale in which privilege is reconstituted in an increasingly constricted golden ghetto. In so doing, Appelfeld provides a portrait, albeit a caricatured portrait, of the superficial pleasures, the status aspirations and the underlying anxieties of assimilation. In contrast, Becker's gentle and affectionate humor immerses us in the residual resources of traditional Jewish culture.

Becker adopted the narrative technique and tone of the Yiddish narrator. His choice implied a justification of the hope kept alive by Heym, and the vitality of the style may be seen as an expression of the writer's own sense of personal security with his chosen society.[13]

Becker's characters approach the Holocaust seeking hope but without illusions or denial. Despite their suffering, their humanity has not been compromised. They emerge as *menschen*. Conversely, Appelfeld's "assimilinski" seem to have sacrificed their humanity and their emotional well-being on the altar of bourgeois citizenship.

2. Into the Abyss: Living within Genocide

The two novels to be considered now, *Fateless* by Imre Kertesz and Ian McMillan's *Village of a Million Spirits: A Novel of the Treblinka Uprising*, immerse their characters in slave labor and death. These unvarnished accounts of the Holocaust at its excruciating worst become the occasion for asking whether, and if so how, it is possible to sustain a will to live while being worked to death as a cog in the apparatus of extermination.[14] The answers provided are unmistakably secular and share Appelfeld and Becker's misgivings about assimilation.

Fateless

> *The drive to survive makes us accustomed to lying as long as possible about the murderous reality in which we are forced to hold our own, while the drive to remember seduces us into sneaking a certain complacent satisfaction into our reminiscences.*
>
> Imre Kertesz[15]

> *For him Auschwitz is not an exceptional occurrence that like an alien body subsists outside the normal history of Western Europe. It is the ultimate truth about human degradation in modern existence.*
>
> The Swedish Academy[16]

Fateless, like *Badenheim 1939*, reveals how and why assimilation leads Jews to lose their bearings and their judgment — deadening their sense of impending danger. It also becomes apparent that because they are morally and culturally adrift, assimilated Jews are prone to identify with the aggressor. Yet assimilation is not portrayed as sapping the will to survive; this will emerges instead from primordial instincts. Nor is religious faith represented as a source of strength — or for that matter redemption. What remains is a bleak spirituality. The unlikely bearer of this message is Georg Kovacs, a young and utterly clueless Hungarian Jew, who survives the Holocaust despite brief stints in Auschwitz and

Buchenwald and a long stay in the provincial labor camp at Zeitz where he is worked almost to death.

Also as in *Badenheim 1939*, *Fateless* depicts the ways in which assimilation deadens the sense of impending danger.

DENIAL AND RATIONALIZATION

Over and over again, Georg evidences a truly staggering capacity to misunderstand what is happening to him. When he and the other young Jewish workers are removed from the bus taking them to their jobs, he tells us, "the general opinion was that the whole business was a mistake" (p. 33). Accordingly, he and his friends wait in "a pleasant, cool, spacious, rather empty room" (p. 34) and welcome this break from the routine of work. "After all, we weren't wasting *our* time" (p. 35. italics in the original). Even when a guard is ordered to lock up "the whole band of Jews" in the stables, his reaction is not fear or foreboding but astonishment and confusion, partly from the feeling that "I had unexpectedly dropped into the middle of an absurd theatre play" (p. 43).

Nor could Georg see, except "for the fun of it . . . any other reason for trying to escape. I think I had enough time but still my sense of honor proved to be the stronger of the urges" (p. 42). Indeed, he willingly volunteers when told that labor is being recruited to work in Germany and is assured that the first to arrive will get the choice assignments. He imagines this as a travel experience with a good job thrown in — a bit of an adventure. He remains in the dark even after arriving at Auschwitz — observing the prisoners and wondering what they had done to have gotten themselves into such terrible trouble (p. 61). He cannot imagine that he and his would-be fellow workers are in the same boat (p. 58).

Georg's detached curiosity makes him a morally obtuse guide to the darkest recesses of the Holocaust. Georg is adrift, Kertesz seems to say, not primarily because he is a self-absorbed teenager, but because he is a Jew only in the eyes of others — largely as a "function of the yellow star" that Jews are forced to wear (p. 27). Georg, much like the Jewish elite in *Badenheim 1939*, sees *his* otherness as a case of mistaken identity, and he shares the anti-Semitic stereotypes of his captors.

He takes an immediate dislike to the emaciated, Jewish-looking prisoners whom he views as a kind of alien species.

Their faces . . . were not particularly trustworthy: they had widespread ears, protruding noses, and sunken, cunning, tiny little eyes. Indeed they looked like Jews in every respect. I found them suspicious and altogether strange (p. 58).

In contrast, Georg looks with admiration at "the German soldiers, with their green caps, green collars, and eloquent hand movements . . . because they seemed well-cared-for, clean, and neat, and in all this chaos they alone seemed to exude solidity and calm" (p. 59).[17]

His inability to distinguish between form and substance is embedded in, and but one sign of, the moral vacuum that precludes any semblance of a conscience. When an old woman dies of thirst on the train to Auschwitz, Georg rationalizes her death. "[W]e knew that she was sick and old; under these circumstances everyone, myself included, thought that the event was completely understandable" (p. 55). His lack of affect and detachment weathers even the awareness that some of "our fellow travelers were burnt" (p. 81). Still, more portentously, Georg is favorably impressed by the well-organized guile of the selection process — during which the condemned are treated with "care and affection" and put through the same routine as those who are selected as workers (p. 81). He likens this ruse to "the same way that a practical joke must be planned" and concludes that "there could be no question . . . concerning the success of the execution" (p. 82).*

CLINGING TO LIFE

So what is to be learned from this tone-deaf teenage tour guide? Georg certainly personifies the hazards of assimilation and of losing touch with his faith. But shallow though he is and despite his estrangement from Judaism, Georg doggedly clings to life in an utterly hopeless situation. It is true that when things become unbearable, Georg expresses a kind of distracted envy for those who find solace in prayer. "This was the first time I regretted *a little* that I wasn't able — if only for a few phrases — to pray in the language of *the Jews*" (p. 119, italics added). For better or worse, however, faith in prayer is beyond Georg's reach and, indeed, his ken.

FINDING IDENTITY: A SECULAR EPIPHANY

Georg does, however, stumble into a bleak and cryptic secular epiphany when, on his return to Budapest after the war, he struggles, largely in vain, to make his ordeal and his survival comprehensible to those who

---

* So powerful is Georg's inclination to identify with the aggressor that he berates himself for reacting angrily to the trivial affront of having the barber shave off both the hair on his head *and* his newly sprouting pubic hair (p. 70). Much later in the novel when he is weak from hunger and overwork and drops a bag of cement, he is beaten and demeaned as, "Arschloch, Shiesskerl, verfluchter Judehund [asshole, shithead, and damned dog of a Jew]" (p. 125). He scrupulously notes that his assailant was not "an official, authoritative SS person, but . . . a soldier attached to some sort of shady work-supervisory organization" (p. 124).

avoided transport to the camps. His reflections lead him in two seemingly unrelated directions. To begin with, he attributes both his initial jeopardy and his survival to the *steps* he has taken — or more specifically to the steps that others have forced upon him.

> The point is in the steps. Everyone stepped forward as long as he could; I, too, took my steps — not only in the row in Auschwitz but before at home. I stepped forward with my father, with my mother, with Anne-Marie, and — maybe the most difficult step of all — with the older sister. Now I could tell her what it means to be 'a Jew': it had meant nothing for me until the steps began. Now there is no other blood, and there is nothing but" — here I got stuck but then I remembered the words of the newspaper man — 'but given situations and concomitant givens within them'" (p. 188).

It is out of these "given situations and concomitant givens within them" that not just his actions, the steps, but also his identity was formed.

> It wasn't my fate, but I am the one who lived it to the end . . . "Why can't you see that if there is such a thing as fate, then there is no freedom? If, on the other hand . . . there is freedom, then there is no fate. That is . . . we ourselves are fate." I recognized this all of a sudden and with such clarity that I had never seen before (pp. 188–9).

He has not chosen to be a Jew, to be swept up in the Holocaust, nor to survive it. Those choices were made by others, but they now constitute his identity.[18] He was imprisoned as a Jew; he survived as a Jew, and he now accepts and embraces his Jewishness — but as a concomitant given rather than as religious *faith*.

The second element of Georg's secular epiphany grows from a compelling but unwelcome nostalgia for the camps. This is a profoundly troubling sentiment to accept — much less explain to his postwar interlocutors in Budapest. However, when he reflects on the camps, he cannot escape the feeling that, "in a certain sense, life was purer, simpler" (p. 190). He thinks back to a "favorite hour in the camp" and to "everything and everyone . . . especially those whose existence I could validate by my presence here [back in Budapest] . . . And for the first time I now thought of them with a tiny affectionate resentment" (p. 190). In short, Georg realizes that he has emerged from his deprivations and degradations with an identity which he now embraces and which enables him to face the future with hope in his heart — albeit precariously so.

I now know, happiness lies in wait for me like an inevitable trap. Even back there, in the shadow of the chimneys, in the breaks between pain, there was something resembling happiness. Everybody will ask me about the deprivations, the "terrors of the camps," but for me, the happiness will always be the most memorable experience, perhaps. Yes, that's what I'll tell them the next time they ask me: about the happiness in those camps.

   If they ever do ask. And if I don't forget (p. 191).

The implications of these concluding words are both counterintuitive and work at cross-purposes to the other novels considered in this chapter. More typically, the Holocaust is seen as destroying identities: hollowing them out and leaving survivors as empty shells. Of course, there are also cases, we shall see, where survivors are portrayed as angry, resolved, or forgiving, but it is unprecedented and seemingly inexplicable to associate the Holocaust with happiness.

   So, it seems that the Holocaust and the camps can give as well as take — not, I hasten to add, that they *will* give but that they *can* give — and that in Georg's case, and presumably in Kertesz's as well, they *have* given. Sicher, I think, has it just right — identifying "the bliss of inner freedom that cannot be taken away by any totalitarian regime."[19] This observation inextricably links the constituent elements of Georg's epiphany together. He not only discovered his identity in the camps but was able to keep it intact under the most extreme circumstances imaginable. In the final analysis, Kertesz seems to read an absurdist meaning, redolent of Beckett, into the Holocaust.[20] Freedom in the post-Holocaust world — at least the post-Holocaust peoples' democracies of Eastern Europe — is not about agency *in the world* but instead about creating personal refuge *from the world*.

Village of a Million Spirits: A Novel of the Treblinka Uprising
Ian MacMillan's novel begins and ends with the uprising — with the desperate effort of Jews imprisoned in Treblinka to revolt against their slave-masters. However, the uprising is only a shadowy presence through most of MacMillan's narrative. The heart of the book is instead an account of the terrible costs of living with death, and trying to maintain a will to survive in a social order permeated by, and dedicated to, systematic, sadistic and categorical extermination. We view all of this through the experiences of a young prisoner, Janusz Siedlecki, whose story is related by a narrator named David Schrhafta.

LIVING WITH EXTERMINATION

Janusz perseveres by distancing himself as much as possible from his own humanity. He notes with flat affect that the corpses of "children pull apart more readily than adults" (p. 61). But he also second-guesses himself. "[H]is attitude should be some kind of grief, but he does not feel grief. He feels hunger, and thirst, and his skin is irritated with dirt and sour body oil" (p. 59). He experiences grief when he thinks of his siblings and his grandmother who were put to death: "The children are dead, the little babies are dead, and Grandmother — she is dead, and he did not say good-bye to her." Nor can he ever "put it right" (p. 68). Janusz must, therefore, devise ways to numb himself to extermination and to his supporting role in it, but he never succeeds — nor does he really want to.

He cannot shake off the shame of his and his fellow inmates' dependence on the food that trickles down from the incoming transports. They are as downcast as the Germans and the Ukrainian guards when the trains come from the east, because these victims are generally without either food or valuables (p. 121). Conversely, they rejoice when a Nazi officer announces that transports will, after a troubling hiatus, recommence the following day and that they will be bringing in relatively affluent Bulgarian Jews who will arrive "carrying fifty kilograms of personal effects" (p. 172).

> Then, as one, their voices rise in a deafening, exultant cheer . . .
> New transports mean food, valuables, the chance to barter for more time. He [David, the narrator] does not know if the man [he seeks to console] weeps because of shame at the obvious absurdity of their situation or because of relief that he may live a little longer, even if it means the deaths of tens of thousands" (p. 171).

Similarly shameful is Janusz's assignment at the "roast" where disinterred corpses are burned wholesale in an attempt to conceal the crime of the death camps. There he and his fellow workers benefit when all goes well, and the Germans share the leftovers of their celebratory meals — everyone dining more or less together in the referred heat of the roasting pits.

DEATH AND LIFE

Responsibilities at least as gruesome and in need of numbing devices, but not shameful, result from Janusz's promotion from carrying corpses to serving as their dentist (p. 180). His job is to extract gold teeth, and initially he "could barely make himself do it" (p. 191). "He hates the smell of dead people's mouths — it is bad breath squared, he thinks" (p. 190).

He manages to suppress his revulsion in part by inventing "pasts and identities" for his patients:

> This old man was a teacher, feared by his pupils because of the size of his nose and ears and because of the emaciated look of his face — he smoked, drank too much coffee. But all of his pupils, in later years, realize how much they learned from him (p. 195).

He also dreams up sexual lives for them (p. 192) and thus for himself.

> She is buxom and has a chubby attractive face, and he is momentarily captivated by her body, the breasts and the belly with fine hair reflecting the sunlight in tiny amber and gold needles (p. 190).

More importantly, Janusz works out a way that he can, through his dentistry, contribute to the uprising.

> Janusz discovered the possibility of storing the teeth in his mouth and told Dr. Herzenberg. The doctor got a slightly nauseated look on his face, and then agreed that yes, it would be an excellent service to the cause. In pockets the teeth would show and would amount to a death sentence if they were discovered (p. 193).

Dr. Herzenberg then passes the dental gold to the leaders of the uprising who use it to bribe the Ukrainian guards in return for arms and ammunition.

BEARING WITNESS

MacMillan thus attributes Janusz's determination to live to the uprising and his service to it. But MacMillan does not leave it there. We are made to realize that Janusz instinctively understands that if he is to survive emotionally he must do it in concert with others. "You must not be alone here" (p. 120). He is prepared to sacrifice himself for them — not just in scavenging for valuables but in passing on food to others even though it jeopardizes his resistance to the typhoid that is devastating Treblinka (p. 119).

Janusz witnesses his closest friend and fellow prisoner shot and hung by the Germans, because he had pulled too vigorously on the leash of a dog belonging to a loathsome Nazi officer, nicknamed the Doll. Janusz is devastated, but this initial reaction is followed by existential truths.

- "Janusz feels soiled and empty, somehow without organs inside his body . . . [but then] it occurs to him that revolt is valid. He had only thought of whether or not it was possible, but now he realizes that it is also valid" (p 100).

- He also decides that he has been left a legacy. "All these people have been made to vanish from the earth, the reality of their existence wiped away, but for one thing: the presence of one person to see and remember" (p. 101).

He believes that he is being ordered to survive and to bear witness on behalf of Treblinka, "the village of a million spirits."[21] As an older inmate put it, Treblinka was "the most heavily populated quarter-square mile on earth, the only difference being that 95 percent of the people were spirits" (p. 81).

Thus, without religious faith or instruction Janusz crafts a rudimentary but deeply held code of social morality. In so doing, he grows from boy to man. He comes to understand that death "is nothing to be afraid of. He feels as if he has lived almost too long [and] . . . he hates the odious [Nazi officer] Schneck but more than that he pities him" (p. 145).*

ENGAGEMENT, ESTRANGEMENT

Fateless celebrates the heroic perseverance of Janusz Siedleki and through him the possibility, even in the most of hopeless of circumstances, of morally meaningful collective action. Even the sadist Schneck evidences a grudging admiration for the uprising (p. 230) and passes up an opportunity to shoot David and another prisoner — allowing them to flee the camp (p. 232). Anti-Semitism is not portrayed as universal even where it might seem most likely. When he encounters a Polish farmer during his flight from Treblinka, David reluctantly admits that he is half-Jewish — fearing that the Pole will turn him in. Instead Tadeusz Chmielewski says: "I have two other boys like you, he said. They are orphans, as I think you must be too. My old wife collects orphans, and if I told her I saw you and did not bring you home, she would not feed me" (p. 254).

The Village of a Million Spirits could, therefore, be interpreted as an affirmation of Irving Howe's conception of a political novel — conveying, that is, a vision of politics as tragically insufficient, eternally disappointing, but nonetheless intrinsic to constructing a more just social order. After all, the uprising is the hub around which everything else revolves and is,

---

* A distinctive element of MacMillan's novel is its depiction of the Holocaust from the perspectives of its perpetrators and its complicit bystanders — Nazi officials, Ukrainian guards, Polish villagers. This provides a glimpse into the black box of anti-Semitism — identifying sadists, opportunists and true believers and offering access to the circumstances, motivations, rationalizations and emotions that enable human beings to inflict physical and emotional agony on defenseless others.

moreover, represented as an assertive and inspiring source of principled political action — thus, steering clear of the alienated vision of politics that emerges in *Fateless*.

Instead, *The Village of a Million Spirits* ends equivocally. In the wake of the uprising, very little changes. Most of the prisoners are recaptured and executed on the spot; new transports arrive and even the imminent closing of Treblinka is represented as pyrrhic, with one of the Nazi officers looking forward eagerly to his new assignment in Auschwitz where he anticipates still greater plunder. The novel concludes with a Ukrainian farmer who arrives at Treblinka in time to see the last trainloads and final acts of genocide. He is part of the demolition team and is then ordered to remain as a farmer (whose "farmhouse," he knows, is the former gas chamber). He cannot sleep and uses vodka to ease his anxiety at having to live in the presence of the million spirits whose scent permeates his home.

When all is said and done, *The Village of a Million Spirits* is not a novel of alienation and isolation. The Holocaust is, instead, portrayed as affirming a transcendent moral imperative. Thus, a recaptured prisoner, Sussman, tells Schneck who wants him to cringe that he is "far less afraid [of death] than I thought I would be . . . But you? You are terrified of death, and each time you kill you become more terrified. You can't stand mortality. No matter how many of us you kill, you will never make peace with . . ." (p. 249). He is shot before he can finish his rebuke, but not before demonstrating that the Treblinka uprising had redemptive powers for individuals.

Still, the hope and moral commitment that sustain Janusz and the other participants, much like Georg's steps, lead ultimately back to the self — leaving intact "given situations and concomitant givens within them" (p. 188). The locus of redemption is in the self, and political action is represented as powerless to alter the *givens* of the Holocaust which follows a trajectory that is largely incomprehensible and, in any case, inaccessible.

3. The Half-Life of a Catastrophe: Survivors and Descendants

The novels considered so far take us up to and through the Holocaust. In this section, we turn to accounts of the lives of survivors and their descendants as they try to cope with the emotional aftermath of the Holocaust and its meaning to those who are, in effect, left behind. First, we will return to the work of Aharon Appelfeld, *The Iron Tracks*, for a survivor's view. The novel is despairing. Its flat prose underscores the emotional devastation wrought by the Holocaust. In sharp contrast the irresistibly poetic prose of Anne Michaels' *Fugitive Pieces* traces the desperate, but ultimately successful, struggle of survivors *and* descendants to construct life in the shadows cast by genocide. Finally in his deeply ironic *Second Hand Smoke*, Thane Rosenbaum, the son of survivors, identifies a life-affirming path out of the barren legacy bequeathed by survivors to their children.

Each of these three novels views the Holocaust and its emotional aftermath as an irresistible force of nature and as unequivocal proof of the futility of politics and the illusion of political agency. Despite all of that common ground, their late-modernist sensibilities take them in three distinctly different directions. For Appelfeld the Holocaust is a dead end — definitively destructive to personality, culture and faith. For him, neither solace nor redemption is possible in a post-Holocaust world. Michaels locates in the consoling bonds of intimacy a quintessentially *private* way out of the personal hell generated by the Holocaust. Rosenbaum looks to faith and to justice for renewal and finds the former resuscitating and the latter barren and hollow. Only Rosenbaum's spiritual quest embraces religion and, to some extent, Judaism. His account of a painful personal recovery from "secondhand smoke" will thus serve as a bridge to the religious revival that is anticipated in Elie Wiesel's *The Oath* — the last novel to be considered in this chapter.

The Iron Tracks
The despair of *The Iron Tracks* is expressed in the post-Holocaust wandering of Siegelbaum, who is without the emotional resources to live a normal life. Siegelbaum's emotional incapacitation is signaled by his lack of affect — indelibly engraved in Appelfeld's impassive account of Siegelbaum's seemingly unending and aimless journey on the "iron tracks." Only slowly and rather cryptically do we learn the purpose of this wandering Jew's solitary pilgrimage. He is out to avenge the murder of his parents by Nachtigel and is salvaging along the way the material relics of Eastern European Jewish culture — a culture that was shattered and scattered by the Nazis.

Are we, then, to understand Siegelbaum's journey on the iron tracks that carried so many Jews to their deaths as meting out justice and recovering Jewish culture? Probably not. Only superficially is Siegelbaum's journey a mission of life (preservation of Jewish culture), death (killing Nachtigel) and justice (avenging the murder of his parents). To think of it in these terms is to ignore Siegelbaum's lost sense of agency and of idealism. He feels compelled to do what he is doing but without any sense of hope. The relics will be rescued but, detached from their cultural moorings which no longer exist, they are but museum pieces.

SIEGELBAUM'S MISSION

Siegelbaum's emotional collapse stems from his experience as a 15-year-old who *witnessed* the murders at "Nachtigel's . . . small, brutal labor camp" where he and his father were sent and where: "To our surprise we found Mother" (p. 144).

> One morning Nachtigel shot him [Siegelbaum's father] because he came late to the lineup. Mother worked in the sewing shop, and at night she would bring me pieces of bread at great risk. I asked her not to do it, but she wouldn't listen. One night she, too, was shot, near the fence (p. 144).

Appelfeld focuses on Siegelbaum's determination to find Nachtigel and kill him. Nachtigel is Siegelbaum's vocation; purchasing and selling relics is his livelihood — a necessary means to his all-consuming end.

> This is my strange way of making a living. I buy antiques whose value no one can estimate, and I sell them to collectors. I guard this secret zealously. I have eager competitors (p. 80).

He sells mostly to Max who lives in a fortress-like house that protects the relics, and he assures Siegelbaum that they will be sent to Israel when the time comes (p. 112). Siegelbaum, however, seems less worried by the fate of the relics than about the possibility of getting so caught up in the search for them as to "distract me from my main goal: the murderer" (p. 81).

His incessant and repetitious travels on the iron tracks bring the embittered Siegelbaum small consolations and modest comforts — about as much pleasure as he can handle.

> The trains make me free. Without them what would I be in this world? An insect, a mindless clerk, or, at best, a shopkeeper, a kind of human snail, getting up early, working eight or nine hours, and in the evening with the remains of strength, locking up and going home to what? A disgruntled wife, an overgrown, ungrateful son, a stack of bills (p. 5).

Instead he has, "an entire continent. I'm at home in every abandoned corner" (p. 4). He also partakes of solitary indulgences: "[F]resh rolls, homemade jam, not to mention a cigarette, have a taste that stays with you for days" (p. 4). "After an hour of string quartets I'm a new man" (p. 6). "A week in his [Max's] fortress renews me" (p. 113).

But Siegelbaum fully realizes that his is a melancholy, driven and ultimately empty life.

> In three years, I amassed a considerable sum. If I'd invested the money wisely, I would be a rich man today. Then suddenly I ran out of energy. I would sleep for days on end, wake up and stand by the window. Emptiness seeped into me down to my toes. Had it not been for the nightmares, I doubt that I would have moved. They were my hidden taskmaster, driving me from place to place (p. 25).

Not surprisingly, his relationships with others are fraught. "Fleeting loves are beneficial and never painful. Love for a station or two is love without pretense and soon forgotten" (p. 9). But does he mean it or is he just making a virtue of necessity? His one true postwar love, Bella, was also in the camps but she sleeps incessantly and obsessively. She does so to forget, and because he will not or cannot forget, they are incompatible (pp. 19–20). Similarly, another love, with Bertha, is doomed because she is determined to mourn. To Siegelbaum this amounts to returning to a cemetery — in search of a life which is lost forever. His mission is to redress the murder of his parents. His prey is Nachtigel (p. 71).

ANTI-SEMITISM WITHOUT JEWS

If memories and vengeance are at the core of Siegelbaum's gloomy wandering, he is also angered by discovering that even without Jews, anti-Semitism remains deeply rooted in Eastern European society and culture. A railway conductor recounts his experiences on the eastern front:

> We killed Jews. It was dreadful work, but very necessary. Work that brought relief to the soul. True, at first you were repelled by the screams, but little by little you learned that you were doing something important (p. 140).

This and other similar encounters drive Siegelbaum to the breaking point. He ends up hitting a *double amputee* who claims: "Extermination of the Jews was a great task, a historical mission. No one could have overcome them. They controlled everything" (p. 158). Siegelbaum goes on to explain his assault on this defenseless anti-Semite. "I didn't beat you for what you did in the past. For that I should kill you. I beat you for your thoughts now. If I were braver, if I had something of you in me, I wouldn't hesitate to butcher you" (p. 158).

Even more unsettling to Siegelbaum is the anti-Semitism of those he esteems. "I have found sensitive people here, dedicated to classical music, who don't hesitate to declare their hostility for the Jews" (p. 16). Then there is Gretchen, the simple peasant woman from whom he regularly rents a room. She comforts him with "cottage cheese in sour cream, a salad of garden vegetables, and fresh village bread" as well as with "words [that] have a kind of hidden wisdom" (p. 90). Gretchen was, however, "stunned" and dismayed to discover that Siegelbaum is Jewish, and he "was angry that Gretchen, whose ways I admired and still admire, had estranged herself from me, as if she had discovered in me an unforgivable flaw" (p. 94). Perhaps it is because he deems the otherwise respectable people as compromised that he is most at ease with smugglers who "breathed life into dry bones" (p. 20).

NOWHERE TO TURN

In his travels, Siegelbaum also learns that politics, at least the idealistic politics of his father, are more likely to replicate than to correct injustice and more likely to generate despair than hope. His father, who was in the leadership cadre of the pre-World War II Communist Party, was assigned responsibility for liberating and recruiting Ruthenian peasants. To do so, he chose to play the anti-Semitic card — that is, to condemn Jewish factory owners and Jewish merchants as class enemies (p. 26).

After the war, Siegelbaum runs into a surviving Communist, Kron, who had admired Siegelbaum's father. Kron remains true to secular humanist values and is still sad about the way the Ruthenians turned on the Communist Jews when the going got tough during the war (p. 148). Siegelbaum also learns of "the famous assassination in which my mother took part" (p. 41) — she, too, being a party militant. But she seems to have become disenchanted with communism as well as morose and withdrawn — thus turning Siegelbaum over to his father. With his father consumed by politics, however, Siegelbaum felt emotionally abandoned (see pp. 50 and 57). "When I was under my father's care, I was entirely his . . . But recently I have felt my mother's muteness more and more. Sometimes it seems that her despair was refined into a new faith" (p. 167).

One of his father's political associates, Stark, the former party secretary, initially approves wholeheartedly of Siegelbaum's mission to kill Nachtigel (p. 44). However, just before he dies Stark returns to his Jewish heritage — although not necessarily his faith (p. 99). Siegelbaum expresses deep affection for Stark but does not identify with him. Even though he is a Jew on a Jewish mission, Siegelbaum, echoing *Badenheim 1939*, has no faith, and is made uneasy and uncomfortable with those who have retained their faith — whether by displaying, rather than concealing, their

Jewishness, or who see Israel as their destiny (pp. 92–4). For Siegelbaum there is only vengeance. Accordingly, Siegelbaum continues to pursue his angry mission.

VENGEANCE WITHOUT SOLACE

Siegelbaum eventually catches up with Nachtigel. As he contemplates the showdown, Siegelbaum is almost undone by his anxiety. "Old fears, fears that I had overcome, returned and made my body tremble" (p. 173). But he encounters an old and broken man who has lost his wife and with it life's meaning (pp. 176–7).

> At that moment it was hard to imagine that this man had once worn a uniform, shouted orders, abused people, and shot them the way you shoot stray dogs. He was completely crushed by his misery, and it was clear that no compliment could rouse him from his depression (p. 177).

Then, however, Nachtigel makes it clear that he is still a Nazi ideologue. "From America. All bad things come from America. All the refuse of the world is piled up there, and all the sick ideas come from there" (p.178). Still, Siegelbaum hesitates to assassinate this shell of a man, this pale of shadow of the tyrant who has lived on in Siegelbaum's memory.

> He raised his hand to wave goodbye. Had it not been for that gesture, it is doubtful that I would have struck him. But that gesture reminded me of Nachtigel's comradeship with his young subordinates in the camp, and the warm paternal care he used to shower on them. He treated them like a father, and within a short time he made them as cruel as he was. The old man walked away, and I opened the valise. I took out the pistol and aimed at his back. The first shot hit him, but he didn't collapse. The second shot knocked him over, and he fell with arms outstretched (p. 179).

Clearly, this climax is anti-climax, leaving Siegelbaum at the end of the novel just as empty and unfulfilled as he was at its beginning.

Siegelbaum has been ever more deeply embittered by traveling the iron tracks. He knows that the preservation of artifacts cannot restore life to a culture which has been uprooted or to the people, now dead or scattered around the globe, who gave and were given meaning by these artifacts. Similarly, the murder of Nachtigel, "a minor murderer" (p. 62), while necessary and justified, in the end rings hollow because this old man is only a pale shadow of his former self. Siegelbaum's mission is thus reduced to a largely meaningless confrontation between two superannuated and hollowed-out adversaries.

The bitterest irony, Appelfeld seems to be saying, is that the Holocaust was a success for the anti-Semites who wanted to purge Eastern Europe of Jews and Judaism. Moreover, they have been able to do so while continuing to nurture the satisfactions of anti-Semitism. It is with this cloud hanging over his head that Siegelbaum turns on a man who offers words of consolation. "The Jewish people won't forget your contribution . . . The Jewish people aren't dust. They're the people of the book who fight for their values" (p. 184).

> "Be quiet. Stop making so much noise. Your words sicken me. You're an empty vessel, not a human being." He must have felt the anger raging within me (p. 184).

For Siegelbaum, so it would seem, Judaism has turned to dust. Why then is he more favorably disposed to the nuns who are gathering and preserving all of Stark's materials on Judaism? It is not on behalf of Judaism but for Stark, who is entitled, Siegelbaum believes, to have these materials "returned to his ancestors" (p. 191).

Siegelbaum can and must mourn the personal and cultural losses of the Holocaust, but redemption, recovery and expiation are out of the question. There is no political, religious or moral meaning to be learned from the Holocaust. Accordingly, the novel ends with Siegelbaum heading for Wirblbahn, the site of unspecified outrages, to burn it down. However he does not so much *choose* to go to Wirblbahn as he is driven there without illusion. "As in all my clear and drawn-out nightmares, I saw the sea of darkness, and I knew that my deeds had neither dedication nor beauty. I had done everything out of compulsion, clumsily, and always too late" (p. 195).[22]

Fugitive Pieces

Anne Michaels intertwines the Holocaust stories of Athos Roussos, a Greek geographer; Jakob Beer, the sole survivor of a Nazi massacre; and Ben, the son of Holocaust survivors. Each is from a different generation. Athos in his fifties rescues and restores Jakob, a young boy, and many years later Jakob provides sustenance to Ben. This is very much a book about redemption and spiritual renewal through intimacy. Religion is evoked but subsumed within the cosmic forces that are seen as generative of both science and culture.

The novel begins with the miraculous emergence of Jakob, the sole survivor of a family and of a Jewish community that has perished. "Bog boy, I surfaced into the miry streets of the drowned city" (p. 5). He wanders aimlessly for days — understanding that he had his "duties. Walk at night. In the morning dig my bed. Eat anything" (p. 9). Eventually he encounters Athos, who is "excavating in the mud at Biskupin . . . [and who] wore me under his clothes" (p. 13).* Thus, the boy and the man, the two as one, succeed in escaping across borders and back to the Aegean island of Zakynthos. "I was numb against his solid body, a blister tight with fear" (p. 13). Athos has a small and isolated house on Zakynthos, where he hides Jakob, who is only rarely allowed out of doors for the duration of the German occupation.

It is unimaginable that Jakob could have found himself in better hands, as Michaels makes arrestingly clear. The first order of business is to restore Jakob's *malnourished body* — no mean feat on a rocky island, given all of the inevitable wartime shortages. In an effort to restore Jakob's *emotional health*, Athos enfolds him in an intimacy which is never intrusive but never in doubt. Also Athos, a Christian, provides ample space and encouragement for preserving the ties that bind Jakob to his family and to his Jewish cultural, linguistic and religious heritage.

> Athos didn't want me to forget. He made me review my Hebrew alphabet. He said the same thing every day: "It is your future you are remembering" (p. 21).

Finally, while Jakob's physical world is confined to the tiny cabin, Athos, a man of voracious intellectual appetites, fabricates from books an expansive world of learning that fires Jakob's imagination. "For four years I was confined to small rooms. But Athos gave me another realm to inhabit, big as the globe and expansive as time" (p. 29). Jakob is filled with a sense of awe and wonder as Athos guides him from "geology to paleontology to poetry" (p. 21).

Nonetheless, Athos is unable to ward off Jacob's demons either on the island or later in Toronto, where Athos takes up an academic appointment. What they both come to understand is that Jakob and Athos were not alone in their flight to Zakynthos. They were accompanied by Jakob's beloved sister Bella, whom the Nazis swept up, along with their father

---

* Biskupin is identified as a prosperous and highly developed ancient Eastern European city which was abandoned to the rising waters of the Gassawka River and remained buried for centuries (p. 50). The Nazis are determined to destroy it in an attempt, according to Efraim Sicher, to "falsify history and master the past as the story of Aryan superiority over other cultures" (2005: 185).

and mother. "We were Russian dolls. I inside Athos, Bella inside me" (p. 14). Jakob experiences an agonizing sense of loss and an unquenchable longing for Bella. Even years after moving to Toronto, Jakob's nightmares continue — haunted by ineradicable and devastating images of Bella, his parents and the Nazi desecration of their lives and culture.

> When I woke, my anguish was specific: the possibility that it was as painful for them to be remembered as it was for me to remember them; that I was haunting my parents and Bella with my calling, startling them awake in their black beds (p. 25).

Jakob is thus afflicted by nightmares of the life he has lost and fearful that his nightmares are afflictions for his lost family.

Jakob's path back to a semblance of wholeness requires that he no longer thinks of the Holocaust as sui generis — that he, in other words, ceases to identify it with the eclipse of civilization and with an irreparable rupture in the fabric of his existence. For a transformation of consciousness of this magnitude to occur, Jakob must discover, embrace, and internalize a cosmology that situates the savagery of the Holocaust within the ebb and flow of history. Both the cosmology and its assimilation are necessary, but only in combination are they sufficient.

Jakob's lifeline is the regenerative rhythms of the natural world drawn by Athos from his research.

> Athos was an expert in buried and abandoned places. His cosmology became mine. I grew into it naturally. In this way, our tasks became the same (p. 49).

This shared cosmology of *"redemption through cataclysm*; what had been transformed might be transformed again" (p. 101, italics added) becomes Jakob's template for hope.

> He [Athos] applied the geologic to the human, analyzing social change as he would a landscape; slow persuasion and catastrophe. Explosions, seizures, floods, glaciations. He constructed his own historical topography (p. 119).

As Michiko Kakutani puts it, "Michaels underscores the continuity of human experience, suggesting that just as we can inherit the pain and guilt of earlier generations, so too can we inherit understanding and beauty and grace."[23] In short, Michaels' narrative is permeated with the paradox of creation and destruction in the intertwined worlds of science and art, culture and nature.

Jakob's intellect readily absorbs and embraces the cosmology of "redemption through cataclysm," with which, after all, Athos nourished Jakob from his earliest days on Zakynthos. But Jakob is only able to weave these truths into his emotional life after he meets and marries Michaela. A first marriage to Alex failed to ease Jakob's burden, because it offered love conditional on *forgetting* the Holocaust. Alex was intent on having Jakob put the past behind him. "Alex wants to explode me, set fire to everything. She wants me to begin again" (p. 144). But to do so would have entailed renunciation of his love for Bella — a love that he could not relinquish without abandoning himself.

> Once I was lost in a forest. I was so afraid. My blood pounded in my chest and I knew my heart's strength would soon be exhausted. I grasped the two syllables closest to me, and replaced my heartbeat with your name (p. 195).

In contrast, Michaela's love is a sanctuary which emotionally replicates what Jakob left behind in the ashes of his origins. She is comfortable with the past — her own, Jakob's, and the world's. She "moves through history with the fluency of a spirit, mourns the burning of the library at Alexandra as if it happened yesterday" (p. 176).

When she "offers her ancestors to me, I'm shocked at my hunger for her memories. Love feeds on the protein of detail, sucks fact to the marrow" (p. 179). "She has heard everything — her heart an ear, her skin an ear. Michaela is crying for Bella" (p. 182).[24] By choosing to draw cosmic meaning from the natural world, *Fugitive Pieces* eschews both religious faith and political ideology. Insofar as the narrative invokes politics (hardly at all), it is politics as a problem — the source of unbearable pain and suffering.

Religion is more of a presence in *Fugitive Pieces*, but for the wisdom that can be gleaned from it as an element of culture — not as a repository of faith. Thus it is that Athos insists on Jakob retaining his religious identity and its cultural truths. He invokes old Hebrew sayings and makes the Psalms available to Jacob (p. 156). In much the same spirit Athos calls Jakob's attention to teachings from the Zohar — teachings that are consonant with Athos' secular belief in the redemptive power of catastrophe.[25] None of this is different, in kind, from the tribute to the power of love and remembrance that Athos extracts from the Greek poet (and Nobel Laureate), Seferis. Thus, on departing Zakynthos for Canada, Athos reads to Jakob: "Here finish the works of the sea, the works of love. You who will someday live here . . . if the blood chances to darken your memory do not forget us" (p. 75). Understandably, then, while Jakob acknowledges his Jewish roots, he does so as a secularist — concluding that he is "a kabbalist only in that I believe in the power of incantation. A poem is as neural as love; the rut of rhythm that veers in the mind" (p. 163).

The book concludes with the example of Jakob's renewal and with his writing providing sustenance to Ben, the child of Holocaust survivors. The survivors have bequeathed their emotional desolation to him. Ben's story is one of the "series of narrative loops, in which a passionate relationship is relived intimately."[26] Ben's parents, in a misguided effort to insulate him, have created an emotional and spiritual vacuum between him and the forces and events that determined the trajectory of his life — more or less replicating Jakob's own devastating sense of loss. Accordingly, Athos's cosmology of redemption comes to Ben through Jakob. Whereas in Jakob's case the cosmology precedes the relationship of intimacy required to convert it into a life force, in Ben's case he is unable to accept the intimacy that Naomi offers until after he fully comprehends and assimilates the cosmology.

In the final analysis, then, the meaning of Holocaust emerges as paradoxical and elusive. It is also intensely private. The urgent presence of the absent Bella situates the narrative in what Sicher terms "absence without knowledge of what has been lost or sometimes of the actual loss."[27] For redemption, it is necessary to leave the dead in peace. "To remain with the dead is to abandon them" (p. 170). But neither should they be abandoned. To resolve that paradox, it is necessary to find meaning in their shattered lives. Jakob, of course, finds such meaning in the "cosmology of cataclysm"* but it comes alive for him only after it is sanctified in the intimacy of his relationship with Michaela. Accordingly, we are left with a cosmology of redemption that is without collective implications, relevance or resonance — entirely outside the realms of politics or religious faith.[28]

Second Hand Smoke

Thane Rosenbaum writes as the son of survivors, and he conveys the psychic devastation bequeathed by Holocaust survivors to their children. The novel partakes of much the same history, geography, sociology and politics as *The Iron Tracks* and *Fugitive Pieces*. However, Rosenbaum's

---

* "At that moment of utmost degradation, in that twisted reef, is the most obscene testament of grace. For can anyone tell with absolute certainty the difference between the sounds of those who are in despair and the sounds of those who want desperately to believe? The moment when our faith in man is forced to change, anatomically — mercilessly — into faith" (p. 168).

sensibilities are different. His characters are larger than life; he seasons his story with sardonic humor; the plot is implausible but emotionally resonant; and his message is preeminently redemptive.[29]

If Siegelbaum's lonely journey demonstrates that Holocaust victims are unable to get past the catastrophic rupture of their lives, Rosenbaum helps us understand that victims-as-parents are all too likely to pass on their affliction to the next generation — even when, as in *Second Hand Smoke*, they are determined to do otherwise. "The children of trauma . . . are not free to choose their destiny because they are 'survivors of survivors' already shaped, bred and maimed by the Holocaust, defined by the damage which has made their families dysfunctional."[30] In part, the measure of Rosenbaum's achievement is that he conveys why it could not be otherwise. But his greater achievement is to make us understand the profound yearning of descendants to be free of this secondhand smoke even though they are deeply addicted to it. In the end, Rosenbaum wants us to understand that authentic Judaism, humane, spiritual and religious, offers a way out of the descendants' conundrum — while a bellicose, secular and ultimately counterfeit Judaism does not.

ONE TOUGH JEW

The central character of the novel is Duncan Katz, whose mother Mila and father Herschel, "a former German intellectual," survived the Holocaust (p. 6). Duncan is therefore of a generation that was both spared the Holocaust and weighed down by it:

> What had killed the survivors had somehow become the oxygen for their children . . . a stunning achievement of the Third Reich . . . There were millions of dead Jews, and there were those who had survived but who still qualified as dead under certain measurements for living. And now the children, the next generation — paralyzed, frozen in time, unable to move forward and hauntingly afraid to look back (p. 83).[31]

Certainly Duncan's father, improbably known as Yankee, fits that description: he survived the Holocaust physically but has been emotionally destroyed by it — not unlike Siegelbaum.

This means that Mila, who is another story altogether, takes over Duncan's upbringing and generates, both literally and figuratively, most of the second-hand smoke in which he is enveloped. Mila is a tough-talking, hard-smoking, confrontational — yes, larger than life — personality. She devotes all of her abundant energy to toughening up Duncan so that he will always be capable of fighting back against anti-

Semites and anti-Semitism. "You must avenge our deaths." "But you're not dead," replies Duncan (p. 32). Under Mila's unrelenting tutelage Duncan comes to personify the tough Jew — a legendary hero of Miami high school football, "a natural linebacker" (p. 35) and a karate expert who never shrinks from a fight. He carries that same obsessively pugnacious personality into his job tracking down and prosecuting Nazi war criminals for the United States Department of Justice.

CHILD ABUSE
Up to a point, then, Mila's strategy succeeds brilliantly. But in order to live up to his mother's expectations, Duncan has paid a price that ultimately becomes unbearable. He has, as Rosenbaum puts it, "received an inheritance that he would have rather done without, the kind of legacy he'd just as soon give back" (p. 1). Most fundamentally, his mother deprived Duncan of emotional sustenance — beginning at his *bris* where she denied him a few drops of schnapps that might have reduced the pain. "I want him to feel it" (p. 16). Many years later, he responds more or less in kind at her funeral where he denounces her as a mother who gave "new meaning" to the term "child abuse" (p. 55).

> So she's dead. And you all feel loss, but let me tell you something: I feel freedom. I am newly liberated. For me, today is not about mourning, but about celebration. No sitting *shivah* — at least not by me. I don't want to remember her; all I want is a fresh start (p. 55).

The other mourners who virtually worship Mila for her irrepressible strength and for her enthusiasms — whether for smoking, gambling, music or friendship — are appalled. One responds: "Finish him off right here!" (p. 71).

The combination of being deprived of his mother's love and being driven into a constant battle against anti-Semitism and Nazi war criminals has created a man who is consumed by hatred. The depth of Duncan's obsession and the lengths to which he seems willing to go are so extreme that he almost is not hired by the Justice Department. "I need to know if you can play by the rules . . . Frankly, you're much more dangerous than any punk Jewish kid with a pipe bomb" (p. 24). As it turns out, Duncan who, like the author, is trained as a lawyer, is unable to behave like one. His fanaticism compromises the mission of his office and he is suspended. Even under suspension he hounds Maloney, nee Malyshko, a Ukrainian immigrant. "We've known each other for some time. Your real name is Malyshko, let's not forget that. Maloney may be your stage name, but you kill under Malyshko" (p. 101).

Duncan's family life is contaminated by his obsession and his hatred. His wife Sharon finds the situation unbearable. In her words: "The environment in this house is polluted with smoke imported all the way from those German ovens. We all need some air to breathe" (p. 84). And later: "It's like you're possessed. Your eyes are burning with rage. It's the look of the Six Million in one fragile, but very frightening, face" (p. 145). Sharon is fearful that the poison will be passed on to their daughter, Milan, and finally demands a separation. "By banishing Duncan and blanketing Milan, Sharon was no doubt taking desperate maternal measures. Quarantine the father; insulate the daughter. Maybe there was hope for the child after all" (p. 83).

Duncan is tortured by the separation from Sharon and Milan while Sharon is also shattered because she thinks of her need to break with Duncan as a betrayal.

> Actually, it was more than just separation. It was abandonment, then exile. How was she supposed to explain this to herself? Knowing what she knew about him and the demons that trailed him, how could she do this? She had married a man who had come from a place of total brokenness. And he had joined with her in the hope of defeating the dire omens of his parents, of restoring a lost world, and in the process rebuilding one for himself (p. 143).

She has done everything that she can think of to help Duncan, all to no avail.

Over the course of the novel, however, Duncan undergoes a spiritual awakening *in, of all places, Poland*. He goes there with anger in his heart and discovers, as did Siegelbaum, that there is no truly living Jewish culture any more — only relics.

> Poland was Krypton; he was familiar with the paralyzing garments of this imploded land . . . the blackest hole in the Jewish galaxy (p. 180). The Germans may have committed most of the crimes, but the soil, and the soul, of Jewish loss was a Polish affair (p. 179).

Duncan's bitterness is amplified by discovering that Poles are now profiting from the Holocaust by using the remnants of the pre-war Jewish community as bait to attract Jewish tourists.

> A nation poor in Jews, but rich in Jewish ruins. And the fish in this case were the Jews themselves — particularly the sentimental and affluent American Jews . . . Suddenly, Poles who hated Jews found

a way to cash in on the absence of Jewish life. A cottage industry in Shtetl revivalism (p. 107).

Duncan, in effect, cannot forget; he is focused on redressing the criminality of the past.

SECULAR JUDAISM

In Poland, however, he comes into contact with a half-brother, Isaac Borowski — Mila's first child.[32] Isaac, the anti-Duncan, chooses to transcend the past rather than to bemoan and avenge it. Despite being abandoned by Mila, Isaac is not bitter nor is he filled with hate.

> "These are good people," Isaac said. "There are many decent Poles, and the two over there are young; they were not here for the Holocaust" (p. 109).

Isaac preserves what remains of Judaism's Polish heritage by working as a caretaker at the Jewish cemetery in Warsaw. He also draws spiritual sustenance from yoga and meditation. Not surprisingly, neither half-brother can make sense of the other. They are emotional, social and physiological strangers — a mystery to one another, with Mila as their only common ground. She has, albeit in different ways, abandoned both of them.

Isaac is appalled by Duncan's plan to wreak vengeance on Poland. "I'm talking Jewish vengeance. When we get through with this place, *aliyah* will take on a whole different meaning . . . Warsaw, Krakow, and Lublin once again overrun with Jews" (p. 211). "Isaac wondered for the first time whether, in not knowing Mila, he had somehow been better off after all" (p. 211). For his part Duncan imagines what Mila would have made of her firstborn and his yoga practice and classes — "not exactly a warrior's sport . . . What a field day the Poles must have had with this dumpy, defenseless, four-eyed Jewish kid. The replay of a pogrom. Motherless. Muscle-less. What possible good could come from seeing inside souls?" (p. 208).

Ultimately, Duncan's tough-Jew, Mila-inspired credo is shaken by Isaac's capacity to achieve what for Duncan is the unachievable. "How," Duncan wonders, "could this short, overweight, double-chinned man, with feet pointed out in reverse Vee formation, contort and balance his body without regard to the laws of physics, or common sense?" (p. 199). Duncan is also stunned when he tries to pick a fight with a Polish policeman who is ready to oblige him until Isaac intervenes. "Seconds later the guns were returned to their holsters . . . 'Who are you?' Duncan asked pleadingly. 'What do these people see in you? What are they afraid of? What makes you so special?'" (p. 236). Isaac explains why the Poles defer to him: "It's not really the yoga or the Zen teachings. They see me as a holy survivor. A Christ child. A baby who survived the camps; the only baby who ever lived through the fire" (p. 243). Accordingly: "Even during the mass pogroms of the late 1940s, Isaac — and Keller Borowski [his father] — were untouchable and protected" (p. 244).

Yet more surprising, Duncan senses himself, like the Poles, coming under Isaac's spell.

> What would Mila have thought about her son? Not the street fighter, but the man at the piano, playing her instrument [and her song, "Someone to Watch over Me"] . . . Everyone in the restaurant was being serenaded, but none more so than the American whose fists and spine and heart were opening with each tap of a musical key (p. 233).

Duncan is sufficiently shaken by these surprises, by the train wreck which his own life has become, and by the peace of mind that he senses in Isaac to give himself over to emotional and spiritual renewal.

Only slowly do the brothers come to understand and truly to know one another. It becomes clear to both of them (and to the reader) that "even without her [Mila], Isaac turned out to be the more resilient brother of the two" (p. 263). Isaac comes to understand that Duncan is physically strong but emotionally weak: "Mila gave you the body, but not the nerve" (p. 261). "You have a life force inside you. It's time to use it for living, and not as a poison" (p. 264).

Duncan remains confused but is able to accept from Isaac, a survivor, what he could not accept from Sharon, "a blond shiksa" (p. 140). He just has to transcend the Holocaust in order to live a normal life. "Duncan wanted to live in his brother's world, but that world was Poland, a place where the nightmares began and where now insomnia ruled. Duncan was becoming totally undone" (p. 263). Yet he still could not break free: "I don't want to heal this wound, it's my birthright, it's a permanent scar" (p. 264). And he is unable initially to respond to Isaac who urges him: "Mourn, Duncan . . . The fight is over; nobody won. Not you, not Mila. Say goodbye to our mother. You should have done it at her funeral, but it's not too late" (p. 272).

Once he goes to work in the Jewish cemetery alongside Isaac, Duncan's transcendence commences. This work "calmed Duncan's spirit. He restored tombs, unearthed graves . . . planted flowers . . ." (p. 285). "All of a sudden, just being Jewish, *independent of his Holocaust credentials,* mattered to Duncan" as it did to Isaac (p. 283, italics supplied). He began to pray, and not only in a synagogue but also in the open air, or even in a Catholic church (p. 285). Later in the US, Duncan, with Isaac at his side, finally finds his own peace of mind when they bump into some African-American nurses who had cared for, and come to cherish, Mila in the last days of her illness. They reveal that Mila "never forgave herself" for abandoning Isaac. "And she took it out on Duncan . . . She was sorry about what she did to you, too" (p. 301).

The book concludes with the nurses and the brothers reciting Kaddish at Mila's grave: "So they huddled in a violent Miami rain, surrounded by tears of atonement and the glare of a flashbulb in twilight. Duncan blinked and then wiped his eyes, which were ineluctably, almost morbidly, drawn to his brother's forearm. Misty streaks of water, as though spiked with acid, were slowly washing away the numbers. Four pebbles and one *pysanka*[33] lined up on Mila's gravestone, silently bearing witness to the memory of the life that stirred within" (p. 303). Thus, Duncan finds peace of mind in Isaac's redemptive and eclectic Judaism and thus he is able to give up his own Mila-inspired Judaism of vengeance. Duncan also reconciles in spirit with Mila who, he came to understand, loved the two brothers, not too little but too much — and in the only way that she knew how. While it was perverse and destructive, this love was all she had to give.

   Second Hand Smoke ends on a religious note, and in its own inimitable way makes clear both how and why religious faith offers a desperately-needed, life-affirming antidote to the Holocaust. Isaac's Judaism is inflected with the new-age sensibilities of yoga and Zen Buddhism. Efraim Sicher puts it this way: "It is a kind of New Age Judaism, mixed up with Zen Buddhism and Catholicism, but it brings peace to the child of survivors whose outrage crippled the ability to function and to raise a family."[34] In any case, Rosenbaum leaves us with a tale of religious and spiritual renewal and perhaps with an understanding of why a disproportionate number of Jews seem to have become Buddhist gurus and New Age devotees. For a more traditional vision of the healing power of Judaism in the post-Holocaust world, we turn next to Elie Wiesel, novelist, public intellectual and winner of the Nobel Peace Prize in 1986.

4. The Renewal of Faith: Judaism as Refuge and Affirmation

   A meaningful metaphor was placed in the center of the Lurianic conception of the tikkun: the captive divine sparks that have to be redeemed by human deeds.

Joseph Dan[35]

The Oath

Ellie Wiesel reveals continuities and discontinuities between pogroms and the Holocaust in chronicling an imagined twentieth-century pogrom in the town of Kolvillag — a "small town, somewhere between the Dniepr and the Carpathians" (p. 14). Kolvillag has ceased to exist because the pogrom led to the destruction of the whole town and all of its inhabitants except for Azriel, the primary narrator (p. 21).

Azriel is now an old man but was then a young boy who had fallen under the influence of the mad prophet, Moshe. He had sworn any Jews who might survive the pogrom never to reveal what has happened. Moshe claims that God has decreed that, after the centuries of bearing witness to anti-Semitic outrages, a new response is in order.

> For centuries now we have given ourselves to Him by allowing ourselves to be led to the slaughterhouse. We think that we are pleasing Him by becoming the illustrations of our own tales of martyrdom . . . The enemy can do with us as he pleases, but never will he silence us — that has been our motto (pp. 241 and 243).

It is now necessary to pursue the "one solution we have not yet tried" (p. 244).

> If suffering and the history of suffering were intrinsically linked, the one could be abolished by attacking the other; by ceasing to refer to the events of the present, we would forestall ordeals in the future . . . Better than our predecessors, better than our ancestors, shall we praise our God. We shall speak of Him so as not to speak of ourselves. What will remain of us? Something of our kinship, something of our silence (pp. 244 and 248).

Azriel does not comprehend but he believes — seeing "in Moshe's mysterious protest a paradox — it incited to joy, to fulfillment through joy, rather than to despair" (p. 245). Because Azriel believes, he obeys.

After decades of obedience, Azriel finally decides to break the oath, not because he has lost faith but because he comes to realize that only in breaking the oath can he truly honor its spirit. He comes to this conclusion as a result of encountering a young boy who is contemplating suicide. The boy is the child of Holocaust survivors and feels that life in a post-Holocaust world is meaningless. He is disillusioned by the war crime trials and cannot understand how God, if there is a God, could have permitted the Holocaust. Azriel shares the boy's despair and understands the attractions of suicide.

> You want to die? How can one blame you. This rotten world is not worth lingering in. I know something about it: I covered it from one end to the other. To repudiate it, you have chosen suicide? Why not, it's a solution like any other, neither better nor worse. I myself have explored all the possibilities (p. 16).

However, it turns out that the two share more than despair and an obsession with the infinite darkness of a world permeated by murderous anti-Semitism.

THE POGROM

The boy is intensely curious about Azriel's experience with the earlier but similarly evil pogrom in Kolvillag. "[T]he story teller, he intrigued and fascinated me. Who was he? A saint? A madman? A Just Man disguised as a vagabond?" (p. 25). Azriel works his way through to the realization that helping this boy choose life over death is his mission. "Have I lived and survived only for this encounter and this challenge? Only to defeat death in this particular case? Could I have been spared in Kolvillag so I could help this stranger?" (p. 41).

The story when it is told is every bit as bleak as the Holocaust itself. The Jewish community disintegrated as the pogrom drew closer.[36] When it came, the pogrom unleashed such murderous fury that it led to an inferno that consumed everything and everybody — Jew and Gentile alike. *The final words of the book*, and of Azriel's lament as he reflects on it all many, many years later, could hardly have been bleaker:

> Only the fire still lived in what was once a town, mine. Charred dwellings. Charred corpses. Charred dreams and prayers and songs. Every story has an end, just as every end has a story. And yet, and yet. In the case of this city reduced to ashes, the two stories merge into one and remain a secret — such had been the will of my mad friend named Moshe, last prophet and first messiah of a mankind that is no more (p. 285).

Yet Azriel believes that there is a life-affirming message to be learned from the catastrophe of Kolvillag — a lesson that is equally applicable to the Holocaust. Only by breaking his oath can Ariel affirm life and *perhaps* save this boy from suicide.

AFFIRMATION OF LIFE

Azriel is well aware that he is taking a gamble. Might not the boy be driven closer to suicide, given the way in which the Holocaust and the Kollivag pogrom seem to replicate one another?

> What if I told you about Kolvillag? It contains a lesson that might benefit you, who are incapable of living simply, or simply living. Kolvillag: contagious hate, evil unleashed. The dire consequences of a commonplace, senseless episode. The importance of unimportant things. Breaking his chains, the Exterminating Angel has turned all men into victims. Moral: it is dangerous to use his services. Do you hear me? Despite innumerable eyes that characterize him, he is blind; he will strike anywhere . . . Moral: whoever kills, kills himself; whoever preaches murder will be murdered . . . Just as every murder is a suicide, every suicide is a murder. Yes, the story must be told (p. 65).

If the oath was Moshe's paradox, the alchemy through which death can be transmuted into life is Azriel's paradox, and it rests on the belief that, despite everything, the affirmation of life is all we have — the quintessential value.[37]

Azriel himself had been tempted, but did not suicide. His salvation was to follow the dictates of the Rebbe who detected his deep despair and the burden of his oath.

> You will leave here this very day . . . You will be a *Na-venadnik*, in perpetual exile, a stranger among strangers . . . I send you on the road to the unknown so that you may lose yourself before finding yourself again . . . Remember that God is everywhere and He is everywhere the same. Not you. In truth, there are thousands and thousands of Azriels inside you. It is your task to find them and to bring them together; when they shall have become one, you shall be free (pp. 52–3).

And as he wanders, he learns and becomes "richer for" this learning (p. 55). Indeed, he connects Jewish communities to one another and so becomes a messenger of Jewish life. "With the years, I became a hyphen between countless communities" (p. 57) — all of them united by their tradition and their rituals.

It is, of course, as a *Na-venadnik* that he encounters the boy and their relationship.

I am not telling you not to despair of man, I only ask you not to offer death one more victim, one more victory. It does not deserve it, believe me. The most beautiful of deaths is hardly that; there is no beautiful death. Nor is there a just death. Every death is absurd. Useless. And ugly. Is that your wish? To add to the ugliness of the world? (p. 20).[38]

While we do not know for certain whether Azriel's gamble worked, the presence of the boy as a second narrator suggests that it did — as do his reflections on Azriel's interventions. "By allowing me to enter his life, he gave meaning to mine; I lived on two levels, dwelt in two places, claimed more than one role my own" (p. 24). In short, Azriel has passed on to the boy what Moshe passed on to him — a kind of Talmudic wisdom, refracted through the lens of the Kolvillag pogrom.

Clearly, the Talmud, according to Wiesel, enables us to see that an affirmation of life can be drawn from death and destruction. Consider the book's Talmudic epigraph:

> Had the peoples and the nations
> known how much harm they brought upon
> themselves by destroying the
> Temple of Jerusalem, they would
> Have wept more than the children
> of Israel.

It is clear enough why those peoples and nations who destroyed the temple might well have wept and why, by implication, the post-Holocaust German literature is so much about grieving. But why would they have wept "*more* than the children of Israel?" (italics added). Perhaps it is because of the rediscovery of Judaism, which Wiesel sees as the lesson to be taken from both the pogrom and the Holocaust.

A COSMOLOGY OF AFFIRMATION

In addition, there seems to be a cosmic lesson in the interpersonal sustenance passed on from Moshe and the Rebbe to Azriel, and from Azriel to the boy. Very early in the novel, Azriel makes the connection as follows:

To hell with principles, vows. The true contest must take place on the level of the individual. It is here, in the present, that the temple is reclaimed or demolished . . . The mystery of the universe resides not in the universe but in man; perfection can be attained only by the individual (p. 22).

There is a striking consonance between this understanding and the cosmology of the Lurianic Kabbalah.

According to Joseph Dan, the Lurianic Kabbalah represents a reconfiguration of traditional Jewish philosophy which emphasized obedience to the specific commands of the Torah and other sacred texts.

> The traditional Jewish concept of mitzvah (precept, commandment) demanded physical action. The list of 613 such commandments, which every Jew was required to perform (or, in case of prohibitions, abstain from performing) hardly included any purely spiritual demand . . . Judaism thus had an image, and a self-image, of being an earthly, physical practice, remote from pure divine spirituality.[39]

The Lurianic Kabbalah changed this. It linked the observation of sacred dos and don'ts to "universal perfection" and the failure to do so to "primordial catastrophe."[40]

> Following the divine demands signifies overcoming the physical and evil within man, and thus denotes the spiritual victory of good over evil. The accumulation of such minute victories enhances the completion of the tikkun, while sins and transgressions strengthen the evil powers and delay the achievement of redemption . . . Every person, every deed, every moment is integrated into the mythical project of the tikkun, whether they know and wish it or not. One cannot resign from this cosmic struggle; such a resignation constitutes a sin, which empowers the satanic forces.[41]

From this perspective, Azriel's struggle against the boy's suicide, even if it is not successful, but especially if it is, represents one of those "minute victories [that] enhances the completion of the tikkun."[42] It is not only a struggle for the life of the boy but an intrinsic element in the cosmic struggle for divine perfection and the quintessential way in which individuals can and must engage the divine. This, when all is said and done, is the spiritual meaning of The Oath as well as Azriel's decision to break it.[43]

5. Conclusions

This chapter is divided between novels which focus on the Holocaust and those that consider its aftermath. The former portray the struggle of those caught in the Holocaust to survive physically and emotionally. We learn that assimilation and citizenship are illusions and that Jews live at the sufferance of, and within boundaries established by, others — according to the unfathomable *raison d'être* of the Nazi state and the whim of its officials, as well as to erratic acts of altruism by righteous gentiles, accidents of time and place and so on. In short, both the prelude to, and the hell of, the Holocaust robbed millions of Jews of any semblance of control over their own destinies.

Similarly, their attempts to reassert political agency through collective acts of resistance are portrayed as largely, if not entirely, futile. Nor is religious faith seen as a source of strength or solace, protection against the Holocaust or, more surprisingly, as a resource that helps prisoners endure and survive the ravages of the death and work camps. Without any other recourse, Holocaust victims cobble together idiosyncratic survival strategies. Recall the ingenuity of Jacob Heyn, the ghetto liar; the selflessness of Janusz Siedlecki in Treblinka; and the robot-like steps of Georg Kovacs into and out of Auschwitz, Buchenwald and Zeitz.

The novels of its aftermath reveal the desolation and alienation left in the wake of the Holocaust, but they also unearth resilience and peace of mind. These consolations do not result from a reassertion of political agency, war crimes trials or vigilante justice. These responses to the Holocaust are viewed as inadequate at best and as betrayal at worst. The negation of political agency is certainly not celebrated in these novels; neither is it mourned. Instead, the loss of secular agency and hence of meaningful political action is accepted as an inescapable and eternal element of the Jewish, and perhaps the human, condition.

Opportunities for solace and perhaps even redemption are found in spiritual engagement with the traditions of Judaism. The spiritual meaning taken from the Holocaust varies widely from novel to novel — from the unequivocal secularism of Anne Michaels, through the eclectic religious vision of Thane Rosenbaum, to Ellie Wiesel's invocation of the Kabbalah. However, each in its own way rejects a modern or a late-modern response to the Holocaust. Instead, they offer a *pre-modern*, intensely personal and unequivocally spiritual refuge from, and antidote to, the inhuman barbarism unleashed and uncovered by the Holocaust.

Perhaps the most startling, and indeed perverse, message of these novels is that the Holocaust is not only a catastrophe to be damned but an agent of deliverance. In having unleashed destructive forces that stripped human experience down to its spiritual essence, the Holocaust has demonstrated, these novelists all seem to say, the quintessential necessity of nurturing the soul.

4 Aftermath of Disaster: The Nazi Legacy

> The entire [German] society . . . had consented to be governed by persons with no respect for the ordinary tenets of law or moral conduct.
>
> Robert Boyers[1]

In their early postwar anti-Nazi novels, three of Germany's most distinguished writers, Gunter Grass, Heinrich Böll and Siegfried Lenz, were haunted by the same question. How and why, each of them asked, could Germany have gone so wrong — giving itself over to the Nazis and to the disastrous defeat that followed? While Böll in *Billiards at Half-Past Nine*, Lenz in *The German Lesson* and Grass in *The Tin Drum* each sought the etiology of responsibility, they came to sharply contrasting conclusions about where to point the finger of blame. Despite their differences, however, all three books read as scathing indictments of democratic politics. They all conclude that the Nazis were *granted* power by the German people.

Upon further reflection, and some years later, German writers turned to the Nazi regime itself and to the havoc that it had wrought within and beyond the borders of Germany. Gunter Grass took the lead with the publication of *Dog Years*, the third novel of his Danzig trilogy,[2] as did the East German novelist, Christa Wolf in *Patterns of Childhood*. Each of these novels looked at the *sins of the Nazi era* — including anti-Semitism, war crimes and totalitarian rule.

Finally, and some 50 years after the fact, German novelists turned to the formerly taboo topic of Germans as *victims* of Nazism. Previously it was considered unseemly, even shameful and irresponsible, to dwell on German suffering and/or the war crimes of the Allies, such as the fire bombing of Dresden.[3] For better or worse, this was no longer the case. Gunter Grass' *Crabwalk* and Bernard Schlink's *The Reader* tackle what was hitherto off-limits.[4] A central theme of these novels is that addressing German suffering is inextricably linked to working out a worthwhile and essential intergenerational discourse among Germans of good will.[5]

While these three themes of post-Nazi literature are intertwined, late-modern German political novels of the last half of the twentieth century tended to tackle them separately — in three distinct, sequential and mutually exclusive phases. That is how they will be taken up in this chapter.[6] Suffice to say that for our purposes, whether these novelists are reflecting, anticipating or influencing the prevailing ethos of the era, they offer distinctly different retrospective visions of Nazism — always probing beneath its surface and drawing collective meaning from intensely personal accounts of the Nazi era and its aftermath.

1. Looking Inward: How did it Happen? Who is Responsible?

The novels considered in this section were written in the immediate wake of Germany's defeat in World War II, its division between the Federal Republic and the German Democratic Republic (GDR), the shaming evidence of the Holocaust, the collapse of the Nazi regime and the repudiation of Nazi ideology. Postwar, post-Nazi German political leaders on both sides of the iron curtain were focused primarily on building new Germanys — rather than looking back to either the Nazi era or to the postwar chaos.

In contrast, the leading German novelists of the 1950s and 1960s did look backward — conducting literary inquests into their country's debacle. As historian Gordon Craig puts it:

> The salient characteristics of the new novels were their contemporaneity, their attention to political and social problems, and their forthrightness in taking a position of the issues of the day.[7]

However, these initial inquests largely ignored the Holocaust, Nazism's paramount evil and, indeed, Nazism itself. If we ask why, the answer is to be found in the belief that the preponderance of ordinary Germans welcomed the Nazi regime for opportunistic reasons — not because they embraced Nazism's evil programs, policies and promises. In short, the acceptance of the Nazis was self-serving rather than ideological. The worst of Nazism is at the margins of these novels, because it was deemed to be at the margins of German consciousness — neither unforeseen nor unwelcome but incidental to the belief that the Nazis would restore German prosperity and prestige.

The novels are first and foremost confined to identifying culprits, affixing blame and, by implication, suggesting how to nurture humane values and reinforce virtue in a new Germany.

- For Böll, it is militarism and the military classes that are primarily responsible for abetting Nazism.
- For Lenz, it is a predilection for authority, order and for doing one's duty that betrayed Germany.

• As Grass sees it, everyone is to blame and, indeed, he comes very close to identifying the descent into Nazism with the human condition.

Their concerted efforts to discover what went wrong were not solely about blaming or just getting to the bottom of the debacle of Nazism. Indeed, it is the present condition and future prospects of the Federal Republic that is their principal worry. Accordingly the focus is on Nazism's considerable legacy to, and continuing influence on, the Federal Republic.

These are novels of personal, not political, redemption — leaving the future of the Federal Republic very much in doubt. Grass does tip his hand in *The Tin Drum*, which is profoundly pessimistic. He is unable to ferret out anything in German culture that is healthy or redemptive. Lenz and Böll are able to locate redemptive elements of traditional German culture — the artistic spirit for Lenz and the respectable professional classes for Böll. While Böll and Lenz blame *the other* in their midst, Grass seems to say that we are all to blame.

Transcending their differences, each of the three novels portrays the German people as political agents — albeit political agents manqué — morally obtuse and politically estranged.

Billiards at Half-Past Nine

Heinrich Böll's *bildungsroman* traces the lives of three generations of Faemels, a family of middle-class professionals. He takes them from the early twentieth century through World Wars I and II to the establishment of the West German Federal Republic in 1958. *Billiards at Half-Past Nine*, although deeply melancholy, is the most politically hopeful of the three novels considered in this section.[8] The ascendance of Nazism is attributed primarily to the support it received from a single, arguably outdated, element of German society: the Junker class, with its military traditions, authoritarian tendencies and imperial ambitions. Secondly, it was the unwillingness of the forward-thinking and respectable middle class to assert its interests that allowed the aristocrats in concert with the Nazi riffraff to take over.

However, the book ends on a note of *civic* and *moral* rather than *political* re-engagement. For thus having his characters "act privately, not publicly," Böll has been criticized as politically naïve — for, in effect, dwelling on the personal at the expense of the political.[9] From my perspective, however, this critique is an unintended confirmation that this is a novel of political estrangement — implicitly at odds with Irving Howe's admonition to political novelists to locate and give voice to a politically resonant and better, if contingent, future.

BOURGEOIS VIRTUES, BOURGEOIS VICES

The Faemels embody the contradictory qualities, the competing impulses, and, thus, the suspect civic reliability of the respectable bourgeoisie. It is not that the Faemels have failed to do their duty to the state. On the contrary! Accordingly they have been rewarded with honors and prosperity. By 1958 Grandfather David Faemel is retired. He was something of a self-made man — with his service in World War I seemingly instrumental in his success. He trained as an architect, became an officer in the Engineer Reserves in 1897, and in his own words: "built siege trenches, I bored tunnels, set up artillery emplacements, faced barrages, dragged wounded out of fire" (p. 99). Winning the commission after the war to build an abbey was career-making because at the time he had no reputation, and his triumph over more established architects was a shock to all concerned. This abbey commission became the foundation of the family's considerable status and prosperity.

On the other hand, the family had been all too likely to elevate personal security and short-term self interest over public virtue. In so doing, they betrayed the very republican principles which are consonant with their long-term class interests. For the Faemels this has meant death and discord. We learn that percolating beneath the placid surface of the family's respectability and material success are desperate divisions rooted in disparate visions of civic responsibility and generations of wartime losses.

VISIONS OF CIVIC RESPECTABILITY

Grandmother Faemel and her son Robert are the dominant voices of personal loss and estrangement from politics. Her suffering is especially intense — stretching across the generations and eating away at the faith that sustains her. She expresses this faith in terms of the perpetual struggle between the Host of the Lamb as Christian virtue residing in the spiritual world and unrelentingly under assault from the Host of the Beast that permeates the material world.

> Men, responsibility. Obeying the law, imparting a sense of history to children, counting money and resolved on political reason, all were doomed to partake of the *Host of the Beast*, like my brothers (p. 139).

She loves her husband, David; she has stood by him; and she believes he is a truly good man. However, she deplores his determination to maintain cordial relationships with a corrupt world. "He's a child, he has no idea how bad the world is, and few the pure in heart. He's one of them. A quiet man, no blemishes on his pure heart" (p. 117).

In contrast, she has always been uncompromising and outspoken about her ideals. As a young bride she refused to "drink champagne when we were invited to the garrison commandant's, wouldn't eat the jugged hare and refused every dance. She said it out loud: 'That fool of a Kaiser.' You'd have thought the Ice Age had come, there in the Wilhelmskuhle Casino" (p. 81). She continued her struggle throughout her adult life and grievous losses. Brothers were lost in World War I and sons as well as a daughter and a daughter-in-law in World War II. To her utter despair, her son Otto became a rabid Nazi and was twice lost — first to the Host of the Beast and then to death in battle.[10]

By the end of the war Grandmother Faemel has been driven to distraction by these betrayals and seems to have lost her grip. As one character puts it:

> His mother went off the beam, lost two brothers and three of her children died. Never got over it. Fine woman . . . Never ate a crumb more than the ration card allowed her . . . Whatever she got extra, she'd just give it all away . . . she went down to the freight yard and tried to go along in the cars with the Jews. Screwball, they said. They locked her up in the looney bin (pp. 26–7).[*]

The narrative suggests that she has not so much been locked up as chosen a kind of *inner migration* — seeking asylum both literally and figuratively (p. 141). Thus, a familiar theme re-emerges: sanity masquerading as insanity and vice versa.

Robert, like his mother, cannot ignore injustice (p. 27) and he too pays a heavy price. In high school he has an experience that transforms him from a much admired athlete and popular student into a pariah. He witnesses the gratuitous violence inflicted on his schoolmate, the anti-Nazi Schrella, and instinctively sides with him.[11] At first, Robert's popularity enables him to protect Schrella. All of that changes, however, when Robert, Schrella and another friend, Ferdi, hatch a plan to attack Vacano, the Nazi gym teacher who has inflamed the school boys to do violence against Schrella. The three are charged with murder, arrested and subjected to brutal interrogation. Ferdi is executed; Robert and Schrella flee Germany.

Robert is able to rehabilitate himself through the efforts of his mother. She compromises her principles this one (and only) time by using family influence to negotiate a deal (p. 122). In return for permission to return from exile, Robert must and does agree to enter military service and

---

[*] It can only be taken as an indication of her extraordinary virtue that the persecution of the Jews figures prominently in her distress.

refrain from engaging in political activity. He is trained as a demolitions expert, is promoted within the officer ranks and receives commendations for his demolition work for a general who demands that buildings standing between him and the enemy be destroyed to provide a "field of fire." Thus, Robert ends up fighting a war he opposes on behalf of an ideology he detests.

Robert's burdens are, unlike his mother's, neither spiritual nor religious, but emotional. He emerges from the war an intensely detached adult who views everything abstractly. His satisfactions are strongly ascetic.[12] But, even in this detached state, at heart Robert remains his mother's son. He takes a young hotel bellhop under his wing and discovers that he, Hugo, has also been beaten by others who take him to be "God's Little Lamb" (p. 60 ff.) — providing us with one of the novel's suggestions that the ugliness of the Nazi era lingers on in the Federal Republic.

THE FEDERAL REPUBLIC

The novel is, however, less about the Nazis and their war than about their poisonous legacy. The Faemels view the Federal Republic as profoundly compromised by a malevolent combination of residual Nazism, imperialism, rampant materialism and corruption. Two characters from Robert's youth, the admirable Schrella and the odious Nettlinger, move to the narrative center and expose the infirmities of the Federal Republic.

Schrella was, of course, one of the three anti-Nazi co-conspirators; he was exiled, but unlike Robert, was not rehabilitated. Indeed when Schrella returns to the Federal Republic he is jailed for the boys' attempt to assassinate the Nazi teacher. Nettlinger, in instructive contrast, had ingratiated himself to the Nazi authorities by the contribution he made to the arrests of Robert, Schrella and the martyred Ferdi. Nettlinger and Schrella return in tandem to the narrative in time for the 1958 festivities commemorating the reconstruction of Grandfather Faemel's abbey and his eightieth birthday, the novel's two culminating events.

The opportunistic Nettlinger is the symbolic representation of all that is unsavory about the Federal Republic. He is readily able to make a seamless transition from the Nazi state by fabricating principled rationales for his self-serving activities during the Nazi era. He proceeds to embrace the opportunities for status and material success afforded by the Federal Republic. Nettlinger also intercedes to arrange a provisional release for Schrella in time for the celebratory events. He does so in a vain attempt to establish his postwar bona fides and in a futile search for absolution from the incontrovertibly virtuous Schrella.

Nettlinger hosts an ostentatiously lavish post-incarceration dinner for Schrella. He promises to plead Schrella's case before the appropriate authorities, in order to get "your name definitively struck off the Wanted List" (p. 169). "I'm a democrat," declares Nettlinger. "A democrat by conviction" (p. 171). Schrella will have none of it; he finds this new Nettlinger more contemptible than the old Nettlinger.

> I hope you understand me — even at that time I never doubted the sincerity of your personal motives and feelings; you can't understand, don't even try; you didn't play your part knowingly — you'd be a cynic or a criminal — and you're neither (p. 163).

But now, "'Your politeness,' he thought, 'is worse than your rudeness ever was. Your always wanting to be Johnny on-the-spot is the same now as it always was. It was that way when you threw the ball in my face'" (p. 164). Nonetheless, Nettlinger has made it possible for Schrella to reunite with Robert and join in the family's celebration. This celebration seems an unlikely occasion for healing the rifts within the family or for establishing the vitality of the Host of the Lamb. However, that is precisely the purpose that it serves.

CELEBRATION, RECONCILIATION AND REDEDICATION

Virtually without exception, the Faemels as well as Schrella approach the family gathering with foreboding. Robert is burdened by a secret that he has kept from the family. Not only had he been in charge of the Abbey's demolition, he had actually rejoiced in this assignment. Grandmother Faemel is apprehensive about venturing into the corrupt world of the Federal Republic which she had fled a decade earlier. Schrella has much the same concerns. He experiences every step that he takes in the Federal Republic as a betrayal of his values. And then there is Robert's son, Joseph, who is in charge of reconstructing the Abbey and has learned to his dismay about Robert's secret. Joseph is also uneasy about a reunion, however brief, with his emotionally distant father.

Despite the general foreboding, the family reunion and the celebratory events lead not only to reconciliation but also to the discovery of a deeply shared sense of moral conviction. Robert makes it clear that his destruction of the Abbey was in truth an affirmation of the Host of Lamb.

> [H]e had waited through five years of war for that moment, the moment when the Abbey would be his booty, lying like a gift of God. He had wanted to erect a monument of dust and rubble for those who had not been historical monuments and whom no one had thought to spare (p. 146).

David contributes to the spirit of family reconciliation by denying any resentment about Robert's role (which appears not to have been a surprise). It turns out that David "never had too much feeling for buildings I designed and put up. I liked them on paper, I had a certain passion for the work, but was never an artist" (p. 157). He saw the rebuilding of the Abbey simply as a professional opportunity for his grandson Joseph. David also reveals that he was not as detached as it may have seemed — and, indeed, was deeply grieved by the same losses that wore down his wife.

Family bonds are further strengthened by Grandmother Faemel's defiant act of violence during the blatant triumphalism of the civic celebration held in conjunction with the reopening of the Abbey.

> I tell you dearest [she confides to her husband], the whole pack of them have partaken of the *Host of the Beast*. Dumb as earth, deaf as a tree, and as terribly harmless as the Beast in his last incarnation. Respectable, respectable. I'm scared, old man — I've never felt such a stranger among people, not even in 1935 and not in 1942 . . . Respectable, respectable, without a trace of grief. What's human without grief? (p. 230).

Her goal was to shoot either Nettlinger or Vacano, but with these targets out of reach, she turns her gun on "M" — a campaigning politician, who happens to be reviewing from an adjacent terrace the "Fighting Veterans' League" parade in honor of "some field marshal's birthday." M serves as a readily accessible symbol of all that is wrong with new Germany. In the wake of the shooting, the family proceeds to reunite around their matriarch — thus validating her moral authority and healing their rifts.

By honoring Grandmother Faemel's resonant return to the material world, the family in effect rededicate themselves to a worldly struggle against the Host of the Beast. They also pledge themselves to the future as personified by Joseph and Marianne and by generations to come. Only the admirable Schrella holds out and decides to exile himself from Germany. In other words, while Grandmother Faemel has decided to re-engage against the Host of the Beast, Schrella cannot bring himself to do so. These two paths emerge as the only two choices open to decent people faced with a homeland firmly in the grip *yet again* of the Host of the Beast. *Note, however, that neither choice is political.*

Schrella explicitly proclaims that his decision to leave Germany is not a political act. He simply cannot tolerate a country full of wolves clothed as lambs. He is offended by the excess, the sheer opportunistic materialism, of the new German state. As he confides in Robert:

> You think I don't want to live here because this country seems to me to have no political future, but I'm more inclined to believe I couldn't live here because I always have been, and still am today, completely unpolitical . . . Those people down there aren't scaring me off . . . I'm not afraid because those people exist but rather because the other kind do not exist. What kind? Those who think the word, sometimes, or perhaps whisper it . . . *Feed my lambs*, Robert — but all they do is breed wolves (p. 246).

In good conscience, then, Schrella concludes that he simply cannot make a decent life for himself in the Federal Republic.

Even though Schrella's moral stance is beyond reproach and his pessimism fully warranted, the decision of the Faemels to remain seems to express Böll's own vision about what must be done. They reunite in affirmation of the Host of the Lamb and seem determined to re-engage with the world. Because the narrative attributes the success of the Nazis to the failure of the respectable classes to act honorably, it follows that the future of the Federal Republic will depend on how many of its natural leaders follow the example set by the Faemels.

Given the return of the Faemels to the world and given their belief that virtue on a large scale can transform the world, is it reasonable to maintain, as I do, that *Billiards at Half-Past Nine* is a novel of political estrangement? Robert Conrad believes that to think in my terms is to conflate "the fictional world with the real world:"

> If one recognizes that the goal of the author and the novel is to change existing society . . . it does not follow that a passive character or a character acting privately cannot effect this as much as a politically active character . . . The novel is as politically active, or socially effective, as it can be, when it raises the necessary social questions in an enlightened manner with philosophic and artistic consistency.[13]

As I see it, Conrad is referring to the novel itself and considers it, as do I, as political. The narrative does portray characters who are themselves politically estranged. Grandmother Faemel's feckless and futile attempt to assassinate M is a political act, but it leads to a spiritual, rather than a political epiphany, with the family uniting around the objective of bearing spiritual witness in the material world to the Host of the Lamb.[14]

The German Lesson

Siegfried Lenz's eloquent meditation on the insidious "joys of duty" also addresses the distressing continuity between the Nazi era and the Federal Republic. The life of Siggy Jepson, the novel's central character and narrator, is blighted by the joys of duty — personified in his father, Jens, "the Rugbull policeman."[15] Siggy comes to see the joys of duty not as an idiosyncratic trait of his father's but as deeply embedded in the blood, in the soil and especially in the insular ethos of rural Germany with its reflexive distrust of *the Other*. Siggy finds refuge from all of this in the home of a neighbor and Expressionist painter, Max Nansen. The core of the novel is to be found in the ever-mounting tensions among these three main characters.

As the novel progresses, the people of Rugbull become ever more accepting of, and complicit in, the Nazi regime. Nansen's paintings, set in Rugbull, mirror the repellent truths about Rugbull society. Also at odds with that society is Nansen's loose and easy lifestyle which clashes in particular with the Rugbull police officer's fixation on duty, on order and on respect for authority. Although the two men had been friends, it was foreordained that their friendship would sooner or later founder — and so it does.

The ensuing drama extends over Siggy's adolescent wartime years and his post-adolescence in the Federal Republic. During the war he is plagued by enmities and loyalties he cannot comprehend. What is unequivocally and elementally clear to Siggy is that the joys of duty are poisonous — riding roughshod over good instincts and standing resolutely in the way of doing the right thing. Understandably, upon coming of age at the end of the war, he indulges his irresistible urge to flee the suffocating cultural milieu of Rugbull. Accordingly, he follows his equally disaffected brother Klaas and sister Hilke to Hamburg. Unlike them, however, Siggy resolves by the end of the novel to return.

How and why Siggy returns to Rugbull is the sustaining mystery of the novel. The mystery is never entirely cleared up, and so we are left with an indeterminate German lesson. However, like *Billiards at Half-Past Nine*, *The German Lesson* strongly suggests that the most important lesson to be learned from the Nazi experience is moral rather than political.

NAZI CULTURE

Siggy's war-time tale begins innocently enough when the Rugbull policeman visits his then close friend, Max, to deliver an official order to stop painting — an order that the puzzled Jens does not understand. "Why, Max?" Jens asks. "Perhaps I talk too much," responds Max (p. 32). And indeed Max, who was at one time a loyal Nazi, has turned against them and refused their offer to head the State Academy of Arts. He announces that he cannot do so because he has been afflicted by a "colour allergy. Brown diagnosed as a source of trouble" (p. 165). However, irrespective of his aversion to the Brown Shirts, we know that as an Expressionist — a practitioner of *degenerate art* — he had no more future in the Third Reich than did the dedicated Nazi, Emil Nolde, who, like Max, was relegated to social and artistic limbo.

While Jens is puzzled and unenthusiastic about enforcing this order, he believes he has no choice but to do his duty. Siggy tells us of his father's "everyday sense of duty, which has become second nature, which forced him to get going: not eagerness, not the pleasure he took in his job and certainly not the mission that had fallen to his lot" (p. 20). Yet to Siggy, Jens' fixation on doing his duty and his seemingly congenital incapacity to question authority is connected to a more fatal flaw in the rural German character. Siggy asks:

> Why is it only among us that everybody seems afraid of confessing there's anything he knows nothing about? The all-out narrow-mindedness in which people are lured by local patriotism probably finds its completest expression in the people's notion that they're called upon to give an expert answer to all questions: arrogance born of narrowness . . . (p. 134).

Only the small circle that gathers around the increasingly isolated Max is immune from this antipathy to *the other* and tuned into cosmopolitan values and virtues.

Jens attempts to drill a sense of duty into Siggy and, unsuccessfully, to make him an informer against Uncle Max (pp. 57–8). His transgressions include not only continuing to paint but harboring Siggy's older brother Klaas, who has chosen to desert his army unit rather than to do his soldier's duty. Moreover, we learn about the price paid by the Jepson family for Jens' obsession with duty from a series of Uncle Max's paintings. That price is clearest in the deep suffering and fear expressed by Klaas' face in "a dozen paintings" including "The Last Supper" (pp. 186 and 190). Each of the seagulls in one of Max's paintings "had my father's face, the long, sleepy face of the Rugbull policeman, and all of them had on their three-clawed feet little boots and gaiters of the sort my father wore" (p. 51).

There are, thus, several strands to the conflict between the Nansen circle and the Jepsons — with Jens' sense of duty only the tip of the iceberg. More fundamental are the clash of values, the alienation of the Jepson children from their parents, and the irresistible pull of the Nansen household. Siggy's mother, the joyless, censorious and fanatical Gudrun, is at least as responsible for the repressed tone of the Jepson's household as is the officious Rugbull policeman. At a birthday party she looks on reprovingly at the festivities and, as Siggy puts it, "only my mother held aloof and I knew nothing would induce her to join us" (p. 70). "There was nothing I enjoyed less than having a meal alone with Gudrun Jepson" (p. 252).

Siggy becomes both a pawn and a player in the cultural conflict among competing conceptions of social, political and family values. First, his father recruits him to spy on the Nansen household. Then when Max is finally arrested by men in leather coats, accompanied by a smug and triumphant Jens (p. 223), Max's final act at home is to give Siggy his painting, "The Cloudmaker," (p. 228) and to ask him to "keep it safe somewhere" (p. 229). The adolescent Siggy is thus drafted into the deadly *adult* contest between duty to art and duty to the state, leading inevitably but many years later to the crime spree which results in Siggy's arrest by anonymous officials, still wearing leather coats, and his incarceration in the progressive penal system of the Federal Republic.

"REPUBLICAN" CULTURE

The symbolism of leather-coated agents of the state is just one of many indications that although things *seem* to have changed radically, in many ways the German Federal Republic and its citizens continue to engage in many of the ostensibly discredited practices of the Third Reich.† Returned soldiers put on a play which seems to repeat traditional patriotic themes (p. 329). The persistence of blood, soil, and duty in Rugbull provide further reason for disillusionment with the new Germany. Gudrun brings her contempt for the mentally ill with her to the Federal Republic. She denounces the mentally ill who are housed nearby after the liberation. "Worthless creatures! They'll be nothing but trouble, you mark my words" (p. 386). When, after a brief postwar internment, Jens is returned to his position as the Rugbull policeman, he is unwilling, indeed unable, to change his ways. He continues to believe in blind obedience — doing his duty, even when it means saluting British occupation officials who have

---

* The Cloudmaker is described by Siggy as "an irresistible relentless brown, a brown occupying the whole of the horizon, a brown streaked and bordered with grey, [which] unrolled and went on growing and growing over a countryside sinking into dusk" (p. 228).

† On the day that the British arrive, the brutal biology teacher provides a lesson on natural selection which stresses the difference between the strong who survive and the "trash" (p. 298) that do not — expressing his contempt for the sounds of nearby gunfire and of planes flying overhead (p. 296). Only after two British soldiers enter his classroom does he finally succumb to depression and dismiss the class (p. 301).

come to award Max a "Diploma of Honorary Membership of the [Royal] Academy [in London]" (p. 374).

I don't ask what good it does a man to do his duty, nor whether it's good for him or not. Where would it get us all if every time we did something we asked ourselves what it was going to lead to? You can't do your duty just according to your mood or by letting yourself be guided by caution — if you get my meaning" (p. 292).

Gudrun thus lives and breathes ideology of racial purity and eugenics into Jens' largely apolitical sense of duty.

Max's intimate friend, Teo Busbeck, is distraught by these ghosts of the Nazi era and urges Max to leave Rugbull with him. The countryside, he laments, "has no surface, only . . . this baleful depth, and everything that's down there is a threat to you" (p. 344). Max himself observes that "the rats are boarding the new ship" (p. 341) when he is approached by an official, Maltzahn, who has thrived during the Nazi era as editor of the journal, "Art and the People." Now he — Lenz's Nettlinger, one might say — claims to have been Max's "patron and anonymous defender" during the war (p. 340) and wishes to view and to reproduce some of Max's work for his *new* journal, "Abiding Things" (p. 338).

The crime spree for which Siggy is ultimately incarcerated is his own response to failings of the Federal Republic — symbolized by the continuing threats to Uncle Max's paintings. Immediately after the war, Jens not only banishes Klaas from the family (p. 363), he also burns Max's sketch book — "with an expression of gloating satisfaction on his face" — much to the horror of Siggy (p. 367). Siggy immediately understands that his father will not stop there but will destroy as much of Uncle Nansen's work as he can. When Siggy confronts his father — "you mustn't confiscate anything any more, you mustn't make fires, you mustn't burn anything," Jens strikes him and knocks him down (p. 368).

The other threats to Nansen are less material than moral — but no less dangerous to Siggy. He is struck by the extravagant superficiality of the art critics. They tend to misinterpret Nansen's work by applying purely aesthetic standards to his Expressionist determination to bare the north German soul and also by drowning it in a contradictory babble[16] — all the while snickering at Uncle Nance's extravagant and anachronistic garb. In doing so, they betray Uncle Nance's truths — the truths that have become fused with Siggy's identity.

Siggy feels compelled to protect Nance's work and does so by stealing his paintings from the galleries and museums of the Federal Republic — even from the painter himself. While seizing one of Nance's paintings,

Siggy tells himself: "Nobody, nobody would ever see this picture again, that was settled, and the other pictures, too, were there only for me now. I had found out something about myself and what I need to live with myself" (p. 413). While Siggy's sole purpose is to protect them, the bitter irony of his intervention is that by secreting them away, he *ipso facto* conceals the truths which Nansen has been so implacably determined to tell.

The "trench coats" are soon on high alert, and when Siggy attends an exhibition of Nansen's work in Hamburg they appear and hustle him out with the intention of arresting him. When he asks whether they have been tipped off by Rugbull, the response is "Shut your trap" and "Get a move on" (p. 430). Siggy manages to escape, to elude the authorities and to find refuge with Klaas who lives in a building of aspiring artists. There Siggy discovers that the artists' ambitions and their unconventional lifestyles are, in their own ways, every bit as reprehensible and narrow-minded as the ethos of Rugbull. He gets into a confrontation with a painter friend of Klaas's who refers to Uncle Nansen as "that great landscape-window-dresser" (p. 437).[17] Hansi attacks Siggy and knocks him out — thus replicating the brutality of his arrest by the police, and of course all of it is redolent of Nazi-era thuggery.

GERMAN LESSONS
Ultimately, Siggy is captured and incarcerated by the new German state in a progressive penal institution for delinquent youth. There he is subjected to what seems, albeit misleadingly, like the final irony — required to learn the lesson of his delinquency by writing an essay on the *joys of duty*. Initially, he cannot bring himself to descend into — or try to make sense out of — the moral and emotional chaos of his wartime youth. "I could not find anything to hold on to so as to descend step by step, into my memories. I told him [the school's director] about the many faces, the chaotic pushing and shoving, all the movements crisscrossing in my memory that frustrated each of my attempts to start" (p. 15).

However, once he finally does get started, he cannot stop even when the prison authorities decide that he has fulfilled the terms of his sentence. Not surprisingly, the correctional authorities and Siggy interpret his dedication to the essay in diametrically different ways. As his fellow inmate, the rebellious Ole, puts it, "I see *the joys of duty* have got hold of you" (p. 159). But to Siggy the essay certainly does not represent a tribute to the joys of duty, nor a way of paying a debt to society for his crimes, nor a step towards his rehabilitation. Instead, he sees the essay as bearing witness — giving his family and his neighbors an opportunity to tell their stories.

The northernmost police station in Germany, the painter, my brother Klaas, Asmus Asmussen, Jutta — was I to deny them the right to state their case and to defend themselves (p. 159)?

As the essay (and hence the novel) progresses, we learn to interpret Siggy's sense of purpose in more intensely subjective terms — to make sense, that is, out of the bewildering tangle of his struggle with, and estrangement from, his family, from his countrymen and from his roots.

Ultimately, Siggy feels compelled to return to Rugbull:

Rugbull is irrevocably there, the place that I have sounded out in so many directions and which nevertheless still denies me so many answers . . . . I ask why they so belittle those who are afflicted in body and mind, and why they regard anyone with second sight with awe, even indeed dread . . . And I ask myself why they leave the stranger there outside, scorning his help. And why they cannot turn back half-way and have a change of heart . . . Their taciturn gluttony, their smugness, their local lore, the element in which they live and move and have their being: to these as well I put my questions (pp. 467–8).

Because, therefore, the mystery of Rugbull continues to elude him and because it is where he belongs, Siggy feels he must return.

Lenz leaves no doubt that Siggy will return, but the book ends prior to that return, so its consequences and even Siggy's objectives are left open to inference. It might be tempting, and politically inspiring, to see his return as taking up where his uncle Max left off — helping the citizens of Rugbull to understand their shortcomings and to change their ways. However, that outcome would be at odds with Lenz's tragic perspective, with the indeterminacy and irony that permeate the novel, as well as with the culminating events of the novel itself.

Consider, to begin with, the last sentence — Siggy's speculation about his exit interview with the Director of the penal institution who has taken Siggy under his wing.

He will make a gesture and we shall both sit down, shall sit facing one another without stirring, each of us thoroughly pleased with himself because he feels he has won (p. 470).

If we work our way back through the events attendant to Siggy's incarceration, it seems possible to believe that they both may have won — or equally likely that neither has won.

Siggy has not, as the authorities wished, learned the joys of duty. Throughout the novel, he derides both the means and the ends of the state's progressive penal practices. He satirizes and patronizes the therapists who indulge in various versions of behavior modification. He believes that they completely misunderstand him. Yet Siggy is acutely aware that during his incarceration he has come to understand himself in ways that are an unintended consequence of, but not necessarily inconsistent with, the methods and goals of the authorities, and has done so by adapting their means to his ends. He puts it this way:

> [I] had been allowed to go on writing because it was clear that I wanted to do the theme justice and demonstrate its possibilities. True, he, Himpel [the director], had also been aware of something else: he had been struck by the way that memory had become a trap [into] which I had fallen, and he had wanted me to extricate myself unaided. And he had also come to the conclusion that the punishment he had imposed on me was a mild one compared with the punishment I had imposed on myself by insisting on completing the task (p. 465).

Put another way, Siggy has, in collusion with the authorities, transformed an exercise in behavior modification into a search for a truly meaningful life.

He concludes that this search must be conducted in Rugbull where he returns to figure out why the joys of duty have so strong and malevolent a grip on the rural ethos and presumably to live his own life according to the humane and inclusive values of Uncle Nansen. In one sense, the essential importance of this moral awakening cannot be exaggerated. If the Federal Republic is to thrive, the cosmopolitan virtues of the Enlightenment must prevail over the insular vices embedded in the joys of duty — especially in their traditional rural strongholds. Moreover, the parochialism of Rugbull also emerges as a metaphor for traditional Germany's deeply entrenched resistance to the contestations and inclusiveness that are hallmarks of modern society and liberal democracy.[18]

In the end, however, this is not a book about social and political change. We know that Siggy has emerged from his encounter with the state's progressive penal practices with his conscience redeemed* — and in so

---

* Lenz's attitude toward progressive penal practices is left unclear. Siggy emerges from the progressive (non-punitive) condition of his confinement as a changed man

doing has discovered the redemptive power of the individual conscience. However, Lenz gives us little, if any, reason, to believe that Siggy will have even the remotest chance of being an agent of reform in Rugbull. He will probably fight the good fight for a while and then end up beaten down by it. In a worst case, but utterly plausible, scenario, Siggy could actually succumb to, rather than transform, the blood and soil which is his heritage and to which he is returning. After all Siggy is drawn back to Rugbull not only by his sense of moral responsibility but also because of the gravitational force of blood and soil.

The Tin Drum

> *[A] wailing infant is 'about the most disturbing, demanding, shattering noise that we can hear.'*
>
> Jerome Groopman[19]

Gunter Grass's masterpiece, published originally in 1959, focuses exclusively on the petite bourgeoisie and the working class — while remaining supremely uninterested in the professionals, the aristocrats, the militarists, the capitalists and the artists who are foci for Böll and Lenz. The central figure, Oskar Matzerath, the eponymous tin drummer, is the omniscient and prescient narrator who "knows," as children are wont to know, that the adult world is corrupt and hypocritical. Of course because Oskar is judging the adult world of Germany in Nazi years — almost literally a world from hell — his judgments cannot be dismissed as a childhood fantasy of narcissistic omnipotence.

The story of Oscar's innocence as well as its corruption is anchored in the child's inarticulate and irresistible capacity to elicit compliance from reluctant adults. The drum is Oskar's *deus ex machina*: it is a source of power and truth, dependent on its capacity to "drum the necessary distance between grown-ups and myself" (p. 59). He also has at his disposal a high-pitched scream with the power to shatter glass, and he deploys it against adults who grow weary of his incessant drumming and attempt

---

with a strong sense of moral responsibility and ready to become a good citizen. He thus lives out what Foucault memorably characterized as the progression of penal practice from punishment to discipline. While both practices, he believed, were directed at suppressing difference, discipline seeks to make the miscreants complicit in their own subjection — thus subverting agency while claiming to nurture it. Michel Foucault, *Discipline and Punish: The Birth of the Prison*, New York: Pantheon Books, 1977. However, it could also be argued, and I suspect Lenz would agree, that Siggy has demonstrated that the open texture of disciplinary practices can be utilized to serve agency rather than to subvert it.

to seize his drum or refuse to replace the drums he regularly wears out. Thus two expressive tools of childhood reinforce one another — keeping adults at bay and compliant.

Nor does Oskar shrink from the desperate implications of his insight. In an inevitably futile effort to preserve his three-year-old innocence, Oskar decides not to grow up. His carefully calibrated plunge down the cellar stairs stunts his growth without otherwise disabling him. As a result, "I remained the precocious three-year-old, towered over by grown-ups but superior to all grown-ups" (p. 56) — while keeping them at arm's length and thus preserving his perspective on adult life.

THE INNOCENT EYE

Absent his raucous intrusions, adults tend to ignore him and thus he is allowed to observe the many sordid aspects of putatively respectable lower middle-class life. Oskar is aware that his mother has carried on an affair with Jan Bronski — both before and after her marriage to the easygoing grocer and cuckold Matzerath.

- "Jan's hand has disappeared under Mama's skirt — communicates nothing but the mad passion of this unhappy pair, steeped in adultery from the very first day of Mama's marriage" (p. 52).
- He also witnesses his mother engaged in lesbian sex during afternoon tea with the baker's wife, Gretchen (p. 88).

All of this monkey business puts Oskar's paternity in doubt, and he is inclined to believe that his father is the adulterous Bronski and not Matzerath whose name he bears and upon whom his legitimacy depends. Of course, legitimacy is for Oskar only a figment of the adult world's hypocritical imagination.

It is, however, not only those adults closest to Oskar who behave badly while hypocritically thinking of themselves as respectable Germans, but also their friends and neighbors. Consider the party in which adults in "an advanced state of intoxication, had paired off strangely . . . As was to be expected, Mama, with disheveled corsage, was sitting on Bronski's lap. It was the opposite of appetizing to see Alexander Scheffler, the short-legged baker, almost submerged amid the billow of Mrs. Greff. Matzerath was liking Gretchen Scheffler's horse teeth. Only Hedwig Bronski sat alone with her hands in her lap, her cow's eyes pious in the candlelight, close but not too close to Greff, the greengrocer" (p. 64).

The hypocrisies of daily life foreshadow and readily accommodate the opportunistic engagement with Nazism observed by Oskar. He calls our attention to the social benefits of party membership with a photo of the Schefflers cruising on "the 'Strength through Joy' ship, the 'Wilhelm

Gustloff'" (p. 53).[20] But Oskar's primary focus is on the Nazi "era of torchlight processions and parades past rostrums and reviewing stands" (p. 110). He notes that children began to wear "uniforms and black ties" (p. 169) and that his friend Meyn, a trumpeter and a drunk, having become a member of the mounted storm troopers, "stone sober in boots and breeches with a leather seat . . . would take the steps five at time" (p. 169). The passive Matzerath, following the line of least resistance, remakes himself from a World War I soldier with "the Iron Cross Second Class" (p. 49) into a minor Nazi functionary. He rejoices in the parades and rallies. "But that was the way he was; he always had to wave when other people were waving, to shout, laugh, and clap when other peoples were shouting, laughing, and clapping. That explains why he joined the Party at such an early date" (p. 147).

So here we have children in uniform emulating adults and adults in uniform reverting to the childish fantasies nurtured by the social solidarity and martial myths of the Nazi discourse and practice. Indeed, one might say that Grass discovered the banality of this particular evil well before Hannah Arendt gave voice to that now resonant phrase. Patrick O'Neill puts it this way: "Oskar's distorted refraction of German society strips away the façade of respectability and reticence veiling the rise of Nazi Germany."[21] Oskar sets himself firmly against all this hypocrisy, duplicity and corruption wherever he finds them and against Nazism in particular. His drumming and his glass shattering are dedicated to preserving and proclaiming truths and exposing deceit and exploitation.

One of Oskar's proudest moments is when he completely transforms the ethos of a Nazi party rally by drumming out a non-military counterpoint to the martial music with which the faithful are saluting Party "martyrs" (p. 115).[22] In so doing he changes the tone of the proceedings, leading to dancing rather than to marching. "Gone were law and order" (p. 117). Another of Oskar's capers is to use his voice to cut through display windows of jewelry shops — thus making valuables available to "the small and medium-sized desires of all those silent walkers in the snow" (p. 125). In their rush to take advantage of this opportunity they engage in behaviors they profess to deplore as "self-righteous citizens who until that hour had looked upon the pettiest and most incompetent of pickpockets as a dangerous criminal" (pp. 125–6).

He drums away ugliness and hopelessness. When his mother dies, Oskar sees his drumming as having "re-created the ideal image of her grey-eyed beauty" (p. 157) — thus erasing her jaundiced ravaged death mask. He also drums for his own lineage and in praise of his grandmother who sheltered a soldier-deserter beneath her ample skirts. "I called forth sounds of October rain, similar to what she must have heard by the smoldering potato plants, when Koljajeczek, smelling like a hot pursued firebug, came to her for shelter" (p. 210). While thus hidden, Koljajeczek begat Oskar's mother. He drums up a reassuring future for Polish patriots overwhelmed by Nazi cultural imperialism and the Wehrmacht: "Poland's lost, but not forever, all's lost, but not forever, Poland's not lost forever" (p 103).

THE CORRUPTIBLE EGO

But the same powers that serve Oskar's idealistic and altruistic impulses are all too readily corrupted. Indeed, the very act intended to preserve Oskar's innocence compromises it. He makes no effort to intervene when his mother blames, and never forgives, the hapless Matzerath for being so inattentive as to allow Oskar to tumble down the stairs. The novel then becomes a lesson in how and why Oskar does not, and cannot, preserve his innocence, and in what he and we learn from his efforts to do so.

As Oscar grows up, reluctantly and in stages, over the course of the novel beginning with the onset of the war, his corruption proves not so much unavoidable as irresistible. Oskar comes to see himself as a soul divided "between Rasputin and Goethe, between the faith healer and the man of the Enlightenment, between the dark spirit who cast a spell on women and the luminous poet prince who was so fond of letting women cast a spell on him" (p. 86). Oskar, like the German people, is torn between virtue and self-indulgence but in the end he finds self-indulgence irresistible, leading to a shameless hypocrisy — the tribute that vice is said to pay to virtue.

With the suicide of Markus, the Jewish shopkeeper, Oskar loses his source of drums: "How was he to preserve his three-year-old countenance if he lacked what was most necessary for his well-being, his drum? All the deceptions I had been practicing for years . . . all this nonsense that grown-ups expected of me I now had to provide without my drum" (p. 206). In his desperation to find a drum, he seeks out his putative father, Jan Bronski, who risks his life and ultimately loses it on Oskar's behalf. In search of a reliable repairman for Oskar's drum, Bronski returns to the Polish Post Office, his place of employment. There, in fear and trembling, he finds himself embroiled in an attack by the German Home Guard. He is captured, tried, convicted and executed by the Germans for having taken part in "irregular military activity" (p. 243).

Oskar is introspective enough to feel shame, but he is more interested in ridding himself of any witnesses to his shame than in doing penance for it. His first love, Maria, becomes enmeshed in his effort to cover up his role in Jan's death. She enters his life as he is furiously drumming "to destroy the last witness to his shameful conduct with the Home Guards"

(p. 252) with the intention "to settle his accounts by Christmas" (p. 253). He destroys the drum, expecting, *in vain* it turns out, that he will be given a new "guiltless drum" for Christmas. Maria then steps in and supplies him with new drums on a regular basis throughout and beyond the war. More to the point, her "vanilla scent" as they pass Jan's burial place "in an instant vanquished the mouldering Jan Bronski" (p. 261). Oskar goes on to develop a bizarre relationship with Maria who, playing the role of a big sister and caregiver, tempts him with access to her body and other less than innocent gestures.[23]

In the end, *The Tin Drum* has little if anything to offer about a better future — only an uncompromising judgment about the past. Grass's bona fides have been called into question since a belated acknowledgment in *Peeling the Onion*[24] that he had been a member of the SS. As I see it, Grass's sweeping indictment of German culture is entirely consistent with his own long-acknowledged youthful support for Nazism, and with his belated disclosure of membership in the Waffen SS at the end of World War II. After all, his novels consistently acknowledge the powerful resonance of Nazism among ordinary Germans. Grass does not spare anyone, including the well-intentioned Oskar.*

Ordinary Germans living ordinary lives are subjected to forces and temptations that are virtually irresistible. The *innocent* Oskar proclaims standards that the *worldly* Oskar cannot meet. He readily discovers that corruptibility is contagious and hypocrisy is at least a tacit recognition of virtue as well a marker of inescapable human frailty.

Conclusions

For all that they have in common the three books considered above offer strikingly different accounts of the nation's capitulation to the Nazis. Grass locates that capitulation in the bowels of German culture — albeit exclusively through the prism of his uniformly petit bourgeois characters. Böll and Lenz look beyond themselves to the internal Other who corrupts an otherwise virtuous German culture. For Böll the true Germans are the moderate middle and professional classes while the internal Other is the militarist Junker class. For Lenz, the internal Other is embodied in those

---

* What is puzzling is why he failed for so long to reveal his brief and hardly com-promising service in Waffen SS. I also have trouble understanding his postwar immersion in SPD politics, given his pessimistic assessment of the German political culture, not only in *The Tin Drum* but in the other two of his novels to be considered in this chapter: *Dog Years* and *Crabwalk*. Suffice to say that only Grass confronts with equal intensity and with exemplary honesty all three of the themes which, as I see it, comprise the literary legacy of postwar, post-Nazi German literature.

committed to unquestioning obedience of authority while he locates the good and the true German culture in an artistic spirit that nurtures humane, aesthetic sensibilities.

It follows that in political terms too, there are parallel differences among the three. They agree that the betrayal of German virtue was about granting power to the Nazis, not about the Nazis seizing it. However, in identifying the intrinsically republican elements of society that betrayed Weimar, Böll and Lenz are *ipso facto* singling out those who can and must take responsibility for the well-being of the Federal Republic. Grass's vision is darker. As Elizabeth Krimmer points out, his characters make subversive political choices but are profoundly estranged from politics.

> It is their inability to conceive of themselves as subjects of history and their failure to create both biologically and artistically that takes them down the path of violence and crime. In the novel's world, human players define themselves as objects, not subjects of history.[25]

So, whereas Böll and Lenz can at least conceive of political paths, however unlikely, to reclaiming German virtue, Grass offers no way out.[26] The three novelists were, however, in heated agreement that the Nazi stain had not been eradicated from German life; that it continued to thrive and to grievously threaten republican prospects.

2. Nazi Anti-Semitism and German Responsibility: A Moral Accounting

In turning from the early postwar novels of Böll, Lenz and Grass to Grass's somewhat later novel *Dog Years* and Christa Wolf's *Patterns of Childhood*, we move to a much higher-stakes inquest into the sins of the Nazi state. Although once again the narratives are about affixing responsibility, these novels are not simply asking who is responsible for bringing the Nazi riffraff to power and keeping them there. They look unflinchingly at the crimes of the Nazis, the price paid by Jews in particular, and the willingness of ordinary Germans to abet those crimes. To what extent, they ask, are ordinary Germans true believers and/or complicit opportunists in the crimes of the Nazi, and/or innocent dupes and unknowing bystanders?

Dog Years

> *'The Germans are a bad love of the Jews,' a Polish peasant woodcarver once observed to a friend of mine.*

Timothy Garton Ash[27]

This novel recounts the star-crossed friendship of two ill-matched boys growing up during the heyday of Nazism. We follow them into the early years of the Federal Republic — through, that is, their maturation and the collapse of the Third Reich. During their school years, Walter Matern, the much stronger of the two, protects the weak and overweight but much more clever Eduard Amsel (p. 37). Eddi may or may not be a "sheeny" (p. 33), but he is made to suffer as one. It is not long before Eddi's rumored Jewish roots (p. 30) and Walter's deep-seated ambivalence about Jews come between them. Still, echoing the historic love-hate relationships between Jews and Germans, the two, as we will see, "remain inseparable blood brothers in spite of the death's-head and the word 'Sheeny'" (p. 80).

However, the novel swells and sprawls beyond simple parable and beyond Walter and Eddi to include an extensive cast of primary and secondary characters, not the least important being three German shepherds, the eponymous dogs of *Dog Years*: Harras, the sire; Senta, the bitch to which he is bred; and their issue, Prinz, who becomes the Fuhrer's dog, just as the breeders intended. Harras is distinguished by his pure black color — blackness, we are told, that resonates with contradictory qualities: Othello-black and more ominously SS-black. Prinz seems created in the image of his sire, a true German shepherd and definitely not "related to the degenerate wolfhound" (p. 154). It turns out, however, that while Harras is of unimpeachable lineage, the bitch Senta is of mixed Lithuanian, Russian and Polish heritage (p. 35). As Prinz goes on to make history over the course of the novel, we learn that his mixed breeding overwhelms the admirable traits passed on by Harras.

The dogs are introduced into the narrative by way of several key secondary characters: Tulla Kynstute, aka Tulla Pokriefke (p. 112), her cousin, Harry Liebenau, Dr. Oswald Brunies, and his adopted daughter Jennie (p. 113). Harry is the narrator; he swims with the tide and becomes the enabler of cousin Tulla. She is a congenitally fickle temptress, who "had taken her [church] vow the preceding March and already broken it twelve times" (p. 64). She is a pervasive presence and a dogged trouble-maker — truly a force of nature. Brunies is a well-intentioned, well-liked and beneficent gym teacher. His stepdaughter, Jenny, a Gypsy orphan, is introduced into the narrative as a pudgy, clumsy and much-maligned young girl — not unlike Eddi.

ANTI-SEMITISM TRIUMPHANT

Throughout the early portions of the novel, Eduard Amsel's putative Jewish origins make him the target of Tulla, the anti-Semite. Her anti-

Semitism is unrelenting — driven by instinct, by envy and by stereotype. Eddi is deemed Jewish *because* he is talented, enterprising, anti-Nazi, and nonviolent. His talent is evidenced by the strikingly effective scarecrows that he constructs. His enterprise is demonstrated by his business acumen in selling these scarecrows which are much in demand by local farmers — thus raising *capital* which he deploys to engineer mechanical scarecrows which give the Nazi salute (p. 188). He proceeds to dress them in Nazi uniforms and gives them the faces of various Nazi leaders (pp. 209–10). Then there is Eddi's subversive relationship with Harras to whom Tulla is devoted. She sees the peaceable Eddi as not only alienating Harras' affections but also bringing out the dog's gentler qualities — all too likely to take the fight out of her dog and her dog out of the fight (pp. 162–3). Eddi compounds his poisonous relationship with Tulla by stealing her limelight. Together, Eddi and Jenny begin to forge artistic careers — she rather badly with piano and he more promisingly with singing.

Tulla proceeds to unleash an increasingly ruthless and brutal campaign of defamation and violence. With Harry, her compliant enabler, standing by, she sets in motion plans to freeze Jenny to death and to unleash Nazi violence on Eddi. The deeply ambivalent, confused and corruptible Walter cannot resist taking part in Eddi's beating (pp. 198–9). A sudden thaw saves Jenny from freezing to death (p. 217). Eddi escapes the beating with his life but without his teeth. The two of them emerge transformed — Eddi, lean and mean; Jenny, lean and lithe (pp. 217–19).

REINVENTING IDENTITIES, REDISTRIBUTING MISFORTUNE

Eddi disappears without a trace and without a word to anyone. He manages to reinvent himself after investing the proceeds from the sale of his mother's estate "on profitable terms in Switzerland" (p. 169). He and the money become equally anonymous; he has himself fitted with 32 gold teeth, a new passport and a new name. Enter Hermann Hasselhoff, aka Goldmouth, of Prague, a chain-smoking impresario (p. 222–3), who flourishes in this role and is hailed throughout the Reich for his fabulous productions. Jenny transforms herself from an ungainly ugly duckling into a dancer of dazzling talents. Without revealing his identity, Haselhoff adds Jenny to his theatre company and she tours the greater German Reich to much acclaim and celebrity.

For the others, things go from bad to worse during the final spasms of the Third Reich. Walter becomes an accomplished actor but he takes to drink and ruins his career. One can only conclude that he is guilt-ridden because of his betrayal of Eddi and, paradoxically, in mourning because of his deep sense of loss now that Eddi has vanished from his life (p. 234). He cannot live with the sheeny, nor can he live without him. With the end in sight, Walter poisons Harras, whom he deems a Nazi (p. 242). The ever-perfidious Tulla is complicit in the poisoning, hoping to exploit the connections between Harras, Prinz and the Fuhrer to bring the law down on Walter. Like just about everything else in Tulla's life, this plan fails. Tulla not only loses Harras, but her life becomes increasingly tawdry — loved by her cousin Harry but impregnated by another.

The final days of the Third Reich are heralded by Hasselhoff's ballet of the scarecrows danced by Jenny; symbolized by an ineffectual home guard aircraft battery, commanded by Walter (p. 302); and sealed by the sordid goings-on in the Hitler bunker. The debacle is too much even for Prinz who is at the Fuhrer's side when the conspirators' bomb goes off and who finally deserts the Fuhrer — generating a desperate search by the authorities, presumably because he is in some metaphysical sense (p. 348) the soul of the Reich. However, Prinz eludes his pursuers and "like everybody else, is headed west" (p. 353). Prinz explains: "Sick of moving all over the place. No fixed dog-here, dog-there, dog-now. Bones buried everywhere and never found again. Not allowed-to-run-loose . . ." (p. 350).

THE FEDERAL REPUBLIC: SELF-RIGHTEOUS, UNREDEEMED AND UNREPENTANT[28]

In the penultimate episodes of *Dog Years*, the "Materniads" of the obtusely self-righteous Walter Matern become our guide to the sins of the Federal Republic. Walter tries desperately to reinvent himself as anti-Nazi, philo-Semite, and socialist, but he, like the Federal Republic itself, is unable to either escape or transcend the past. He sets out to denounce the sordid excesses of the Federal Republic, to expose the Nazi past of many of its unrepentant but now respectable citizenry, and to show the way to a republic of social justice.

Not surprisingly, Walter ends up succumbing to, rather than battling against, the corruption he vows to root out. Only by leaving out his participation in the attacks on Eddi, minimizing his membership in the mounted storm troopers and exaggerating the nature and extent of his discord with the Nazis (pp. 357–60) is he able to get clearance from the British occupation authority to make his "Materniad." There is also the matter of his traveling companion, Pluto, the renamed but unreconstructed Fuhrer dog.

Once underway, Walter discovers that, when confronted, the former Nazis offer excuses for their behavior that are much the same as those he offered to the de-Nazification screeners. "We were brainwashed," claims his old Nazi buddy (p. 439) Capt. Hufnagel, now a well-fixed official in the Canadian Occupation Authority. Yes, he had court-martialed Walter, but he did so for a lesser crime and thus saved Walter's life (p. 380). Then there is Sawatzki, for whom everything is history and if Walter exposes him, he will do the same to Walter (p. 373). Walter ends up settling scores by cutting a sexual swath through the Federal Republic — bedding the willing daughter of Capt. Hufnagel (p. 381), becoming part of a *ménage à trois* with the Sawatzkis (p. 374), and bringing gonorrhea to the former Hauptbannfuhrer, Uli Gopfert (p. 388). In sum, it becomes abundantly clear that Walter is primarily concerned with confronting those who have wronged him — that this journey has more to do with settling personal grudges than with truth telling.

SHEENY TRUTH

In the beginning there was the pre-war scarecrow maker, Eddi, who reinvented himself as the wartime Czech impresario Hasselbach aka Goldmouth. In the postwar period, he becomes the mining magnate, Brauxel, whose firm, Brauxel & Co., takes the lead in developing visual aids to counteract memory loss concerning the Nazi era. There are the "little mica mirrors" that force people to look themselves in the eye, but none of the adults is interested (p. 453). Then there are "recognition glasses" that allow children to see their parents clearly — so-called "family unmaskers" (p. 454). "Episodes which are kept from the younger generation for one reason or another are made palpably clear" (p. 455). As a result, parental figures come under pressure, but these pressures peter out as the children come to terms with what a rupture of family relationships would mean (p. 456). "The past flares up for a few months and then blacks out — forever it is to be hoped" (p. 457).

Brauxel's recognition glasses expose Walter's hypocrisies for all to see when he returns to acting and participates in a radio play — a dramatization of a political discussion with the younger generation. Wearing recognition glasses, these younger Germans readily see through Walter's anti-Nazi, philo-Semitic façade. They confront Walter with his role in the beating of Eddi and in exasperation he blurts out: "Hasn't it been made clear enough? — The sheeny got beaten up. Shoilem boil 'em! He got it square in the puss" (p. 505). Walter stands condemned: "Then we may characterize Walter Matern, the topic under discussion, as an antifascist who feeds Adolf Hitler's legacy, the black shepherd Pluto — formerly Prinz" (p. 505).[29]

While the younger generation is eager to wash its hands of Walter, the sheeny is not. Director Brauxel takes Walter on a personally guided tour of the deepest recesses of the Brauxel & Co. mines — in effect, into the circles of Hell populated by scarecrows, the sole product of the mines. Each circle inculcates a specific human trait or emotion in the scarecrows — laughter, anger, fear, sexuality, metaphysics, etc. All of these traits are in one way or another hellish (p. 544) in their artificiality — e.g. sexual gratification is frustrated (p. 550); philosophy is degraded (p. 551); laughter is devoid of human warmth (p. 545).

Each circle has set itself a different tear-promoting yet desert-dry task . . . Wailing, crescendo and decrescendo, dents and distends each circle. Muffled weeping . . . [b]lubbering . . . [s]nivelling . . . Misery is contagious (p. 544).

Over the protests of Walter, they haul the dog along with them down into the bowels of the mine. Walter fears for Prinz's delicate constitution. "This is hell, indeed! We ought to have left the dog up top" (p. 543). But Brauxel knows better. "Every hell has its climate. The dog will have to get used to it" (p. 537). And, indeed, while the still redeemable Walter frets and sweats, the dog remains "as chipper as ever" (p. 542).

The tour of production facilities concludes with scarecrow graduation exercises — complete with graduation ball (p. 559). Walter is troubled because the scarecrows, "guided by remote control, 'soulless automats' . . . take the oath to the firm of Brauxel & Co. [and] . . . have the audacity to babble: 'So help me God'" and end by swearing "never to deny their origin, namely the pit below" (p. 560). And yet the ever-confused and troubled Walter would have these ersatz humans without souls endowed with various kinds of civic responsibilities and rights — including for example the responsibility "to preserve our national and political scarecrow unity . . . the right . . . of scarecrow personality to develop freely . . . the right to assemble peacefully" (pp. 548–9). After graduation the "scarecrow collections are packed up in crates for export" (p. 560) — presumably to populate the Federal Republic.

When they ascend to the surface, Brauxel and Matern strip off their mine outfits and repair to the bathtubs drawn for them. Walter, now aware of Brauxel's true identity, ends the novel on a wistful, bittersweet and inconclusively conclusive note: "I hear Eddi splashing next door. Now I too step into my bath. The water soaks me clean. Eddi whistles something indeterminate. I try to whistle something similar. But it's difficult. We're both naked. Each of us bathes by himself" (p. 561).

Is Eddi a sheeny? Certainly not by religion. Perhaps he has some sheeny blood; perhaps not. However, it does not really matter. If he is deemed to be a sheeny, then he is a sheeny. And he is deemed to be a sheeny, because he is different, gifted and therefore vulnerable. Is Walter anti-Semitic? Indeed he is; anti-Semitism seems to be in his blood. It is, then, *Walter's* blood which is impure. However, Walter is also philo-Semitic. He admires Eddi — perhaps even loves him. He does Eddi's bidding; he risks his well-being to protect Eddi, and he is at his best when they work in tandem. When Walter turns against Eddi, it spells ruin for Walter who becomes both self-destructive and self-deluded. His betrayal of Eddi dooms Walter just as German anti-Semitism paved the way to Nazism, to the disasters of the Nazi era, and to the corrupting ethos of the Federal Republic.

Eddi's story is more complex and elusive. He not only survives his victimization but emerges triumphant. In a sea of opportunism, he of necessity becomes the supreme opportunist. As Goldmouth the impresario, he is celebrated for his theatrical extravaganzas of the Nazi era and subsequently for The Morgue, his trendy nightclub in Dusseldorf. For Brauxel, he becomes an affluent and successful mining magnate. But his real triumph is in seeing the truths that escape other Germans which he sees precisely because of his outsider status. Eddi's mechanical Nazi scarecrows reduce Nazism to its artificial essence; Goldmouth's ballet dances the destruction and defeat of World War II; and Brauxel's scarecrow factory deep in the bowels of German soil illuminates the corrupt foundations of the Federal Republic.

Just as we are left with serious doubt about whether Walter is able to accept or even to comprehend those truths, so too are we left with serious doubts about the prospects for German democracy.

> Is there a hell? Or is hell already on earth? . . . If man was created in God's image and scarecrow in the image of man is the scarecrow not the image and likeness of God? . . . Of what race are scarecrows members? . . . Is a German scarecrow allowed to buy from a Jewish one? . . . Is a Semitic scarecrow even conceivable? Scarecrow sheeny, scarecrow sheeny! (p. 552).

So long as Germans are unable to transcend their penchant for anti-Semitism — for victimizing the Other and blaming the victim — they are, Grass tells us, beyond redemption and incapable of building a new and truly democratic Germany. Nor is it entirely clear that the postwar, post-Nazi Eddi, for all of his truth telling, can be a reliable partner in the democratic process. Is it not reasonable to conclude that victimization has transformed Eddi into an unscrupulous opportunist — an impresario of sordid cultural diversions, an oppressive employer and the creator and exporter of hell on earth?[30] Or do his hell on earth and its scarecrow products symbolize the determination of a true German to refuse to allow his countrymen to forget the lessons of the past, their impact on the present, and their implications for the future?

Patterns of Childhood

> *The soul is race seen from within. Race is the soul seen from without.*
> Christa Wolf[31]

Christa Wolf's *Patterns of Childhood* explores the moral burden borne by the conscience-stricken Nelly Jordan.[32] She had embraced Nazism as a girl and after many years of holding her conscience at bay feels compelled at the age of 43 to understand why. Her moral inquiry is conducted during a trip that she makes in the 1970s with her younger brother and her teenage daughter Lenka to the pre-war family home in what is now Poland. In order to discover the extent of her moral culpability, she asks whether she was an innocent dupe or whether she should have known better. Worse yet, *did* she know better? She asks these questions for her own sake; in order to make amends to her mother, Charlotte, who warned Nelly not to become entangled with the Nazis; and in an effort to rescue a foundering relationship with the insistently judgmental and disapproving teenaged Lenka.[33]

Nelly recalls how distraught she was towards the end of the war — vacillating between denial and despair. She refused to accept the unmistakable precursors of defeat and disintegration — most notably the first refugees arriving from the East — and remained loyal to her Fuhrer. "The Fuhrer, as one can see, is invulnerable" (p. 278). Even as it occurs, she is unwilling to acknowledge the collapse of the Nazi state and expresses her anger at those who do — not only her mother but also her grandfather (p. 296) and her brother (p. 313). She is inconsolable.

> "Collapsed horizon of events" . . . Nelly's state in those months couldn't have been described more aptly. She believed that she wouldn't return home ever again, yet at the same time she still considered the final victory possible" (p. 296).

In the refugee camp when all is manifestly lost, she harbors thoughts of joining "a Werewolf group" (p. 305).*

---

* Only in looking back from the vantage point of the 1970s is Nelly able to fully appreciate Charlotte's heroic efforts to save the family while slowly bringing a sleep-walking Nelly to her senses. "The fatherland is finished," she declares (p. 330) and concludes that the family must flee the chaos of their home town. "Well, my dears, here we are in the asshole of the world" (p. 333). Unlike others who wallow in anger and self-pity, Charlotte acts. As the practicalities of survival impose themselves on the family, Charlotte wills Nelly to accept life over the dead end represented by the werewolves.

She manages to pull herself together with the help of her postwar teacher, the "devout Christian" Maria (p. 389). Nelly learns that "she'd been living under a dictatorship for twelve years, apparently without noticing it" (p. 394). Maria absolves Nelly of blame for succumbing to the specious allure of Nazism. She blames those like Nelly's teacher, Julianne, a fervent Nazi. "Who can absolve them for having sent their minds on a vacation?" (p. 391). Julianne betrayed Nelly and her other students by corrupting them.

> [Julianne] has made your conscience turn around, against yourself
> . . . She's made it so that you can't be good, that you can't even think
> good thoughts, without feeling guilty (p. 391).

Maria thus helps Nelly gain perspective on her fanatical devotion to the Fuhrer. She was simply overpowered by a politics of which she was largely unaware and could certainly not comprehend. She was, therefore, fully entitled to begin anew.

Nelly's hard-won peace of mind is, however, too fragile to survive her daughter Lenka's disbelief and contempt. Nelly comes to the realization that she has been repressing, rather than facing up to her Nazi past, and putting off the inevitable day of reckoning. The trip back home and into her past becomes the occasion for Nelly to search her conscience in an effort to come to terms with her sins of omission and commission. She wants to comprehend as much as possible about the bewildering complexity of growing up in Nazi Germany — both the exculpatory and the incriminating. To do so, she must summon up the child that she had been:

> the child that had been abandoned by the adult who slipped out of her and who managed to do to her all the things adults usually do to children. The adult left the child behind, pushed her aside, forgot her, suppressed her, was ashamed and proud of her, loved her with the wrong kind of love, and hated her with the wrong kind of hate. Now in spite of all impossibility, the adult wishes to make the child's acquaintance (p. 7).

Nelly believes that only by recovering the totality of her Nazi past can she get through to Lenka and indeed come to terms with the extent of her own culpability. She must cross a threshold that most Germans of her generation, including her own brother, refuse to cross. He believes that Nelly probes too deeply about the responsibility of the German people; he wants simply to blame the Nazi regime, its propaganda machine and its system of terror (p. 326).

THE EXCULPATORY

As she evokes the child she was, Nelly comes to realize that Nazism was her emotional sustenance. Among Nelly's earliest memories is her five-year-old sense of Hitler. "The Fuhrer was a sweet pressure in the stomach area and a sweet lump in the throat which she had to clear to call out for him, the Fuhrer, in a loud voice in unison with all the others, according to the urgings of a patrolling sound truck" (p. 45). Nelly also remembers how uplifting it was for her to view Nazi war victories and how difficult it was to hear her mother's skepticism about the Fuhrer and Nazis. "Nelly had sat by the loudspeaker listening to the delirium of joy bursting forth in a city named Vienna, a jubilation that could no longer be distinguished from a howl, which rose as though a force of nature were exploding, but which moved Nelly's inner depths in a way no force of nature had ever moved her before" (p. 164).

Nazism's "truths" had become Germany's civic culture — the "fascism in everyday life."[34] What was put on offer in popular culture was reinforced in school through an unremitting indoctrination. The affective allure of Nazism was thus lent a kind of academic legitimacy. She is taught by and "loves" Herr Warsinski. He is very strict and deeply committed to the Fuhrer and to Jesus Christ.

> A German girl must be able to hate, Herr Warsinski said: Jews, and Communists and other enemies of the people. Jesus Christ, Herr Warsinski said, would today be a follower of the Fuhrer and would hate the Jews (pp. 128 and 130).

And for good measure, Warsinski explains that it was the Jews who betrayed Germany at the end of World War I. Under the tutelage of the likes of Warsinski and subsequently Julianne Strauch,[35] Nelly came to believe that the plight of Jews was of their own making. Not only were they "weird" and "different from us," they "must be feared, even if one can't hate them. If the Jews were strong now, they would do away with all of us" (p. 160).

Also leading her astray in the prosaic and opportunistic "fascism in everyday life" were adults — most of whom were caught up in cultures of opportunistic complicity and patriotic duty. Uncle Emil Durst, otherwise a failure, bought a candy store from "the Jew Geminder" cheaply, because he "was sitting on hot coals" (p. 95). Her own father Bruno's complicity begins innocently enough as his business thrives under the Nazis.[36] His association with Nazis becomes ever more incriminating.

Bruno succumbs to extortionate pressure from "Standartenfuhrer" Rudi Arndt, who promises to ignore the "regrettable rumor [that] . . . the

wives of certain Communists had unlimited credit with Jordan" (p. 41) —
but only if Bruno pays Arndt off with various products from the Jordans'
store. Subsequently, Bruno calls on an old friend and committed Nazi,
Leo Siegmann, who "pulled every string possible" (p. 167) to get his wife
Charlotte off the hook for having said in 1944: "We've lost this war, even
a blind man can see that" (p. 165).

Bruno's accommodation changes from passive to active when he joins
"the Navy storm troops." Membership in this "comparatively harmless
organization . . . could not have been refused without consequences."

> What consequences? That's too precise a question . . . the bliss of
> conformity (it isn't everybody's thing to be an outsider, and when
> Bruno Jordan had to choose between a vague discomfort in the stom-
> ach and the multi-thousand-voice roar coming over the radio, he
> opted, as a social being, for the thousands against himself) (p. 43).

Finally, Bruno marches off to the Eastern Front even though he detests
war. His experiences in the trenches of the First World War had taught him
that "any human being can be turned into an animal" (p. 41). Still, when
called upon, he does his duty for the fatherland. Looking back, Nelly
speculates that had Bruno not been away fighting, he probably would
have joined others who became war criminals by killing Polish hostages
— that, in other words, "her father had missed becoming a murderer by
a hair's breadth" (p. 181).

THE INCRIMINATING
Yes, Nelly was certainly a victim of the cultural forces in which she was
enmeshed. However, even at the time, Nelly had doubts: serious reservations about young girls making themselves available to SS men to produce
"racially pure" children (p. 223) and about Nazi eugenics more generally
(pp. 196–7).[37] She also recalls how shamefully she dealt with the cognitive
dissonance she experienced from the persecution of the Jews. She was
aware that Lehmann, a former teacher, was available as her tutor because
he lost his job as a teacher — having been accused (falsely, he says) of
having non-Aryan blood. She persuaded herself that her sadness about
the destructive violence of *Kristallnacht* was misplaced because it was the
Jews' own fault. Even more troubling was her failure to ask herself why
she was unable to hate one of the Jewish boys in her class. Instead, she
found refuge in "'[b]lind hate,' yes, that would work, would be the only
way. Seeing hate is simply too difficult" (p. 134).

And why had she closed her eyes to these warning signs? To have
followed her conscience would have excluded her from the status and

emotional sustenance that Nazism provided: an honored place among her peers and the approval she craved from her teachers. She recalls wishing that she could completely free herself of any second thoughts. She desperately wished that she could be more like a girl in her class who at Christmas time refused to sing the words "Born is the King of Israel" because she sees it as "glorification of Judaism" (p. 158).

As Nelly's moral quest unfolds before her and us, it becomes clear that her beneficent pre-adolescent and adolescent instincts had been subverted by forces that were beyond her control. Still we come to understand why the adult Nelly is unwilling to let young Nelly off the hook without exploring every nook and cranny of her surrender to Nazi values and to her Fuhrer. She owes it to the memory of her mother, to Nelly's own self-respect, and perhaps most urgently to Lenka.

In the end, Nelly finally recognizes her mother Charlotte's indomitable will, her courage and her integrity. Only Charlotte's intensely practical instinct for survival during the precarious flight westward enabled Nelly and her brother to survive.[38] Still more admirable was Charlotte's unwavering sensitivity to the plight of other refugees, despite her own family's dire circumstances. Unlike the others who had taken flight, Charlotte was "almost the only person equipped with prerequisites for a conscience: the possibility to be sensitive toward people who didn't belong to her own narrow circle" (p. 327). Most tellingly, she shares her food with a concentration camp survivor (pp. 331–2). Nelly recalls that she, in shameful contrast, was not even able to think of survivors as victims. To her they were lesser beings, scarcely human, for whom she had no feelings.[39] Nelly is finally able to acknowledge and pay tribute to her mother's moral courage — albeit much too late and therefore less a comfort than a lamentation.

As for Lenka, she sees Charlotte's moral courage less as a tribute to her grandmother than as a rebuke to her mother. Lenka simply cannot understand why *only* Charlotte was willing to share food with the starving (p. 324). Accordingly, Lenka judges Nelly and everyone else as morally corrupt — thus reinforcing the Manichean instincts that are especially alarming to Nelly. Nelly is convinced that after all is said done, what made the Nazis so dangerous was the way they exploited ideals — transforming them it into mindless idolatry. Paradoxically, then, the unthinking *anti-Nazism* that has made Lenka unable to grasp Nelly's moral dilemma was no different in kind from the Nazism that made Nelly unable to grasp Charlotte's moral courage in opposing the Nazis. This is the lesson she wants most desperately to pass on to the obstinately oblivious Lenka.[40]

What, then, *has* Nelly learned from her soul searching? She has gained self-knowledge but not peace of mind. Was she simply a naïve and gullible child — in effect a victim of circumstances? Or did she knowingly betray right and embrace wrong to serve her own selfish interests? As befits the complexity of her inquiry and her own unflinching honesty, moral clarity evades her.[41] We as readers are consoled by the realization that, although she cannot answer these questions, she is a better human being for having pursued them with absolute integrity. Nelly, however, is not consoled. In the final pages of the book, she wonders whether her effort to recapture "the child who was hidden in me" has been successful or has she simply "proven — by the act of misleading — that it's impossible to escape the mortal sin of our time: the desire not to come to grips with oneself" (p. 406).

This is in the end a melancholy narrative of political estrangement. Clearly, the young Nelly was enveloped in, and overwhelmed by, her relentless and intense immersion in Nazi culture. At the same time, her parents' generation (Charlotte excluded) were succumbing to the Nazi manipulation of sticks, carrots and racial antipathy. While it might be argued that that was then and this now, Wolf will have none of it. Lenka's tunnel-vision morality symbolizes how and why the present could fall prey to sins and temptations of the past. In short, Wolf is profoundly concerned and deeply pessimistic about the continuity between past and present. Indeed, *Patterns of Childhood*, she has said, "attempted to describe everyday life at that time and everyday life of today to show: those are the same people who were living then and now."[42]

Conclusions

Dog Years and *Patterns of Childhood* are first and foremost novels of moral accounting. To their credit, once this Pandora's Box is opened, Grass and Wolf do not shrink from its shameful implications. Nor do they simply don hair shirts. Instead, they dig deeply and subtly into the underlying psycho-social pressures that suppress conscience and lead a nation to turn a blind eye to the bestial practices of the Nazi state.

By implication, then, Grass continues to affix blame at least as much on the German people who abetted the Nazis as on the Nazi regime itself. *Dog Years*, much like *The Tin Drum*, suggests that German democracy is, if not an oxymoron, a profoundly suspect aspiration. Put another way, Grass finds in *Dog Years* that the German political culture is not simply self-serving and opportunistic, but morally debased as well.

Christa Wolf takes us in a different direction: she undertakes an inquiry into the emotional vulnerabilities that led so many young Germans to sell their souls to Hitler's far-right demagoguery. She seems just as deeply troubled by the postwar temptations of rigid left-wing idealism. In other words, the gravitational force and Manichean truths that steal one's conscience are, Wolf seems to be saying, if not irresistible then arguably exculpatory, especially for the impressionable and vulnerable young.

We are left with little doubt that Grass sees true-believer tendencies pathologically embedded in German culture. Wolf is more ambivalent, in part because her focus is almost exclusively on the volatile sensibilities of intrinsically troubled adolescents and post-adolescents. Nelly seems to conclude that she both had and did not have choices. Moreover, Wolf leaves us with the strong impression that it is especially, if not exclusively, in Germany that demagogic politics are likely to thrive.

3. Thinking the Unthinkable: Germans as Victims

People's ability to forget what they do not want to know, to overlook what is before their eyes, was seldom put to the test better than in Germany at that time.

W. G. Sebald[43]

Although virtually all Germans suffered in the latter stages of the war and in its aftermath, there seemed to be a tacit understanding that it was inappropriate to complain — much less to point the finger of blame at those who inflicted this suffering. W. G. Sebald, more than any other literary figure, has been insistent on calling attention to the devastation experienced by Germans in the wake of the war.* Paraphrasing Air Commodore E. J. Kingston-McCloughry, Sebald underscores the depth of postwar devastation: the "sheer nausea of existence . . . the terrible and deeply disturbing sight of the apparently aimless wanderings of millions of homeless people amidst the monstrous destruction [which] makes it clear how close to extinction many of them really were in the ruined cities at the end of the war."[44]

Sebald also points to the conspiracy of silence that swallowed up the grim realities of the immediate postwar world — attributing this silence to an unlikely convergence of shame and defiance. To "keep quiet and look the other way," served a "quasi-natural reflex, engendered by feelings of shame and a wish to defy the victors."[45] From a more pragmatic

---

* Sebald seems to have been among the first to articulate the necessity of incorporating German suffering into the public discourse. He does so most directly in *On the Natural History of Destruction*. Because it is not a novel, I do not take it up directly in this section, but it does inform my understanding of *Crabwalk* and *The Reader*, and more broadly my understanding of the consequences of evading for so many years an essential element of Germany's mid-century national trauma.

perspective, it seems undeniable that there also had to be within the Federal Republic an understandable reluctance[46] to bite the hand that was, through the Marshall plan, *literally* feeding them.[47] It seems that there was a tacit understanding that, whether as sinners or losers, postwar Germans were not entitled to indulge in recriminations or even to mourn their own losses.

Only much later, toward the end of the millennium, were the burdens borne by Germans at the end of the war and in the immediate postwar period considered to be legitimate topics of literary inquiry. The two novels that will be considered in this section confront the causes and consequences, especially the intergenerational consequences, of a half-century of silence: Gunter Grass in *Crabwalk* speaks as the voice and the conscience of the Nazi generation; in *The Reader*, the much younger Bernhard Schlink speaks to the postwar generation's understanding of German sins and German suffering.

Whereas Grass invites us to think about the suffering of ordinary Germans, Schlink asks much more of himself and his readers, because his focus is on the suffering of a Nazi concentration camp guard — almost literally one of Hitler's "willing executioners.'"[*] As John E. MacKinnon said of *The Reader*, "Schlink commits himself to eroding, if not collapsing, the distinction between Nazis and those who assisted or accommodated them, on the one hand, and 'second generation' Germans, 'the lucky late-born,' on the other."[48] In neither novel is the burden borne by Germans in the wake of the national catastrophe of Nazism presented as some kind of cosmic justice, or as redemptive. They are offered as facts of national life with important consequences for the present and the future of the German people.[49]

Crabwalk

As the war ended, the *Wilhelm Gustloff*, crammed with refugees fleeing westward, was sunk by a Russian submarine. For Grass, this tragic event symbolizes what the German people had to endure during the war and in the immediate postwar period. Allied bombing devastated many areas of Germany; the occupying powers dismembered the German State; millions of fearful Germans fled westward from their ethnic enclaves in states

---

[*] *Patterns of Childhood* also addresses intergenerational disconnect, but speaks in the retrospective voice of the Nazi generation. The postwar generation, represented by the opaque Lenka, is largely silenced. Postwar privations are introduced but only toward the end of the narrative and are, in any case, subordinated to Nelly's moral vocation. The intergenerational theme in *Billiards at Half-Past Nine*, unlike the others, treats the disconnect as a family misunderstanding rather than as an existential condition of national defeat and dishonor.

liberated from Nazi rule in a desperate effort to escape retribution from the advancing Soviet army. The Germans also suffered from shortages of jobs, fuel and food — not to mention the injuries and indignities inflicted upon them — including the rape of German women by Allied soldiers.

To Grass, this havoc typifies the inevitable costs of war, and there is certainly an anti-war narrative woven into *Crabwalk*. However, it is not primarily an anti-war novel. It is instead a novel of intergenerational estrangement — revealing the costs, both personal and political, of the failure of Germans to come to terms with the entirety of the Nazi experience. Specifically, Grass asks us to consider how and why Nazism — disowned, disavowed and discredited in the wake of the catastrophic defeat of Germany in World War II — could prove appealing to members of the millennial generation, coming of age in the 1990s.

He invites us to ponder this problem through the cleavages that divide and disrupt one family. Its matriarch is the volatile troublemaker of *Dog Years*, Tulla Pokriefke. She represents the wartime generation, *Grass's generation*, who were nurtured by, and took to, Nazism. Her son Paulie is the narrator; he speaks to us in the voice of a wishy-washy, vaguely left-ist but mostly apolitical, member of the immediate postwar generation.[50] Konny, Tulla's grandson and Paulie's son, is the combustible neo-Nazi product of his opportunistic and ideological grandmother and his dif-fident and detached father. Konny is the apple of his grandmother's eye while Paulie is her despair.

Grass's narrative attributes the re-emergence of neo-Nazi proclivities to a tacit agreement between the political leaders of the Federal Republic and ordinary Germans to close the books on Nazism — including the burdens borne by a defeated Germany. The inevitable curiosity of succeeding gen-erations about these matters became an invitation to construct their own history from the detritus available to them. It is precisely in this way, we shall see, that Konny — *Crabwalk*'s incarnation of neo-Nazism — comes under the influence of his opportunistic grandmother.

THE ALLURE OF MARTYRDOM

At the end of the war Tulla found herself in the GDR and not only chose to remain there but also to become an influential official in, and an enthusiastic supporter of, the "socialist" state. We know Tulla too well to believe that she underwent an ideological conversion from Nazism to Marxism. Tulla had always been, and continued to be, drawn to power. Better to think of her, as Elizabeth Krimmer suggests, as the "classic survivor."[51] Her commitment (if that's the correct term) to the GDR was thus indistinguishable from her commitment to Nazism — a means to her self-absorbed ends.

However, for the impressionable Konny, united with his grandmother by the reunification of Germany, Tulla represents a forceful and ostensibly idealistic contrast to the apolitical Paulie and to the West Germans, among whom he had been raised when Paulie and Konny's mother Gabi fled the GDR. In particular, he was receptive to the harrowing tale of Tulla's narrow escape from the sinking of the *Wilhelm Gustloff*. Pregnant and already in labor as the ship went down, Tulla was rescued by another German ship where she immediately gave birth to Paulie who was named after the captain of the rescue vessel. Prompted by Tulla, Konny undertakes a rudimentary inquiry into this hallmark family event.

The sinking of the *Gustloff* was for Konny inextricably linked to his very being. His grandmother and his father only narrowly escaped the fate of the vast majority of the refugees who went down with the *Gustloff* or perished in the freezing waters of the Baltic Sea. They were martyred, and he is in effect a *survivor* who, like his father and his grandmother, is indebted to those victims. Germany's wartime enemies, and especially the Russians whose submarine had sunk the *Gustloff*, became *ipso facto* Konny's enemies.

UNINTENDED CONSEQUENCES

However, Konny also stumbles on a broader political theme linking both Gustloff the man and the ship named after him to Gregor Strasser's *socialist* wing of the Nazi's national socialist movement. The ship was itself a vestige of the Nazi left wing — built to serve as a cruise liner without class distinction and priced to provide ordinary Germans with the kind of cruises that had been hitherto the province of the wealthy and the aristocratic.[52] Gustloff was a Strasser protégé who was assassinated in Switzerland where he was working as a Nazi organizer. The killing was an act of retribution by a young Jew, David Frankfurter. The confused Konny seems oblivious to Hitler's purging of Strasser and his followers during the infamous "night of the long knives" even though Gustloff had fled to Switzerland precisely because of Hitler's crackdown on the socialists among his followers.[53] Konny's ignorance of all of this is, however, entirely understandable, because his school essay on "The Positive Aspects of the Nazi Organization Strength through Joy" was simply suppressed — without explanation and certainly without any effort to introduce Konny to the bigger picture (see p. 202).

Paulie, too, is obsessed with the sinking of the *Wilhelm Gustloff* — albeit for dramatically different reasons. To begin with, he is seeking to clarify his own origins. He hopes against hope that he is not Tulla's son after all but another person entirely — specifically a second child who escaped the doomed ship.* His search is conducted "in a crabwalk, seeming to go backward but actually scuttling sideways, and thereby working my way forward fairly rapidly" (p. 3). Yes, he is seeking to affix responsibility for the event that almost ended his life before it began. Unlike Konny, however, Paulie wishes to expose the *Gustloff*, not to commemorate it. For Paulie, the *Gustloff* represents a cynical ploy — the neutralization of socialist workers by absorbing them into the Nazi's German Labor Front (p 38). He also wants to track down Germany's postwar Nazis — "old unregenerates but also freshly minted neo-Nazis . . . venting their venom" (p. 3).

Their preoccupation with the *Wilhelm Gustloff* does bring Paulie and Konny, father and son, together — but not in a good way. Konny's blog becomes a site for rallying a movement to honor Wilhelm Gustloff, ship and man. Meanwhile Paulie's effort to track down unreconstructed Nazis and their neo-Nazi protégés leads directly to Konny's website. There Paulie is treated to a heated war of words between "Wilhelm" (aka Konny) and his antagonist, the mysterious David (Frankfurter?). They struggle with one another over who is truly the martyred hero. Is it Wilhelm Gustloff who was gunned down while in Switzerland seeking converts to National Socialism? Or is it David Frankfurter for striking back at the Nazis who were persecuting his people? As he follows the extended struggle between Wilhelm and David, Paulie comes to realize with horror that "Wilhelm" is in fact his son.

As for "Wilhelm" and "David," over the course of their lengthy clashes in cyberspace the two adversaries come to develop a kind of grudging respect for one another — bordering on affection. They agree to meet at the ruins of the Wilhelm Gustloff memorial site.[54] Their encounter ends calamitously, with Konny shooting and killing Wolfgang Stremplin, the *virtual* David Frankfurter (p. 184). What is so jarring about this climax is that almost to the last minute the two of them seem to be getting on so well — "two bosom enemies" (p. 186) who were "both passionate about table tennis" (p. 187) and who talked "amiably" (p. 186). What set them off? Paulie, our narrator, explains that at the monument site for Wilhelm Gustloff, "David" feels compelled to act on behalf of his vision: "'As a Jew, I have only this to say,' whereupon he spat three times on the mossy

---

* His grievances with Tulla are endless — beginning with the uncertainty about which of Tulla's many sexual partners is actually his father. Was it Tulla's chameleon cousin, Harry Liebenau? He could be Paulie's father but probably is not (p. 17). More likely it is one or another of the *Dog Years* characters who gathered around the anti-aircraft battery as the war ended — including Walter Matern (p. 18).

foundation — thereby as my son later testified, 'desecrating' the memorial site.'"

After shooting David, Konny "turned himself in with the words, 'I fired because I am a German'" (p. 188). Of course, Wolfgang Stremplin is also a German — the son of a physicist father and a piano-teacher mother (p. 186). Nonetheless, Konny readily confesses, because he is proud of having done his duty as a true German. At trial Konny is found guilty of manslaughter and is sentenced to seven years of incarceration. He is outraged because he believes that the sentence is much too lenient and demonstrably inequitable. After all, as Konny puts it: "They slapped eighteen years on the Jew Frankfurter" (p. 213). In other words he feels that the light sentence, in effect, devalues his heroic and selfless act — presumably depriving him of the martyrdom to which he feels entitled.

Not surprisingly, the book ends in frustration, hopelessness and alienation. Paulie visits Konny in jail and finds him without remorse: "I fired as a matter of principle" (p. 196). Indeed, he has painstakingly built a replica of the *Gustloff* and waits until Paulie arrives to mark with red dots the places, the "stigmata," where the torpedoes hit (p. 226). Paulie marvels at the way Konny, after willingly taking responsibility for his actions and paying the price, now has job offers even while in prison and faces a promising "future in the new century that was just around the bend" (p. 228). Konny's followers remain loyal: "'We believe in you, we will wait for you, we will follow you . . .' And so and so forth. It doesn't end. Never will it end" (p. 234).

It might seem that the obvious lesson to be drawn from all of this is that raking over the coals of Nazism is bound to rekindle the enmity on which it thrived. However, there is another way of looking at the murder — a way that is much more consistent with the general thrust of the book. After all is said and done, the sinking of the *Gustloff* is a legitimate symbol of German suffering and its story must be told. Grass himself puts in an appearance as "the old boy" (p. 103). The old boy is said to feel that he should have written about this long before and now he wants to make absolutely certain that Paulie, his narrator, does so in the correct way.

This means laying out in detail the full story of the sinking of the *Wilhelm Gustloff* — not the ideological half-stories that fueled the resentments of both Wolfgang and Konny. On the one hand, the old boy prompts Paulie to put in context both the sinking-of-the-*Gustloff* story and the broader tale of "hardships endured by the Germans fleeing East Prussia: the westward treks in the depths of winter, people dying in blinding snowstorms, expiring by the side of the road" (p. 103). We learn that the Germans fled because they feared Russian retribution — fear fed by the discovery of Russian atrocities when the German army briefly retook Nemmersdorf (p. 106). On the other hand, we learn through the intervention of the historian Heinz Schon that the sinking of the *Gustloff* was not an atrocity as the die-hard Nazis and Konny's neo-Nazis would have us believe. The Russian submarine captain, Aleksandr Marinesko, had not known about "the four thousand children who had drowned, frozen to death, or were sucked into the depths with the ship" (p. 101). The captain thought of the *Gustloff* as "stuffed to the gills with Nazis responsible for launching a surprise attack on his homeland and leaving scorched earth when they retreated" (p. 101).[55]

The full story thus turns out to be not about heroes and villains but about victims caught up in the fog of war, the xenophobia and devastation it inflicted, and the hate and fear it engendered. We learn that hate feeds on itself — far outliving its precipitating events. Over and over again in this chapter our attention is directed to the awful symmetry of suffering which is, despite all of the triumphalism of the adversaries, the inevitable result of war and ideological conflict. We are, in short, made to see that the sinking of the *Gustloff* is not the story of a war crime but a story of the crime of war — exacerbated by ideological fervor and nativism.

It goes without saying that die-hard Nazis for whom "the war had not ended" (p. 101) would find the full story of the sinking of the *Gustloff* totally unacceptable.[56] In contrast, the old boy and Paulie are convinced that the full story is unimpeachable evidence of the impermanence of political truths and the monuments erected to celebrate them (see pp. 177–81).[57] Why is it, we are finally encouraged to ask, that Konny and his neo-Nazis refuse to understand what is so readily apparent? Why, in short, is the half-life of hate extending into a new millennium?

Crabwalk does not fault the new generation's embrace of hatred, but their elders, who persistently and catastrophically failed to address either what Nazism provided for Germans in the 1930s and the 1940s or the suffering that went along with Germany's defeat. The new Nazis were deprived of robust political discourse and thus easily led astray by the malevolence of the die-hards (symbolized by Tulla); the diffidence and neglect of parents (symbolized by Paulie and his never-written book, *Between Springer and Dutschke*, p. 41); and the failings of the educational system (symbolized by the fate of Konny's essay, "The Positive Aspects of the Nazi Organization Strength through Joy"). Simply put, the neo-Nazis see themselves as reclaiming their national patrimony from their evasive, pusillanimous and politically apathetic elders.

Crab Walk thus emerges as an ode to the cost incurred by the repression of the collective memory of German sins and German suffering. The Federal Republic followed the path of least resistance — both fostering and abetting the public's inclination to put the Nazi experience behind them. The unintended but inevitable cost of repression was a festering unconscious that was easy prey for ideological demagoguery. Ironically, then, forgetting about the victims of the *Wilhelm Gustloff* inevitably led to remembering them for the wrong reasons.[58]

The Reader

Bernhard Schlink's narrator, Michael Berg, is, like the author himself, from the generation that was bequeathed the silences of German sins and of German suffering. Michael has managed to avoid the neo-Nazi refuge that sheltered Konny and his followers from a reckoning with the past. Instead, Michael and his classmates in law school have found their own hiding place. They have chosen, not unlike Lenka, to distance themselves as much as possible from the past. To that end they condemn their parents' generation, deciding that all of this has nothing do with them and that their only moral duty is to hold the elders responsible. Not even Michael's father, who had lost his job in the Holocaust and was not implicated in it in any way, was spared. "[H]e too was under sentence of shame?" (p. 92).

Enter Hanna Schmitz, a former concentration camp guard who unwittingly but inexorably forces Michael into a moral reckoning that he, along with others in his generation, had been evading — leaving him with his own sense of shame.

But even once he has understood his moral responsibilities he, as we will see, continues to evade them.

The book opens well into the postwar period with Hanna's seduction of Michael. He is 15 years old and she a woman in her 30s, many years removed from her service as a concentration camp guard and now working as a streetcar ticket taker. Michael is oblivious to Hanna's past, which catches up with both of them as their lives diverge and subsequently reconnect, when Hanna is put on trial for crimes that she committed as a camp guard.

THE NARROW LEATHER BELT

The love affair between Michael and Hanna, at least at the outset, is an oddly symmetrical exchange relationship. She provides Michael with sex and in return he reads aloud to her. As the novel unfolds, it becomes apparent that much more is at stake for both of them. Predictably Michael is entranced, fascinated and emotionally enthralled. "The next night I fell in love with her . . . Did I fall in love as the price for her having gone to bed with me?"

Hanna's stake in their relationship is more obscure. Most of the time she seems to be securely in charge. She invariably refers to him as "kid;"

she bathes him; and her affect is more that of a stern mother than a lover. It is unclear how seriously Hanna takes the relationship. When Michael complains about his schoolwork, Hanna is incensed. "'Out.' She threw back the coverlet. 'Get out of my bed. And if you don't want to do your work, don't come back. Your work is idiotic? Idiotic? What do you think selling and punching tickets is?'" (p. 35). When he worries that he has hurt her feelings, she retorts: "You don't have the power to upset me" (p. 48).

The emotional texture of their relationship — an incongruous combination of tenderness and cruelty — is deeply troubling to Michael. "Whenever she turned cold and hard, I begged her to be good to me again, to forgive me and love me" (p. 49). After a misunderstanding stemming from a note he had left for her, she turned on him: "'Don't touch me.' She was holding the narrow leather belt that she wore around her dress; she took a step backwards and hit me across the face with it" (p. 55). She strikes him once; begins to swing again but instead: "She let her arms fall, dropped the belt, and burst into tears . . . then clung to me . . . Then she gave a deep sigh and snuggled into my arms" (p. 55).

Following that outburst things changed dramatically between them.

> The fight made our relationship more intimate . . . She began to show a soft side that I had never seen before . . . We made love in a different way. For a long time I had abandoned myself to her and her power of possession. Then I learned to take possession of her (p. 57).

Michael attempts to convey their new intimacy — and in particular that they "no longer merely took possession of each other" (p. 57).

> *When we open ourselves*
> *you yourself to me and I myself to you,*
> *when we submerge*
> *you into me and I into you*
> *when we vanish*
> *into me you and into you I*
>
> *Then*
> *am I me*
> *and you are you* (pp. 57–8, italics in the original).

Somehow, against all odds and in the cruel shadow cast by "the narrow black leather belt," they seemed to have both found and lost themselves in one another.

Then suddenly and without a word, Hanna disappears from Michael's life, leaving him bruised and bereft.

MORALITY AND RESPONSIBILITY

Michael and Hanna's lives reconnect many years later when he is among a group of law students attending a war crimes trial as part of their training. For Michael, the trial is transformed from an academic exercise into a moral and emotional awakening by the discovery that Hanna is one of those on trial. She is accused not simply as a concentration camp guard but for her complicity in the death of camp survivors as they were force-marched westward in the final days of the war. One night during their ordeal, the prisoners were locked in a church while the guards spent the night in the empty house of the parish priest. When the church is set afire by a rocket, virtually all of the prisoners perish.

At first Michael manages to distance himself from the plight of the love of his life — the woman who to that day intruded into all his efforts to connect *emotionally* with others. He tells us that he "felt nothing. Nothing at all" (p. 95). Michael looks the other way because, correctly it turns out, he senses that to do otherwise would open a Pandora's Box. Accordingly, he rationalizes her custody as justified: "Not because of the charges, the gravity of the allegations, or the force of the evidence, of which I had no real knowledge yet, but because in a cell she was out of my world, out of my life" (p. 97).

As the trial proceeds and he becomes aware of Hanna's illiteracy, Michael is no longer able to maintain his moral and emotional distance. Her illiteracy explains not just the importance of Michael as reader and her fury at his complaints about schoolwork but much, much more. He comes to realize how not being able to read had impinged devastatingly on her life. She had taken dead-end jobs as a prison guard and a streetcar ticket taker. The former had made her into a war criminal and she fled the latter rather than accepting a promotion that would have exposed her illiteracy. So begins the blurring of the bright line that Michael had always drawn between the innocent and the guilty, between victim and victimizer.

Michael does not retreat without an internal struggle — falling back on incredulity about her choices and their implications. "But could Hanna's shame at being illiterate be sufficient reason for her behavior at the trial or in the camp? To accept exposure as a criminal for fear of being exposed as an illiterate . . . Was she simply stupid? And was she vain enough, and evil enough, to become a criminal simply to avoid exposure" (p. 133)? It is at once inconceivable and incontrovertible that she was more shamed by her illiteracy than by her participation in the "final solution." Maybe her illiteracy did drive her to become both a victimizer and a victim.

The line between the moral and the immoral is further blurred for Michael as it becomes clear that Hanna is willing to take responsibility for what she has done, but that in return she wants the judges to acknowledge her plight — to understand, that is, not only what she was *up to* but also what she was *up against*. In the work camp, she was responsible for choosing which women would remain and which would be sent to the death camps as fresh prisoners arrived, thus making a comparable number of those already there redundant (p. 111). She implores the judges: "I . . . I mean . . . so what would you have done?" (p. 112). She is similarly prepared to "be called to account" (p. 133) for the deaths of the prisoners who perished in the church fire. But here too Hanna implores the judges to recognize that her sense of duty [once again German duty] and her moral sensibilities were in irreconcilable tension — "a conflict between two equally compelling duties that required action" (p. 129). "We couldn't just let them escape! We were responsible for them" (p. 128).

Once the bright line that has protected Michael for so long is blurred, he begins to understand his own moral culpability — culpability that becomes ever more inescapable through the trial, Hanna's imprisonment, and her subsequent release.[59] Even though he comes to understand his own moral responsibilities, he persists in evading them. In the end, he has to acknowledge that, not unlike many in his father's generation, dilemmas, not bright lines, are intrinsic to moral choice and that when faced with these dilemmas, he had temporized and become complicit in legal and moral injustices — injustices that lead inexorably to Hanna's suicide.

All of this plays out in stages. As a budding lawyer, Michael believes that if she had been properly defended it would have been possible "to cast reasonable doubt on whether these defendants were the actual ones who had done the selections" (p. 113). He finds himself facing moral ambiguity — *his own* irreconcilable moral responsibilities. Should he step in to mitigate the injustices of the trial where Hanna is taking the fall to avoid being outed as an illiterate? More broadly, was he "guilty of having loved a criminal" (p. 134)? Should he allow her to conceal her shame even if he finds her actions inexplicable? He turns to his philosopher father for counsel — that act in itself constituting a retreat from Michael's post-Nazi, anti-Nazi moral hubris. His father leads Michael where he does not want to go — that is, to trying to persuade Hanna to tell her story, but if that doesn't work, to allow her to live by her own sense of "dignity and freedom" (p. 142). He does not talk to Hanna but settles for a predictably unsatisfactory discussion with the smug and self-satisfied judge (pp. 158–60).[60]

After she is found guilty and imprisoned, Michael attempts to make amends. He records readings for her. The readings he chooses are from the cornerstones of, and "testify to a great and fundamental confidence in bourgeois culture." He also presents his own writing to her — thus making her, in effect, "the court before which once again I concentrated all my energies, all my creativity, all my critical imagination" (p. 185). He is gratified when she calls upon her newly achieved literacy to write to thank him, because he interprets this literacy as evidence that "Hanna had advanced from dependence to independence, a step toward liberation" (p. 188).

Once again, however, the self-involved Michael has gotten it all wrong. Yes, he sent her tapes, but no letters. Nor is Michael willing to grant her redemption in the only way that counted — to allow her back into his life. He is all too obviously ill at ease with the old woman she has become during her imprisonment (p. 196). Finally, although he has made post-prison living arrangements for her, they are not meant to include him. He certainly cannot imagine bringing Hanna, the elderly ex-concentration camp guard, along with him on a planned visit to the United States (p. 211).

Only subsequent to her suicide does Michael learn the full import of what he has done *to her* in the guise of doing things *for her*. She became, he is told by prison authorities, an old woman precisely because he has provided tapes but no letters (p. 208). To be sure, Hanna's successful pursuit of literacy did, as Michael believed, have to do with independence and liberation — but not from Michael. On the contrary, she sought independence and liberation so that they might make a life together on a basis of rough equivalence. "I had granted Hanna a small niche, certainly an important niche, one from which I gained something and for which I did something, but not a place in my life" (p. 198).[61]

As a typical German of his generation, Michael begins with a deep and judgmental sense of shame for the Holocaust and for his country's evasive efforts to come to terms with it. He is appalled "that so many old Nazis had made careers in the courts, the administration, and the universities, that the Federal Republic did not recognize the State of Israel for many years, that emigration and resistance were handed down as traditions less often than a life of conformity" (p. 170). No wonder when it came to the fate of concentration camp guards, Michael and his fellow law students "placed no reliance on legal scholarship. It was evident to us that there had to be convictions" (p. 91). They came to the trial not in order to weigh the evidence, much less to learn, but simply to condemn the self-evident evildoers. Doing so "did not free us from shame," but it "converted the passive suffering into energy, activity, and aggression" (p. 170).

It follows that the trial and its aftermath were profoundly painful experiences for Michael. Prior to the trial he had kept the crimes of the Nazi state at arm's length — the crimes of others, somebody else's problem and thus entirely separate from himself and from his German identity. Michael's sense of immunity was, however, shattered by Hanna's role in the Holocaust. She brought the Holocaust into his life and in so doing drove a wedge between him and his generation. "How could it be a comfort that the pain I went through because of my love for Hanna was, in a way, the fate of my generation, a German fate, and that it was only more difficult for me to evade, more difficult for me to manage than for others" (p. 171). He decides that their, and hitherto his, compulsion "to assimilate the horrors and our desire to make everyone else aware of them was in fact repulsive." (p. 93).

This does not mean, as Jeremiah Conway points out, that Michael eschews moral judgment or that by recognizing the constraints of choice he is expressing a position of moral equivalency.[62] In the end, all of this is too much for Michael. He gives up, retreating into himself or, more specifically into the consolations of history. "Doing history means building bridges between the past and the present, observing both banks of the river, taking an active part on both sides. One of my areas of research was law in the Third Reich, and here it is particularly obvious how the past and present come together in a single reality" (p. 180).[63]

But history yields its own frustrations. It is, he concludes, "the story of motion, both purposeful and purposeless, successful and futile. What else is the history of law" (p. 182)? He finds himself losing faith in a progressive view of history. In its stead, he adopts a "different image . . . In this one it still has a purpose, but the goal it finally attains, after countless disruptions, confusions, and delusions, is the beginning, its own original starting point, which once reached must be set off from again" (p. 181).

Taking into account the whole picture brings Michael to a tragic view of human life bordering on but not necessarily leading to political estrangement. Does it rob him of a sense of agency or simply impress upon him the limits of political agency as well as the powerful tendency of human beings to evade their political responsibilities and to take self-serving refuge in strategies of rationalization?[64]

Conclusions

To deny this freedom [of choice] means to deny guilt that everyone who didn't use his freedom to decide against humanity has taken upon himself.

Rolf Hockhuth

In the clownish spectacle of our century, in the collapse of the white race, there are no people who are guilty or responsible any longer. Everyone couldn't do anything about it and didn't want it to happen.

Friedrich Durrenmatt[65]

This chapter traced the progression of postwar, post-Nazi German novels through three stages. The first dealt with the efforts of novelists to explain how and why the Nazis were able to engender consent and support for their repressive regime and its threadbare ideology. The novels of the second section confront German and Nazi anti-Semitism — the road to the Holocaust. Finally, in the third section German literary imagination refocuses away from the damage done by Nazis to others and toward the damage inflicted on the German people — as the tide of World War II turns from ostensibly decisive victories into the finality of unconditional surrender. This three-stage account has so far directed attention to the distinctive interpretation each novelist brings to life in Germany during and after the Nazi regime.

It is now time to assess not what divides these novelists, but their abundant common ground. To begin with, all of the novels are overwhelmingly about ordinary Germans — not about the Nazis or those who resisted them. These ordinary Germans emerge in shades of grey, readily distinguishable from die-hard Nazis and some heroic anti-Nazis who can readily be colored in black or white. Nazism serves primarily as a shadowy, pervasive and malignant backdrop to an inquiry into why so many ordinary Germans supported the Nazis through thick and thin. This "why" question leads to competing narratives of choice and destiny that are embraced by virtually all of the novelists.

Choosing an illusion
In earlier chapters the catastrophes of war and the Holocaust descended upon people who were without the capacity to comprehend, much less to influence, the course of events. In contrast, Germans are mostly represented, at least at first reading, as choosing to embrace Nazism. If the victims of war and the Holocaust were without voice or choice, the German people made sinful and ultimately disastrous choices — disastrous for themselves and others. The sins were venial and mortal — venial insofar as they served immediate self-interest and mortal insofar as they were associated with, and sustained by, anti-Semitism, which was taken for granted in Germany.

Of course, anti-Semitism has been and still is a fact of life elsewhere in the world. Only in Hitler's Germany, however, did a "final solution" become operative and unchallenged national policy. In any event, the bulk of the German people are represented as exercising political agency, albeit to obliterate political agency — *one person, one vote, one time*, as it is frequently put. Perhaps they were gullible or opportunistic or felt themselves bound by a sense of duty to their fatherland (or to duty itself). Nonetheless, in choosing the Nazis, they rejected and scuttled Weimar's republican democracy.

The illusion of choice
On closer examination, however, these novels are at least as much, and often simultaneously, about the illusion of choice — about, that is, "the powerful constraining conditions, within which we exercise our moral judgments and responsibility."[66] Certainly, the principal characters in these novels are portrayed as victims of choices made by others and of events and forces that were beyond their control. Postwar generations — personified by Konny, Lenka, Michael and others — were victimized by events that pre-dated them. They bear the burdens of crimes committed by their parents and grandparents but somehow attributed to them as Germans. They resist being held responsible for evil done by others but somehow in their name as Germans — their birth right, their birth wrong.

Indeed, they were multiple victims of their parents' choices compounded by the *secretive nature of their parents' generation* and the deeply flawed Federal Republic bequeathed to them. To a lesser extent, their parents too — the generation that came of age as enthusiastic Nazis in the 1930s — are also portrayed as without choice. These youngsters were engulfed in a cultural and political tidal wave. Nelly, Walter and Oskar — but Nelly above all — are shown as largely defenseless against powerful socializing mechanisms of state and society. This was, Christa Wolf makes abundantly clear, a generation compromised — made suspect to their own children and generating spasms of guilt and expiation. Even the concentration camp guard and war criminal Hanna is portrayed as in the grip of forces that were arguably beyond her control.

In the final analysis, then, the most celebrated novelists of post-Nazi, post-World War II eras leave us with competing, unreconciled and, by implication, unreconcilable narratives of choice and destiny. They all seem deeply pessimistic about the future of the Federal Republic, which is deemed compromised by the legacy of Nazism and by the persistence of the values and forces that made it possible and sustained it.* This

---

* Tellingly, the novels tend to express ever more skepticism about the political future as the years go by and the influence of the Nazi era might be expected to wane.

chapter leaves us with a deep skepticism about the prospects for German democracy.

In the next chapter, the perspective will be broadened beyond the suspect prospects of German democracy to examine novels of democracy in the United States and the United Kingdom. To what extent, the question will become, does estrangement extend beyond the catastrophic events of the twentieth century, total war, the Holocaust and Nazism — to everyday democracy in its acknowledged safe havens?

.

Among the host of factors identified as accounting for this paradox, the one that emerges paramount is the powerful intergenerational inclination of Germans to repress the Nazi years rather than learn from them.

5   The Contradictions of Democracy: Political Estrangement in the U.S. and the U.K.

Democracy was tested and found wanting during the first half of the twentieth century. The well-established democracies of France and England were unable to avoid, and indeed entered enthusiastically into, the futile savagery of trench warfare in World War I. In the aftermath of the war, the collapse of fledgling democratic regimes in post-World War I Italy, Germany and elsewhere led directly to Nazism and at least indirectly to the Holocaust and to World War II. Novelists, as we have seen in previous chapters, portrayed the despair and political estrangement engendered by these epic failures of democracy. Those were, of course, tumultuous times that presented arguably insurmountable challenges to democratic regimes.*

This chapter turns *from* that unsettled and unsettling ethos when democracy was at risk — threatened by the last vestiges of aristocratic rule and pre-modern values. It turns *to* the relatively tranquil and prosperous post-World War II period; to the mature democracies of the United Kingdom and the United States; and to English and American novels of that period.† By this time there were widely accepted social contracts in

---

* World War I, the last dynastic war, was largely a product of personal rivalries among monarchs who may or may not have seen the curtain coming down on their aristocratic prerogatives. They were readily able to enlist *public* support for these *personal* misadventures. They did so by preying on a deep-seated romanticism about war and on the rampant nationalism of the late nineteenth and early twentieth centuries. After the war the many unresolved tensions between embattled traditional societies and emerging modern societies paved the way for a fascist backlash. Authoritarian-populist demagogues tapped into the anxieties of those who were being displaced by the convergent pressures of industrialization, urbanization, and secularization.

† The choice of novels for this chapter was especially difficult. In previous chapters, it was a relatively simple matter to identify and to include the books that really matter — be they anti-war, Holocaust or anti-Nazi novels. Here my choices are necessarily more idiosyncratic and open to challenge, because they are derived, not from historical *events*, but from the *idea* of democracy imperiled. This difficulty is exacerbated because I am, of course, not selecting conventional political novels that focus on the

both countries, symbolized by the welfare state in the United Kingdom and the New Deal in the United States. Democracy and modernity were widely recognized as essential carriers of, indeed as prerequisites to, human achievement, humane values and personal freedom. This would seem to have been the ideal time and place for the modern and the democratic to demonstrate both their compatibility with one another and their capacity to serve as agents of peace, prosperity and virtue.

However, the lives constructed by celebrated novelists continue to reveal contradictions between democracy and modernity exacerbated by cultural cleavage — leading to a sense of hopelessness and estrangement from politics. Among the culprits uncovered by the literary imagination are such hallmarks of modernity as the tendency of wealth and consumption to trump other aspirations; the pervasive reliance on bureaucratic organizations both public and private; and the privileging of abstract rationalities of professional knowledge. Novelists give voice to these contradictions as they play out in the daily trials and tribulations of society's winners as well as its losers — both of whom are portrayed as disconnected from, and/or despairing of, the politics of democracy.

Among novelists in the United States, estrangement is inextricably linked to the false promises of the American dream — both to those who have seemingly realized the dream, as in Philip Roth's *American Pastoral*, and those who have been excluded from it, as in Ralph Ellison's *The Invisible Man* and Russell Banks' *Continental Drift*. Each of these novels is arguably an American classic, which traces distinctive iterations and perverse intrusions of the American dream into the lives of the mainstream or the marginalized. The *Invisible Man* won the National Book Award in 1953 and, in 1965, some 200 authors, editors and critics polled by *The New York Herald Tribune* picked it as the most distinguished novel written by an American during the previous 20 years."[1] *Continental Drift* was a finalist for the 1986 Pulitzer Prize and in it, according to Michiko Kakutani, "Russell Banks created a visionary epic about innocence and guilt and in doing so, he also set down a shattering portrait of contemporary American society."[2] Ms. Kakutani praised *American Pastoral* in similarly expansive and politically evocative terms "as "one of Mr. Roth's most powerful novels" and "a resonant parable of American innocence and disillusion."[3]

Estrangement in the English novels of this period is also about unredeemed promises — the shortcomings of the British welfare state. The

institutions and processes of governance and political action — a relatively concrete and well-established classification. Instead, I have sought novels in which politics are, as I explained in Chapter 1, an absent presence — meaning in this chapter, novels that trace the perils of democracy into the culture of the everyday.

English novels are less literary classics than cultural representations of politically consequential segments of English society — each with its own distinctive iteration of estrangement. In *Saturday Night and Sunday Morning*, which was awarded Author's Club Prize for the Best English First Novel of 1958, Alan Sillitoe, as Julian Moynahan puts it, "is working class" and (along with Margaret Drabble) provides the "the most reliable reports of what life is really like in England today."[4] Zadie Smith's *White Teeth* is noted for its depiction of multiculturalism in 1990s England; for its sparkling prose; and, in the words of Anthony Quinn, the "provisional and undogmatic" way in which it confronts "large themes — migration, cultural identity — and knows to stop short of haranguing the reader."[5] Perhaps only Ian McEwan's novels can be seen as well on the way to becoming classics. With *Saturday*, in particular, "Mr. McEwan has," according to Michiko Kakutani, "not only produced one of the most powerful pieces of post-9/11 fiction yet published, but also fulfilled that very primal mission of the novel: to show how we — a privileged few of us, anyway — live today."[6] In short, we learn how and with what consequences the shortcomings of the welfare state intrude into the lives of the affluent *and* the afflicted in Ian McEwan's *Saturday*; the working class in Alan Sillitoe's *Saturday Night and Sunday Morning* and the ethnic Other in Zadie Smith's *White Teeth*.

For all the parallels between British and American novels of this period, what is perhaps most striking and in need of explanation are the contrasting textures of estrangement — with estrangement in America portrayed as predominantly angry and bitter, and in England for the most part, as wistful and resigned. The exception to these generalizations and indeed to the late-modern ethos of the novels of political estrangement is Zadie Smith's *White Teeth*. Smith's novel expresses modern rather than late-modern cultural truths. This is because, I will argue, she tests modernism not in relationship to its tarnished ideals but against the sectarianism of traditional Islam. *White Teeth* also reaffirms the contrast between the obsessive milieu of the American dream and the more open, eclectic and culturally receptive ethos of the British welfare state.

1. The American Dream: A Deceptive Obsession

Jennifer Hochschild argues in *Facing Up to the American Dream: Race, Class, and the Soul of the Nation*[7] that increasing inequality among the classes in the United States tends to exclude those in the lower strata of the racial and class structures from realizing the American dream of earned upward mobility.

By the American dream, I mean not merely the right to get rich, but rather the promise that all Americans have a reasonable chance to achieve success, as they define it — material or otherwise — through their own efforts, and to attain virtue and fulfillment through success.[8]

For Hochschild, this dream is a "central component" of the glue that holds us together as a nation. It is our "dominant ideology" — our "shared world view."[9] It follows that if substantial elements of the society are excluded from partaking in the American dream, the society and polity are put at risk.

The novels considered in this section portray the powerful, virtually irresistible, pull of the American dream on the lives of their characters and in so doing reveal just how devastating it is for society's marginalized to be excluded from the promise of the American dream. But these novels go well beyond Hochschild to expose the American dream as a social centrifuge which, far from providing unity, divides society against itself. Whereas *she* associates the American dream not only with material success but with virtue, *the novels* tend to see the American dream as a pernicious, irresistible and intrinsically alienating temptation that stretches across the socio-economic spectrum. It follows that to be liberated from the spell cast by the American dream is a social, personal, and political blessing.

The Invisible Man

> *I found out all about white people, that's what they were like, alone where only a black girl could see them, and the black girl might as well have been blind as far as they were concerned. Because they knew they were white, baby, and they ruled the world.*
>
> James Baldwin[10]

Ralph Ellison's nameless narrator clings to marginalized versions of the American dream — marginalized by the unique dispossession of African-Americans in the pre-civil rights era.[11] At the outset of the novel he dreams of joining the Southern black bourgeoisie. When that dream is thwarted, he moves north where he becomes the spokesperson for a Marxist political movement whose goal is represented as ending capitalist exploitation of the African-American minority. Neither of his dreams is realized, suggesting that a multicultural American democracy is, or at least was, an illusion, both in the traditional South and in the modernizing North. As the novel proceeds, it becomes increasingly clear that the dreams of ascent into the black bourgeoisie and of a color-blind society are not the narrator's own dreams, but intrinsically alienating dreams imposed on him by others. Only in the final pages does he come to realize that *he is simultaneously black and invisible in a color-obsessed society where color is an indelible signifier*. How is this possible? That is the question that drives the novel.[12]

THE BLACK BOURGEOISIE

The narrator's earliest dream is simply to rise above his rural dispossession. He gets the ball rolling in an ostensibly promising direction by parlaying his talent for oratory into access to a genteel and pretentious black college. Success at the college guarantees upward mobility — albeit within the confines of a relentlessly segregated society. The college thrives on the patronage of wealthy whites and is, in effect, an island of comfort, civility and privilege in a sea of black poverty and oppression. The students are frequently reassured by visiting speakers of their good fortune, "to belong to this family sheltered from those lost in ignorance and darkness. Here upon this state the black rite of Horatio Alger was performed to God's own acting script, with millionaires come down to portray themselves; not merely acting out the myth of their goodness, and wealth and success . . . but [personifying] themselves, these virtues concretely" (p. 111).

At the college he is immediately introduced to its can-do, American dream-like culture of hope, faith, endurance, ceaseless struggle and ultimate triumph. This culture is traced to the mythologized "founder" and to his loyal acolyte and immediate successor, the current president, Dr. Bledsoe, who proved himself capable of picking up just where the founder left off. The wily, obsequious and autocratic Bledsoe (p. 114) understands that the white benefactors of his college are reassured about their own virtue by the college's replication of polite society and that they do not want to be reminded of the squalor outside the cloistered institution.

Accordingly, Bledsoe is horrified to learn that the hapless narrator has taken a well-meaning college trustee, Mr. Norton, for a drive through the no-go area beyond the college grounds. Norton literally goes into shock when he is exposed to the squalid poverty and moral depravity of the rural blacks who lead lives that discredit the reassuring message of the college's tranquil gentility. President Bledsoe is so enraged and, yes, terrified by the possible repercussions of Mr. Norton's misadventure that the narrator is made to undergo a black-on-black ritual of degradation.

He is banished from the college and sent up north with letters of introduction to wealthy and influential New Yorkers. Ostensibly these are letters of recommendation meant to secure a job, which will enable the narrator to prove himself and get back into the good graces of President Bledsoe and regain entry to the college. However, the narrator learns more or less accidentally (p.190) after much futile job hunting that these are letters of condemnation, not recommendation. So much for racial solidarity! The President has warned the business leaders neither to give him a position nor to divulge that he will never be readmitted the college.

THE MULTICULTURAL ILLUSION

Left to his own devices, the narrator struggles to gain a foothold in New York City. He finds a job but immediately becomes a pawn in a conflict between labor organizers and his angry and insecure black supervisor who is determined to protect his privileged position and his white employer-benefactor from the union reformers. The narrator is clueless and distrusted by both sides. The paranoid supervisor, imagining a plot, contrives an explosion that nearly succeeds in killing the narrator (pp. 119–30).

After a long period of recuperation the narrator finds himself once again without a job and without any prospects. In this deeply confused and conflicted state he roams the streets of Harlem, where he experiences a transformational moment. He comes upon an incident of injustice — a black tenant being turned out into the streets with all her possessions. On the spur of the moment, he feels compelled to speak out and quickly stirs the sullen crowd with his eloquence. "Tell 'em about it brother," the old man interrupted, "It makes you feel you ain't a man" (p. 279). A near riot ensues and Brother Jack, a senior official in The Brotherhood, a left-wing, multi-racial political movement, is struck by the narrator's resonant way with words and recruits him.

The narrator is provided with a paid position, an apartment and access to the wealthy uptown Manhattan radicals who fund the Brotherhood (p. 301). He is gratified to be treated so well by whites, and in particular by white women — less like an object and more like a person. He muses about one woman's interest in him:

> It was not the harsh, uninterested-in-you-as-a-human-being stare that I'd known in the South, the kind that swept over a black man as though he were a horse or insect; it was something more, a direct what-type-of-mere-man-have-we-here kind of look that seemed to go beneath my skin (p. 302).

Then there is the irresistible attraction of the Brotherhood's inclusive, multiracial aspirations which stand in stark contrast to the insular visions of the African-American community (p. 316).

There are, however, costs that come to weigh ever more heavily on the narrator. He is assigned a new name, subjected to a rigorous regime of study to learn the Brotherhood's foundational principles of scientific revolution and admonished to refrain from contacting his family (pp. 308–9). He is also required to get new clothes and wearing them begins to feel that he is "becoming someone else" (p. 335). But who?

When the Brotherhood brings him back to Harlem to speak to a gathering he captivates the audience and is himself transported.

> "Look at me!" The words ripped from my solar plexus . . . "Something strange and miraculous and transforming is taking place in me right now . . . As I stand before you!" (pp. 344–5).

He ends up with the audience eating out of his hands. "The applause struck like a clap of thunder" (p. 346).

The members of the Brotherhood are both impressed and troubled. Yes, he is an outstanding rabble-rouser, but they are a *scientific* organization. They are modern and on a modern mission — disciplined by historical truths derived from the laws of dialectical materialism. He is a loose cannon who spontaneously, instinctively and unselfconsciously rises to the occasion. In other words, just as the narrator is discovering and giving voice to an unknown but gratifying element of his identity, the Brotherhood demands obedience and adherence to its scientific and intellectually rigorous agenda. "'You were not hired to think.' He was speaking very deliberately and I thought, 'So . . . So here it is, naked and old and rotten'" (p. 469).

Things go from bad to worse when the Brotherhood changes course. It turns from local injustices to "those more national and international in scope, and it was felt for the moment the interests of Harlem were not of first importance" (pp. 428–9). When the narrator protests, he is told that the Harlem campaign is being subordinated to the goals of the revolution. This is not an instance of the weak being sacrificed for the good of the strong, as the narrator charges. "No, a part of the whole is sacrificed — and will continue to be until the new society is formed" (p. 503).

Accordingly, the Brotherhood turns a blind eye to the surge of grassroots Black Nationalism that is feeding off local grievances — the secret of the narrator's rhetorical success. Black Nationalism in Harlem was, of course, anathema to the Brotherhood's multiracial, anti-capitalist aspirations. "We do not shape our policies to the mistaken infantile notions of the man in the street. Our job is not to ask them what they think but to tell them!" (p. 473). The resultant political vacuum is quickly filled by "Ras the Exhorter," whose Black Nationalism readily trumps the Brotherhood's revolutionary abstractions. Ras successfully demonizes the Brotherhood in general and the narrator, its voice in Harlem, in particular.

THE INVISIBLE MAN

The Brotherhood turns out to be no different from the other whites who have betrayed him. "And now I looked around a corner of my mind and saw Jack and Norton and Emerson merge into one single white figure" (p. 508). Multiracialism is a façade; the Brotherhood exploits Harlem-ites for their own purposes. And he may well have been "part of a sellout" (p. 480). Of course, it has not only been whites who looked through him — seeing him as a means to their own ends. In this sense, President Bledsoe and his black supervisor in Manhattan were no different. To all of them he was a cipher whom they were determined to recreate in their own image or destroy.

"Everywhere I've turned somebody has wanted to sacrifice me for my good — only they were the ones who benefited" (p. 505). Making it all worse, the decisions were made to sacrifice him without knowing him. Everyone looked through him, not at him. "Well, I was and yet I was invisible, that was the fundamental contradiction. I was and yet I was unseen" (p. 507). "Outside the Brotherhood we were outside history; but inside of it they didn't see us. It was a hell of a state of affairs" (p. 499). Also discredited for the narrator is the Brotherhood's constricted, modernist vision of history. History he concludes is "a gambler, instead of a force in a laboratory experiment . . . What if history was not a reasonable citizen, but a madman full of paranoid guile" (p. 441).[13]

However, on the run from Ras the Exhorter the narrator discovers that invisibility in Harlem imparts a kind of freedom, and he resolves to use that freedom as a weapon against the Brotherhood. To evade Ras he takes on the guise of a Harlem hipster with glasses, "so dark that it appeared black" (p. 483). Not only does this disguise work better than he ever could have imagined, it also serendipitously *seems* to open a whole new world of possibilities. He is mistaken, even by those who know him well, for Rinehart, Harlem's celebrated and notorious, chameleon.

"What you sayin', daddy-o," they said.
"Rinehart, poppa, tell us what you putting down," they said.

Rinehart, it turns out, was everything to everybody. "Rine the runner and Rine the gambler and Rine the briber and Rine the lover and Rinehart the Reverend" (p. 498).

What Rinehart knew instinctively and what the narrator had now discovered is that in Harlem a life "without boundaries" was possible — in effect, the freedom of modernity (p. 498).

In the South everyone knew you, but coming North was a jump into the unknown . . . You could actually make yourself anew. The notion was frightening, for now the world seemed to flow before my eyes. All boundaries down . . . Then I looked at the polished lenses of the glasses and laughed. I had been trying simply to turn them into a disguise but they had become a political instrument (p. 499).

He resolves to parlay his invisibility and the supreme indifference of the Brotherhood to the well-being of Harlem into a strategy to subvert the Brotherhood. He would simply reinvent himself so as to appear to be just what they wanted him to be.

I would hide my anger and lull them to sleep; assure them that the community was in full agreement with their program. And as proof I would falsify the attendance records by filling out membership cards with fictitious names — all unemployed, of course, so as to avoid any question of dues. Yes, I would move about the community by night and during times of danger by wearing the white hat and the dark glasses. It was a dreary prospect but a means of destroying them, at least in Harlem (p. 510).

So even as Harlem is coming under the sway of Ras, the narrator assures the Brotherhood that all is well. He resolves to preach to the choir of modernity. To be "a justifier, my task would be to deny the unpredictable human element of Harlem so that they could ignore it when it in any way interfered with their plans" (p. 514).

Alas, in the culminating event of the novel, a full-blown insurrection, the narrator's strategy backfires. Initially he is buoyed by the fellowship among the rioters who take him in and do their best to care for him (p. 538). However, with Ras the Exhorter becoming Ras the Destroyer the uprising quickly gets out of hand. Windows are smashed; goods are taken from shops; and the streets become boiling cauldrons of pent-up anger — in effect, an open invitation for the civil authorities to crush the rioters. Only then does it dawn on the narrator that this was the Brotherhood's plan all along, and he had abetted it. In effect, the Brotherhood didn't really care whether Harlem was on its side or not. The Brotherhood had actually wanted "the streets to flow with blood, your blood, black blood and white blood, so that they can turn your death and sorrow and defeat into propaganda" (p. 558).

With the riot out of control and blood flowing, the narrator realizes that he is defeated. Nothing had worked. He is overmatched; the Brotherhood is always one step ahead of him, and he is absolutely powerless to affect the course of events — with "no possibility of organizing a splinter movement, for what would be the next step?" (p. 510). Before he can work through this dilemma, he once again becomes the target for Ras's destructive wrath. To escape hanging he takes refuge beneath the streets of the city.

> [T]hat I a little black man with an assumed name should die because a big black man in his hatred and confusion over the nature of a reality that seemed controlled solely by white men whom I knew to be as blind as he, was just too much, too outrageously absurd. And I knew that it was better to live out one's own absurdity than to die for that of others, whether for Ras's or for Jack's (p. 559).

Crawling into his hole is then his last desperate effort to seek his own destiny, preserve his integrity and keep alive his passion and quest for social justice.

A PUZZLING EPILOGUE

The book concludes with the narrator in his underground refuge. Once and for all he has come to terms with the inescapable fact that when he is out in the world he has "been called one thing and then another while no one really wished to hear what I called myself. So after years of trying to adopt the opinions of others I finally rebelled" (p. 573). All of his efforts to fit in led to the eradication of his authentic identity. They loved him. "Oh, yes, it made them happy and it made me sick. So I became ill of affirmation, of saying 'yes' against the nay-saying of my stomach — not to mention my brain. There is, by the way, an area in which a man's feelings are more rational than his mind" (p. 573). "So I took to my cellar" (p. 573). Only there in "hibernation" is there an opportunity to figure out who he is and what meaning his life might have.

He quickly comes to understand that whites as well as blacks are implicated in, and burdened by, the injustice of race in the US. "One of the greatest jokes in the world is the spectacle of the whites busy escaping blackness and becoming blacker everyday, and the blacks striving toward whiteness, becoming quite dull and gray" (p. 577) — and presumably transparent. However, because they have been on the outside looking in and unobserved, they are less corrupted and more attuned to the way in which the "human greed and smallness" of white society has betrayed its own principles.

This ending seems very much like a u-turn — reversing the trajectory of the hundreds of preceding pages. Suddenly the narrator turns his back on the bleakness that animates and indeed defines the vast bulk of the novel. An invisible man decides surprisingly and very much in the spirit of Irving Howe to reject the despair of political estrangement — hoping against hope and against all odds that he can make a difference.[14] In a subsequent introduction to the book, Ellison put it this way:

> Even if true political equality eludes us in reality — as it continues to do — there is still available that fictional vision of an ideal democracy in which the actual combines with the ideal and gives us representations of a state of things in which the highly placed and the lowly, the black and the white, the Northerner and the Southerner, the native born and the immigrant combine to tell us transcendent truths and possibilities.[15]

The problem is that *The Invisible Man* offers no such representations of an ideal democracy — only the unending torment of a well-meaning young man searching for a respectable niche in a society which manipulates him while denying him even a semblance of authenticity. Indeed, he might once more lose his bearings in returning to the corrupt world from which he fled and the indignities that he suffered as a still-invisible man — overwhelmed once again by the definitive sense of futility that he gained while holed up underground.

Continental Drift

> *Florida, in some ways, resembles a modern Ponzi scheme. Everything is fine . . . if a thousand newcomers come tomorrow. The problem is . . . no one knew what would happen if they stopped coming.*
> Gary Mormino, quoted in George Packer, "The Ponzi State: Florida's Foreclosure Disaster,"
> *The New Yorker*, February 9 and 16, 2009: 83.

Russell Banks takes the reader to the emotional core of Bob Dubois' futile struggle to build a satisfying life in the small and economically depressed town of Catamount, New Hampshire.[16] We then follow Bob, the novel's main character, and his family to south Florida, the land of sunshine and opportunity, where he and they believe that it is still possible to realize the American dream of striking it rich. But it is not only northern whites who migrate to Florida in search of their American dream. There are also refugees from poverty and oppression, outside US borders, who have an American dream and risk their lives for it. They are exemplified in *Continental Drift* by a young Haitian woman, her infant son and her nephew.[17] As we accompany them on their perilous flight from Haiti, we come to understand their benighted island lives, their inner spirituality and their American dream.[18]

The novel brings Bob Dubois and the Haitians together in a catastrophic conclusion that underscores how ordinary people, both Americans and Haitians, are the unwitting victims of American dreams that pit them against insuperable odds and one another. Thus, these are narratives of physical and emotional struggle in a world in which choice is so constrained as to be illusory. The Americans believe they have choices, but when all is said and done, they have almost as little control over their destiny as do the Haitians who put themselves in hands of the voodoo spirits.

AMERICAN MIGRATION

Continental Drift opens with a depressing depiction of Bob Dubois' drab life in the cold and largely lifeless New England town of Catamount. He does have a wife he loves, a steady job delivering fuel oil, two young daughters who adore him. He owns a, "seventy-five-year-old duplex . . . [and] a boat, a thirteen-foot Boston whaler he built from a kit" (p. 12). To his wife, Elaine, all this adds up to a gratifying combination. "Oh, honey, we have a good life. We do." (p. 25).

Bob, longing to realize his American dream, looks at everything differently and is desperately frustrated. He hates the grimly cold winters in Catamount; the struggle to make ends meet on his meager salary; his trade as "an oil burner repairman for the Abenaki Oil Company (p. 3)". His life seems crushingly routine. "He's alive, but his life has died" (p. 13). He is desperately ashamed of his inability to take control of his life — as have his brother, Eddie, and his best friend, Avery Boon. Those two along with so many others have moved south to Florida and taken full advantage of the burgeoning opportunities afforded by the Sunshine State. Eddie, the insatiable entrepreneur, has opened up a thriving liquor store which he sees as the just the beginning. Avery has followed a more laid-back path — chartering his boat to tourists who want to fish the Florida Keys.

Ol' Ave, he's probably right this minute walking ashore with a case of Canadian Club or Chivas Regal on his shoulder, and my brother Eddie is down there dancing cheek to cheek with his wife in a fancy nightclub while his accountant works late figuring out another tax dodge for him. And what am I doing? Sitting in Catamount in a fucking chair with the stuffing come out so bad it has to be covered with slipcovers because I can't afford to get it upholstered or buy another one (p. 26).

While Eddie and Avery are living their American dreams, Bob, ineffectual Bob, can neither seize the dream nor abandon it, and it festers inside of him like a cancer.

Elaine Dubois, Bob's wife, is the down-to-earth counterweight to Bob's determination to make it big. She tries to console him. "We love each other, Bob. We don't *need* all those material things . . . to be happy." (p. 28). However, once she comes to realize the depth of Bob's despair, Elaine sees no alternative to giving voice to Bob's unspoken yearning. *She* suggests that they leave Catamount and seek their fortune somewhere in the Sun Belt.

> Let's move, Bob. Let's start over . . . Let's just sell the house, sell the car and the boat, and even sell the furniture, and start over some-place else. *Lots* of people do it. Bob screws his face into a question mark. "Move?" He's never really put the possibility to himself, never truly thought of it. Moving was what other people did, people who were just starting out in life . . . without family responsibilities (p. 29, italics in the original).

This is music to the timorous Bob's ears. But move where in the Sun Belt? Elaine would prefer the Southwest, but Bob insists on Florida where Eddie has promised his younger brother a leg up and where Ave Boone is also living the dream.

Not long after their arrival Elaine and Bob discover the seamy side of Eddie's entrepreneurial endeavors, and they sense the ominous implications of their move to Oleander, Florida. Eddie presents Bob with a gun and bullets. In explaining why the gun is necessary, Eddie reveals things about himself and about life in Oleander that rattle Bob and Elaine and prefigure the tragedy that will envelop the Dubois family.

> You bet your ass things are different here. We got niggers with guns and razors here . . . We got Cubans who cut your balls off. We got Haitians with their fucking voodoo sacrifices and Jamaicans with machetes as long as your fucking arm. We got dark-skinned crazies of all kinds, all hopped up on their fucking pot and cocaine, riding around in brand-new Mercedes-Benzes without enough pocket money to put gas in their tanks. We got Colombians, for Christ's sake, with fucking *machine guns!* (pp. 58–9, italics in the original).[19]

Eddie assures Bob that the knowledge that he has a gun is the best assurance that he will not have to use it. "It's like dealing with the fucking Russians. The second those suckers think you're not ready for them, ready and able to nuke their eyes out, you're a dead man. You got to let these people know you're serious, Bob" (p. 62). But should a crazed, drug addict who is behind in his BMW payments challenge Bob: "You blow the bastard away" (p. 61).

As it turns out, the store is robbed, and Bob does blow one of two "bastards" away, while allowing the other to escape. The older and more professional of the two robbers demands cash while he dispatches his young, angry, indeed, bloodthirsty accomplice to get some liquor out of the storage room. Bob would have been willing to turn over the money, but he has previously emptied the till and deposited its contents. Bob kills the older man but is unable to turn his gun on the young accomplice who is no longer bloodthirsty or threatening, but a quivering boy who has lost control of his bowels. While Bob is calling the police the boy escapes. Of course, Eddie is incensed that one of robbers escaped. Then, in a twist of fate, Bob subsequently crosses paths with the boy and is barely able to contain himself from taking advantage of a second chance to gun down the boy. Bob is aghast at the way he has lost control of his emotions and what this says about the life that he is leading.

The gun is, however, only the final straw, because it has become ever clearer to Bob that working for Eddie is a mug's game. Eddie has vastly overstated what he is willing and able to do for the Dubois family. Bob "works twelve hours a day, six days a week, and except for a part-time stock clerk . . . he is alone in the store. Though he's paid in cash, with no taxes or other deductions taken out, his weekly pay is only seventy-five dollars more than it was in Catamount" (p. 65). Eddie is exploiting him, and the promises of partnership are pie in the sky. Eddie has put Bob's American dream yet further out of reach.

Working for Eddie also exposes Bob to legal jeopardy. Eddie is not a successful businessman. He has constructed a house of cards sustained by expensive capital supplied by threatening mob figures. Dealing in cash keeps Eddie ahead of the tax collector. Staying ahead of the lone sharks who will not take no for answer is another matter. Eddie lives in constant fear, running harder and harder but falling ever further behind — being pushed down the slippery slope towards ever more serious violations of the law. In the end, Eddie loses everything: his businesses, his family, his home, his boat and so on. After fruitlessly turning to the impoverished Bob for money, Eddie recognizes that he is doomed and commits suicide (p. 266).

In contrast to Eddie, Avery Boone journeyed to south Florida in search of easy living, not fast living. He took his boat, the Belinda B, south with him and started a charter fishing business in Moray Key. The now jobless Bob turns to Avery who proposes that the two of them become partners in the Belinda B. To make it happen, Bob will have to sell what little he has left — mostly the trailer home he bought with proceeds from the sale of the house in Catamount. Then, Bob will become the captain of the Belinda B and they will split the profits — although not down the middle. Ave will then use the money invested by Bob to purchase a bigger and faster ship that will allow him to take the more free-spending tourists farther out to sea for the big game fish.

Ave has thrown Bob a lifeline, although it is not long before he has well-founded buyer's remorse. The offer is irresistible because Bob can think of no more appealing way of earning a living than being out on the water in command of his own fishing vessel. Bob can hardly believe his good fortune. However, it turns out that his one-quarter share of the Belinda B's profits provides much less than a decent living for the family. Bob Dubois is thus no closer and arguably farther from his American dream than when he was working for Eddie or, indeed, when he was leading a drab life in Catamount.

One other idea occurs to Ave, and it leads to the fatal convergence of Bob's journey south and the Haitian journey north — both in search of their American dreams. Ave tells Bob that he can make some relatively good money by bringing Haitian refugees to south Florida.

> Five, six hundred a head, whatever the market bears. It's easy. You just drop them off along the beach somewhere — Key Largo, North Miami, they don't give a shit. You can load up with ten or twenty of them over at New Providence [in the Bahamas], drop them off before daylight and be home by breakfast. Tyrone knows the lingo. He can set it up for you. All you do is drive the boat. And what you make is yours, less the twenty-five percent or whatever you work out with Tyrone. Look, I owe you, Bob (p. 283).

Bob is hesitant, but his desperate financial circumstances lead him to undertake what turns out to be the culminating calamity of the novel; the definitive end to Bob Dubois' American dream; and the exposure of the intensely problematic and ultimately lethal character of the American dream itself.

HAITIAN FLIGHT

The Haitians flee a world that is wildly different from anything Bob Dubois could comprehend — a world in which hunger and oppression are a constant for the poor and powerless. The harrowing flight northward from Haiti of the young mother, Vanise, her baby Charles and her adolescent nephew Claude is driven by these inexorable forces that obliterate all semblance of agency. Claude happens upon a truck that had been overturned in a storm. The side of the truck has been ripped off in the accident, revealing, irresistibly, a "large ham, the entire smoked leg of a pig, the kind of ham we had never seen before except in pictures in magazines" (p. 46).

Claude doesn't hesitate; he makes off with the ham; and dutifully brings it home to his hunger-wracked family. They tear into it with desperate relish. Only afterward do they have second thoughts. Because the truck and the ham belong to Aubin, a ruthless local notable, they have no doubt that he will find out about what Claude has done and will be merciless in punishing him. Aubin is not only cruel but also omniscient. "When you deal with people like Aubin, people who have power over you, it's not enough to lie. You also have to be believed" (p. 49).

The family decides Claude must leave Haiti and that Vanise must accompany and take care of him. The family has been saving money, so that they could all go to America, but they now turn it over to Vanise who is in charge of getting her nephew, herself and her baby to America.

> Then they were gone. The boy, who was stepping into manhood sooner than he was ready, was gone. The girl and her baby were gone. The money was gone (p. 51).

They believe that if they can make it to the village of Le Mole, a fisherman named Victor will take them in his boat to America.

They find Victor who promises to take them to "Miami, Mee-ah-mee" (p. 111). He brings them on board and off they go — eventually arriving at a beach where Victor puts them ashore and collects their money. They soon discover that this is not Miami Beach but "North Caicos Island, six hundred miles from America" (p. 109) — the first, and hardly the worst, of many deceptions in their excruciating journey which ultimately leads to Bob Dubois and the Belinda B. As they work their way across North Caicos and ultimately manage to gain passage to the Bahamas, they encounter men who promise to protect Vanise, Charles and Claude from the authorities. But it turns out that the real purpose in each case is to extract work from Claude and Vanise and to subject Vanise to indiscriminate sexual violence.

All of this sexual violence culminates in the Bahamas with one Jimmy Grabow, a sexual sadist:

> His penis hung limply between his legs. Then he hit her a second time, and her eyes filled with water from the force of the blow. A third time he hit her, and a fourth and fifth, back and forth, until

at last she began to weep, and suddenly his penis was erect and Grabow was panting with excitement . . . and then he would . . . force his way into her (p. 199).

Grabow also prostitutes Vanise. Claude immediately sees the handwriting on the wall and flees. Vanise, however, adapts and even develops a fatal fondness for one of her customers, "Tyrone, who spoke some Creole and always rolled and smoked a cigarlike spliff of ganja before making love to her" (p. 198). This is the same Tyrone who works for Ave and Bob, and he tells her that his fishing boat is regularly used to bring illegal Haitians to America. "Tyrone's job was to round up the Haitians. The white man just drove the boat" (p. 204).

When Claude returns to rescue Vanise and Charles, he confronts Grabow and kills him with a machete, "slicing the man across the midsection, opening him up like a piece of fruit" (p. 205). They take Grabow's money and find their way to an encampment of "off-islanders, most of them illegal immigrants" (p. 208). The authorities tolerate these illegals because they are a source of cheap labor, and the illegals nurture the hope that they will be able to buy their way onto Tyrone's boat. With Grabow's money, Vanise, Claude and Charles have no trouble making the necessary arrangements with Tyrone who does, we know, at least intend to take them to south Florida.

THE FATAL VOYAGE

Predictably, the enterprise is an unmitigated disaster — in part because the Belinda B is so slow that getting back and forth in the darkness leaves little or no leeway to account for any delays or glitches. But delays and glitches there are.* Accordingly, the return is delayed in order to pass through the heavily patrolled areas in darkness. Then disaster strikes: they are blown off course; realize that they will have to put the Haitians ashore north of Miami where they will not be able to melt into the Haitian community; and then the Belinda B is discovered by the Coast Guard. Tyrone determines to save himself, Bob, and the Belinda B in the only way he knows how. At gunpoint he proceeds to force all the Haitians into the sea where they flounder. While Bob is appalled, he goes along with the plan —

---

* To begin with, Bob, the ever-cautious Bob, is unwilling to run the Belinda B at full speed even though Tyrone is very well acquainted with these waters. Bob delays things further by insisting on stopping to take on unnecessary fuel. Then, Tyrone discovers that the Haitians he has signed up are not in their village because they have decided that they need a Voodoo ceremony. Tyrone, "with the help of an old man" (p. 296) finds them off in the bush, but realizes he cannot interrupt the voodoo ritual — thus losing still more valuable time.

rushing down below to throw all of the Haitians' belongings overboard. With the Coast Guard boat occupied, trying — without success, we later learn — to pluck the refugees from the water, Bob and Tyrone return as directly and unobtrusively as possible to the marina.

As they ease the Belinda B into her slip, they discover Florida State Patrol officers awaiting them. Bob sees his impending arrest not so much as just deserts as a return to normalcy. He has been living beyond the edge ever since he agreed to bring these refugees into the country, but that is now over. There are, however, things that Bob does not yet know. The Florida State Patrol officers are not at dockside because of the Haitian refugee fiasco, but because Ave has been caught in a big drug bust and Bob is therefore under suspicion. Nor does Bob know that Vanise has survived and been taken in by Claude's father. She is in shock and only some days later recalls through voodoo ritual how she and the others were left to drown by Bob and Tyrone.

Bob, ostensibly home free with the much-needed money, which was overlooked by the Florida State Patrol, is wracked by guilt. He devours the newspapers for every detail of the refugee fiasco, and discovers that 15 bodies have washed up on shore, leaving one of the Haitians unaccounted for. He finally shares his guilt with Elaine, and together they decide to return to Catamount but without the blood money. As an act of contrition, and against Elaine's advice, Bob decides to venture into Little Haiti to turn the money over to anyone in the Haitian community who will use it to do some good.

Bob is completely out his element in Little Haiti and has great difficulty finding someone reliable who will take the money. He gets wind of Vanise's survival and manages to find some young Haitians who agree to take him to her. She remembers Bob and, in particular, his friendship with Claude. She especially recalls that Claude had been the first to leap overboard because he so admired Bob and thought of him as a true friend. Therefore while Bob pleads with her to take the money, she denies him this redemption. Once she departs, the young Haitians feel free to demand the money for themselves. Bob is unwilling to give them the money and, with tragic irony, his last words before they kill him are "This money is mine" (p. 363).[20]

The Dubois and the Haitian narratives are intertwined and deeply *personal* — laying bare the desperate circumstances, both emotional and material, that drive individuals and families from the known into the unknown.[21] They are willing to risk everything in pursuit of American dreams that live misleadingly in their imaginations and that in the end they learn are both out of reach and deceptive. But these are also *political* narratives that illuminate the structural forces that both drive and constrain the search for a better life.

Clearly, the balance between choice and constraint is different for the Haitians from what it is for the North Americans. For the refugees from the northern US, the American dream is of material affluence, enhanced social status, and self-respect — all inextricably linked and infinitely expansive in their aspirations. The Haitian refugees, in contrast, are driven by desperate life-and-death choices, and their dream is survival — south Florida as a haven from hunger, tyranny and lethal violence. Tragically south Florida pits its "immigrants," each in the grip of its respective dreams, against one another. Just as the weak, marginalized and upwardly striving Bob Dubois is exploited by those above him in the social hierarchy, so, too, does he find himself, more or less unwittingly, preying on the utterly powerless young Haitians, who have risked everything to get to south Florida.

But what do the Haitians know about America and to what extent do they *choose* to pursue their dream of America? They are prepared to go through hell to realize it, and both Vanise and Claude reveal themselves as resourceful and relentless. But are they making choices? Indeed, do they even think of themselves as making choices? They flee Haiti precisely because they do not believe that they have any choice. They are in effect driven out by hunger and danger. Nor do they think of themselves, as do Bob, Eddie and Avery, as free to choose. When all is said and done they put their faith in voodoo gods and rituals. Only the spirit world is a constant in the lives of Haitians who have no control over their lives.[22]

Bob Dubois does believe that he is free to choose. His models, at least at the outset of the book, are Eddie and Avery who have begun appealing new lives in south Florida — lives that seem, from the outside looking in, the apotheosis of the American dream. As it turns out, Bob could not have picked two more inappropriate role models or a more ill-suited milieu than south Florida. Although Bob wants the fast buck, he has neither the drive nor the streak of malevolence that is required to compete among would-be entrepreneurs who start from scratch and must live by their wits at or beyond the margins of legality — and in Eddie's case, a willingness to prey on and to demonize the dark-skinned Other. While Eddie and Avery do find material success in south Florida, its satisfactions prove hollow and ephemeral — sparking ever-expanding ambitions that force them into self-destructive behavior, culminating in Eddie's suicide, Avery's imprisonment and Bob's death.

In the end, then, none of them is truly free to choose. Bob, Eddie, Avery and, for that matter, the Haitians are all in the grip of forces that they do not understand and to which they are largely oblivious. For the

Americans, it is the deindustrialization of the north which drives them south, attracted by its rewards and largely oblivious to its risks. But they are also obsessed by the American dream — making them hostage to these outside forces. The Haitians live lives of unremitting and inescapable terror and hunger. They are inexorably drawn to the United States, about which they know next to nothing, as a land of plenty and opportunity.

Thus, when Bob Dubois agrees to bring Haitian refugees from the Bahamas to south Florida, he becomes part of an intrinsically predatory cycle. Both Haitians and Americans are, Banks reveals to us, part of a seemingly endless chain of situational afflictions imposed by the relatively powerful on the relatively powerless. Moreover, while power differentials define relationships among the characters, they are all, exploiters and exploited, living marginal lives and in the mesmerizing grip of an American dream.[23] *Continental Drift*, then, is an account of unrelenting exploitation of those at the bottom of the social ladder by those perched precariously just above them — society's losers unwittingly locked in mortal conflict over equally irresistible and inevitably competing visions of the American dream.

American Pastoral

> *When he tried to imagine a just social order, he could not do it. A non-corrupt society? He could not do that either. There were no revolutions that he could remember which had not been made for justice, freedom, and pure goodness. Their last state was always more nihilistic than the first.*
>
> Saul Bellow[24]

Philip Roth's novel recounts the storied life of Seymour Levov (aka the Swede) from World War II into the post-Vietnam years. Roth infuses those years and that life with "a mixture of rage and elegy."[25] By refracting these years through a storied life, Roth has provided access to a portrayal of political estrangement among Americans who have ostensibly realized their American dream. As Michiko Kakutani puts it, *American Pastoral* takes on:

> what happened to America in the decades between World War II and Vietnam, between the complacencies of the 50's and the confusions of the 60's, 70's and 80's. With the story of Seymour (Swede) Levov, Mr. Roth has chronicled the rise and fall of one man's fortunes and in doing so created a resonant parable of American innocence and disillusion.[26]

The Swede is a Jewish-American prince who seems to have realized the American dream. However, *American Pastoral* looks beneath the glowing surface — the Swede's progression from outstanding high school athlete through his marriage to Dawn Dwyer (an Irish-Catholic and former Miss New Jersey) and on to a successful career in business. What is revealed is the dark underside of the Swede's life and the unstable foundations and illusory promises of his American dream.

Almost immediately, Roth provides us with a glimpse of what is to come. We learn that the Levov's bright and attractive daughter, Merry, developed an incurable stutter which was the bane of her existence; which resisted all forms of treatment; and which transformed her into an over-weight outcast. We also learn that the post-adolescent Merry, in a protest against the Vietnam War, set off a bomb which resulted in the death of a local doctor. Finally, we learn of Merry's flight; she simply disappears without a trace. Her father and mother are devastated, because they in effect have lost their daughter twice over — first through her aggression against civic life and second through her decision to sever all ties to the family.

But how are we to understand Merry's betrayal? In unraveling the mystery, the novel reveals a volatile amalgam of personal and political forces, including Merry's emotional instability, the see-no-evil personality of her father, the Swede, the shattering impact of the Vietnam War and the deterioration of the inner city — all converging into an indictment of the American dream.

PARADISE REMEMBERED

The Swede is tall, blond, athletically gifted and handsome and was incongruously to become a Marine drill instructor during World War II. He, a Jew, was able during the war to mix with and gain the respect of Americans from all walks of life, unencumbered by anti-Semitism. "Accents from all over the place. The Midwest, New England. Some farm boys from Texas and the Deep South. I couldn't even understand. But got to know them. Got to like them" (p. 211).*

His postwar marriage to the beautiful Dawn Dwyer and his successful entry into and subsequent taking of the lead in his family's glove business was indisputable evidence to him that: "Something is shining down on me" (p. 201). The business succession from father to son was seamless, and

---

* Perhaps, the Swede was not entirely unencumbered by anti-Semitism. He recalls: "Another Jewish guy, Manny Rabinowitz from Altoona. Toughest Jewish guy I ever met . . . Manny was money in the bank for me. Nobody gave us any Jewboy shit" (p. 211).

the growth of the business enabled the Swede and Dawn to move from Newark to the pastoral countryside — to Old Rimrock. For the Swede the rural area is bliss, and Dawn, although somewhat apprehensive about life among the WASPs, settles in quite nicely — establishing a successful cattle breeding business on the Levov's 100 acres.

Nathan Zuckerman, the narrator, is a close friend of the Swede's younger brother,* worships the heroic Swede, identifies with the Swede's aspirations, and views him as an authentic expression of the unlimited promise of the postwar United States.

> Let us remember the energy. Americans were governing not only themselves but some two hundred million people in Italy, Austria, Germany, and Japan. The war-crimes trials were cleansing the earth of its devils once and for all. Atomic power was ours alone. Rationing was ending, price controls were being lifted; in an explosion of self-assertion . . . laborers by the millions demanded more and went on strike for it (p. 40).

In this heady setting, the future was there for the taking, and young people were admonished accordingly. "You must not come to nothing! Make something of yourselves! . . . The goal was to *have* goals" (p. 41, italics in the original). And these admonitions were irresistible — in no small measure because they were accompanied by tales of "parental self-sacrifice . . . It would have taken a lot more courage — or foolishness than most of us could muster to disappoint their passionate, unflagging illusions about our perfectibility and roam very far from the permissible" (p. 42).†

The Swede is also viewed by the young Zuckerman as an exemplar of the temptations and opportunities suddenly open to American Jews coming of age in the postwar years. He had married a beautiful "shiksa . . . He'd done it" (p. 15). "[O]ur very own Swede, a boy as close to a goy as we were going to get" (p. 10).

The Jewishness that he wore so lightly as one of the tall blond

---

* He is also Roth's long-time alter ego.

† While the elders conveyed a message of opportunity and achievement to their offspring, they were much more guarded in their appraisal of the welcoming beneficence of American culture. They harbored memories of exclusion. "The shift was not slight between the generations and there was plenty to argue about: the ideas of the world they wouldn't give up; the rules they worshiped, for us rendered all but toothless by the passage of a couple of decades of American time; those uncertainties were theirs not ours" (p. 41).

athletic winners must have spoken to us too — in our idolizing the Swede and his unconscious oneness with America. I suppose there was a tinge of shame and self-rejection . . . Jews who want to fit in and want to stand out, who insist they are different and insist they are no different" (p. 20).

Only in retrospect does the middle-aged narrator Zuckerman come to understand how the Swede's faux "goyness" blinded him to the ultimate barrenness of his American dream.[27]

THE FALL

During the turmoil over the Vietnam War, as Merry's outrage turns violent, the Swede discovers that his pastoral idyll is built on quicksand and compromised by contradictions. "The 'Rimrock Bomber' was Seymour's daughter. The high school kid who blew up the post office and killed the doctor" (p. 68). How this could have happened to a "girl blessed with golden hair and a logical mind and a high IQ and an adultlike sense of humor even about herself, blessed with long, slender limbs and a wealthy family and her own brand of dogged persistence" (p. 95)? It is this question that drives the novel — exposing bit by painful bit the Swede's deeply repressed responsibility for what he is emotionally compelled to blame on Merry and her enablers.

To begin with, there is the odious Rita Cohen. Claiming to be a friend and resistance comrade of Merry's, Rita tells the Swede that Merry would like her scrapbook and other childhood memorabilia. However, she also admonishes the Swede for his mistreatment of the working class and then for his mistreatment of Merry. Rita claims that Merry never wants to see her mother and her father who are both "fakes" in Merry's eyes. Dawn is obtuse, vain and full of hatred, and the Swede has left Merry without protection from her mother (pp. 138–9).

He is stunned by the "unreality of being in the hands of this child! This loathsome kid with a head full of fantasies about 'the working class!'" (p. 134). Nothing that Rita says makes sense to him, but he is so desperate he agrees to meet at a hotel where Rita tries crudely, salaciously and ultimately unsuccessfully to induce the Swede into a sexual encounter (p. 145). And with that Rita disappears for five years.

PARADISE LOST

These are the worst five years of the Swede's hitherto charmed life. There is the terrible not-knowing of where Merry is, what she has done and what she is doing as the anti-war protests grow ever more violent and lethal. Each time a bomb explodes he is tormented by the possibility that Merry has taken another human life. Each time he hears of a bombing gone awry, killing a would-be bomber, he fears that she has become her own victim. Unbearable either way.

Escalating the misery of these five years, he and Dawn become emotionally estranged from one another. She has turned morose, withdrawn and uncommunicative. When, after a time, she returns to the quotidian, she does so with a perverse and self-indulgent vengeance. She splurges on extravagant cosmetic surgery. She decides that the Levovs need a new home and commissions local architect, Bill Orcutt, to design a modernistic antithesis of their house, which the Swede loved because of its local pedigree and traditional charm.

As his life thus comes apart at the seams, the Swede angrily points the finger of blame at Merry. She becomes the villain with her "violent hatred of America" (p. 206) — the America that he loved. "Stuttering, spluttering little bitch! Who the fuck did she think she was" (p. 207)? For her, being an American was loathing America, but loving America was something he could not let go of any more than he could have let go of loving his father and his mother, any more than he could have let go of his decency"(p. 213).

MERRY REAPPEARS

When after five years he is finally is brought together with Merry through the intervention of the odious Rita, things go from worse to appalling — worse than he feared, more appalling than he could have ever imagined. She rushes into his arms crying "'Daddy! Daddy!' faultlessly, just like any other child, and looking like a person whose tragedy was that she'd never been anyone's child" (p. 231). She is dressed in rags, "a scarecrow's clothes" (p. 239) and lives in a burned-out portion of the city in a dangerous and pestiferous "hovel" — virtually begging to be preyed upon by the dregs of society. This place, "where his daughter lived [is] even worse than her greenhorn great-grandparents had, fresh from steerage" (p. 237).

He learns that she gave herself over body and soul to the "revolutionary thinkers" of the era: Marx, Marcuse, Malcolm X and Franz Fanon and to the Cuban revolution itself (pp. 260–1) — culminating in a second bombing in which three people were killed — a homicidal act that finally cured her stuttering (p. 259). It turns out that she is living in this hovel not because she is underground but because she has become disillusioned with political action. She is now a Jain, and has renounced all that is worldly:

I renounce all killing of living beings, whether subtle or gross, whether movable or immovable.

I renounce all vices of lying speech arising from anger, or greed, or fear, or mirth.

I renounce all taking of anything not given, either in a village, or a town, or a wood, either of little or much, or small or great, or living or lifeless things.

I renounce all sexual pleasures, either with gods, or men, or animals.

I renounce all attachments, whether little or much, small or great, living or lifeless; neither shall I myself form such attachments, nor cause others to do so, nor consent to their doing so (p. 239).[28]

Accordingly, it is not surprising that although Merry has in the course of these events been brutalized and raped, she is fully accepting of her degradation. Facing Merry, the Swede feels himself drawn into "chaos itself" in direct opposition to all that he had stood against his whole life. "Once Jews ran away from oppression; now they run away from non-oppression" (p. 255).[29]

The tentative efforts of Merry and the Swede to reason with one another across a cultural and emotional chasm are inevitably to no avail — simply exasperating each and driving them further apart. She condescends to him — "the condescension of a lunatic" (p. 244). Her "words sickened him, the flagrant childishness, the sentimental grandiosity of the self-deception" (p. 250). He tries to convince her to come home with him and even considers removing her forcibly, but decides that he has no right to do so.

THE RECKONING

These shattering assaults on the Swede's sensibilities finally lead him toward the terra incognita of introspection. He begins by recalling the many warning signs that he ignored in his determination to repress any second thoughts that might roil the surface of his placid realization of his American pastoral. The Swede had rejected Dawn's and his father's doubts about the acceptance of the parvenu Levovs in Old Rimrock. He saw these doubts as an anachronistic vestige of an outdated way of understanding the new and now beneficent postwar, post-sectarian United States.*

However, his disastrous meeting with Merry brings to mind his own repressed uneasiness about the people and culture of Old Rimrock. He had had his doubts about Orcutt. The Swede recalls that he instinctively

---

* Dawn was convinced that entrenched WASP culture could never truly welcome a "lace-curtain Irish" wife married to an erstwhile Newark Jew.

viewed the architect's paintings as incomprehensible — and yet suggestive of a depressive streak which belied the ideal life that he imputed to WASP Americans. It subsequently becomes clear that Orcutt is a hollow man and his wife Jessie hopelessly alcoholic. All of this should have, the Swede realizes belatedly, led to the unavoidable conclusion that, when all is said and done, even the fully realized American dream is a seductive illusion. Of course, to think in these terms would have made a lie of his entire life. Only now, with the lie of his American pastoral inescapable, can he face up to his own responsibility for all that has happened — in particular to his determination to get along by going along.

The full measure of the Swede's fall from grace emerges during a bizarre dinner party which includes in addition to Dawn and the Swede, Lou and Sylvia Levov, Bill and Jesse Orcutt, Sheila Salzman, Merry's speech therapist, as well as the Swede's good friend, Barry Umanoff, and his wife, Marcia, the so-called "professor of transgression" (p. 365) — the detested *bête noire* of the party. Early in the evening the Swede stumbles on a compromising scene between Dawn and Bill Orcutt, and subsequently he discovers that Sheila Salzman had betrayed the Levovs by facilitating Merry's flight.

The centerpiece of the ever more raucous dinner is Lou Levov's disjointed, eclectic, eccentric and yet somehow cunning diagnosis of all that ails America. He is set off by a discussion of the popularity of *Deep Throat* which, as Lou sees it, desecrates the culture and should have been resoundingly rejected by the intelligentsia. Lou goes on from the cultural rot evidenced by the popularity of *Deep Throat* to the implosion of life as he had known it in Newark. "Streets aren't cleaned. Burned-out cars nobody takes away. People in abandoned buildings. Fires in abandoned buildings. Unemployment. Filth. Poverty . . . Schools a disaster. Police on the take" (p. 345). He refuses to blame it on a reshuffling of the political class. "Look, the Irish ran the city, the Italians ran the city, now let the colored run the city. That's not my point. I got nothing against that" (p. 345). The real problem has been the loss of good jobs as business failed and production moved overseas — driven out by high tax rates, union piecework, and by manufacturers who didn't understand either" (p. 346).*

LOOKING INWARD
Only as this perfect storm breaks over his head does the Swede finally begin to see the light.

---

* Lou's disquisition does not leave him unblemished. As he recounts the good old days in the neighborhood he mentions a restaurant on Mulberry Street "where we used to go with the kids to eat at the Chinks" (p. 347).

His daughter was an insane murderer hiding on the floor of a room in Newark, his wife had a lover who dry-humped her at the sink in the family kitchen . . . and he was trying to propitiate his father with on-the-one-hand-this and on-the-other hand-that (p. 358).

With the prompting of others, he comes to understand his own role in the family debacle. His aggressive younger brother Jerry excoriates the Swede for leaving Merry in her hovel. "Get in your fucking car and get over there and drag her out . . . Sedate her. Tie her up. But get her" (p. 273).

When the Swede refuses to do so, Jerry denounces the Swede's equivocation, and the shell that he has constructed around himself. "You don't reveal yourself to people, Seymour. You keep yourself a secret. Nobody knows who you are" (p. 275). For Jerry, Seymour is Dr. Frankenstein and he has created a monster by inventing an American dream that ignored the seamy side of life and then by sealing himself, his wife and his daughter into this illusion (p. 277). "Admit that there is something very personal about you she [Merry] hates and bail the fuck out and never see the bitch again" (p. 280).

So, there it is. The Swede meets the enemy and it is he. The Swede is forced to confront the consequences of blindly ignoring the seamy side of life in post-World War II United States. Unlike Dawn or his father, he embraced his new life among the landed gentry. He was oblivious to so much.

The Swede surveys the emotional carnage around him and ends up realizing that in refracting his life and the American century through a rose-covered lens, he has been too determined to palliate and pacify, too conflict-averse to stand up for what really matters. In destroying herself Merry had finally driven home to him what had been, for so long, so apparent to others (p. 418). His determination to see no evil created an ethos against which Merry instinctively rebelled (p. 386).

Even with all this hard-won self-knowledge and with all of its social implications, the Swede clings wistfully to those ideals that sustained him throughout his life. The dinner party has exposed the hollowness of life in Old Rimrock; its "fortification" has been breached. "They'll never recover. Everything is against them, everyone and everything that does not like their life. All the voices from without condemning and rejecting their life! And what is wrong with their life? What on earth is less reprehensible than the life of the Levovs?" (p. 423). With these words the novel ends.

2. The Mixed Blessings of the British Welfare State

Every six months she received a visit from the social security people, to find out if her circumstances had changed. The humiliation of these visits, the posh voices, the questions, the eyes everywhere, only strengthened her determination to preserve her independence at all costs.

Pat Barker [30]

The origins of the postwar British welfare state can be traced to the late nineteenth century when the state became increasing "interventionist."[31] There were, however, precursors under Churchill's wartime coalition government — most notably the Beveridge Report of 1942 which called for "security from the cradle to the grave" and specific statutes such as the 1944 Education Act and the 1945 Family Allowance Act.[32] But the construction of the welfare state began in earnest only after the 1945 victory of Clement Atlee's Labour Party. Its centerpiece was the National Health Services Act of 1946, which was touted for the efficiency that it would bring to the fragmented British health care system.

The Health Service and other elements of the welfare state were seen as agents of social justice, which would ameliorate class divisions, enhance equality and reinforce democratic values. The welfare state did indeed become the foundation of British social policy and had notable successes. Still there were shortcomings and unintended consequences that generated critiques from policy analysts.

Mainstream critiques of the welfare state have been rooted in its fiscal contradictions and its moral hazards. The most systematic analysis of fiscal matters by Claus Offe seizes on the welfare state's problematic impact on taxes and investment.[33] As John Keane, the editor of Offe's essays, put it in his introduction to that volume, the fiscal crisis of the welfare state results from "the continuous expansion of state budgets . . . [while] the borrowing and taxation powers of the state tend to impinge upon the profitability of the capitalist sector."[34] Moreover, because the capitalist sector is the source of the funds that sustain the welfare state, it is necessary that the "Keynesian welfare state must 'positively subordinate' itself to the capitalist economy."[35] What this means, in effect, is that the welfare state is under constant fiscal pressure to reduce its benefits and/or under political pressure from an electorate which experiences a combination of higher taxes and reduced benefits.

The moral hazard associated with the welfare state begins with distinctions between the deserving and the undeserving poor. While the former are entitled to social assistance, the latter are not. This moral critique then goes on to claim that welfare tends to transform the deserving poor into the undeserving poor as they follow the line of least resistance into a disabling dependency on the state, leading to a loss of productive labor and a reduction in the tax base even as the fiscal costs of the welfare state are increasing. It was, of course, this argument that held sway during Margaret's Thatcher's neo-liberal reign as Prime Minister. Further enhancing the resonance of Thatcher's neo-liberalism were the 1981 riots in British cities expressing the political estrangement of those most directly afflicted by the failing political economy of the United Kingdom.[36]

The novels of estrangement from the welfare state focus on its unredeemed promises. We learn from these novels how shortcomings of the welfare state weigh on daily lives of the working class in Alan Sillitoe's *Saturday Night and Sunday Morning*; the ethnic Other in Zadie Smith's *White Teeth* and the affluent and the afflicted in Ian McEwan's *Saturday*.[37]

Saturday Night and Sunday Morning

Twenty-one-year-old Arthur Seaton (p. 25), the central character of *Saturday Night and Sunday Morning*, is an angry young man estranged from politics — indeed from any civic engagement whatsoever. Arthur is self-absorbed and self-indulgent. He is the personification of the post-World War II sensibility of "I'm all right, Jack"* attributed in particular to factory workers and boiling down to every man for himself.[38] In Arthur's case this meant a life devoted to drinking, smoking and screwing other men's wives — a lifestyle sustained by his relatively well-paid and reasonably satisfying job as a skilled lathe operator in his local bicycle factory. Why, then, is he so angry, so self-indulgent and so estranged from civic engagement?

SATURDAY NIGHT: "CRIMES" WITHOUT PUNISHMENT
The novel begins with Arthur drinking himself into a paralytic stupor on Saturday night and tumbling down a flight of pub stairs. As the scene unfolds it seems that there is a tragedy in the making. In Sillitoe's telling, however, Arthur is simply participating with exemplary exuberance in a weekly working-class ritual. "Piled-up passions were exploded on Saturday night, and the effect of a week's monotonous graft in the factory was swilled out of your system in a burst of goodwill" (p. 4). Arthur escapes uninjured and ends up in bed with Brenda, his mistress and the wife of Arthur's fellow worker, Jack, who works the night shift. They

---

* "I'm all right, Jack" was a popular film send-up of post-World War II factory life. In its original, rawer formulation, according to *The Urban Dictionary*, "Fuck you, Jack, I'm all right" conveyed the disillusionment of returning servicemen who felt insufficiently appreciated and entitled to do whatever it takes to get ahead, irrespective of the cost to others.

awaken Sunday with fond memories of Saturday night as having been quite grand — both because of the drunkenness and the sex afterward. An air of ersatz domesticity ensues, with Brenda's young son Jacky eager for a romp with "Uncle Arthur" (p. 16). Brenda prepares breakfast, and Arthur eats heartily while being ready to bolt out the front door as Jack enters the back door.

This is but the first of Arthur's many narrow escapes from hazardous situations of his own making. The common denominator of these adventures and misadventures is Arthur's thirst for danger and his determination to flout convention — drinking, casting insults, picking fights; sleeping with married women; and lying to all about what he is doing. He understands that he is often not believed but either bluffs or charms his way out of trouble with these lies.

What are we to make of Arthur's determination to defy social and moral convention and of his self indulgence at the expense of others? Arthur's own view is that in lashing out in anger whenever his own prerogatives are threatened, he is asserting his independence — that he's all right, Jack. He never backs away from a fight, takes offense easily, and always has a chip on his shoulder except at home and with Brenda with whom he is tender and caring — in part because as a married woman she poses no threat to his independence. His contempt for men who are not real men is palpable; they are incomprehensible to him. He has no qualms about his affair with Brenda, because Jack is too weak and indecisive to take care of his own. In besting Jack and bedding Brenda, Arthur is proving his manhood.

There is a distinct *anti*-social element to Arthur's combative personality.[39] From his nuclear and extended families he has learned that civic responsibility is for suckers. His father boasts: "'When I went for my medical in the war they were A1, but I swung the lead and got off 3C,' he added proudly" (p. 22). The sons of his favorite aunt, Ada, have followed a more wayward path. While "on the run from the army during the war," they had sustained themselves on "loot" from their crimes (p. 76). Arthur has thus been raised to ridicule civic responsibility. He sums up his bitter outlook on life with the old adage: "Don't let the bastards grind you down" (p. 37) — and the bastards, those with social and political leverage, will surely try. These sentiments lead him to a distinctly non-political appreciation of Communists, but not of Communism.

> I tell you. I like 'em though, because they're different from these big fat Tory bastards in parliament. And them Labour bleeders too. They rob our wage packets every week with insurance and income tax and try to tell us it's all for our own good (p. 32).

Even if Arthur's anger is loosely tethered to a sense of injustice against the bosses, this working-class anger is the product of political estrangement and certainly does not lead towards political action. "Me, I couldn't care less if the world did blow up tomorrow, as long as I'm blown up with it" (p. 37). Notably missing is any trace of class solidarity that might lead to political engagement and preclude Arthur's predatory attitudes towards Jack.

Arguably, Arthur's is the voice of hard-left British anarchism and the novel, by its conclusion, can be read as a lament for this dying tradition sapped of its vitality by the meager comforts of the welfare state. Consider Arthur's self-proclaimed, decidedly suspect independence of social constraints and social convention. He has only minor complaints about his job as a skilled and well-paid lathe operator. He also takes comfort from the relatively good life of his parents and from his father's own secure job in the same factory.[40] He has made a separate peace, albeit grudgingly, with the postwar welfare state. Arthur is smug, complacent and comfortable. His paycheck allows him to indulge himself with the clothes that he fancies, with an overabundance of alcohol and cigarettes, as well as the capacity to spend freely on his affairs.[41]

SUNDAY MORNING: TAMING ARTHUR SEATON

Arthur fancies himself a rebel, but his rebellion is a veneer which is mostly a rationale for pursuing his own sophomoric pleasures. As the novel progresses we see Arthur's taste for rebellion soured by "the stick" of angry husbands and "the carrot" of a would-be wife.

His downfall begins with Brenda's unwelcome pregnancy. Although they agree that aborting the fetus is the only option, the process of doing so proves so harrowing that it puts Arthur's affair with Brenda in jeopardy. This is when he turns to the next available target of opportunity, Brenda's married sister Winnie. Further complicating Arthur's chaotic love life is Doreen, who captures his fancy and is determined to make him her husband — to bring him to heel. She is unaware of Brenda and Winnie, and Arthur experiences yet again the thrill of taking chances, of defying social convention and of indulging his own whims at the expense of others.

This time, however, his high-wire act proves unsustainable, and Arthur is made to pay for his transgressions. Winnie's army husband Bill discovers that Arthur is having an affair with his wife as well as with Brenda. Bill sets out to track down Arthur. After a number of near misses, with Jack's help, the two of them find their way to Arthur. A fight ensues and Arthur is mercilessly beaten in this two-against-one battle. It is Doreen who finds Arthur unconscious and manages to get him home.

Arthur takes to his bed, a beaten man. He is unable to rouse himself out of a consuming lethargy. He tries to convince himself that he really is all right: "Me, I'll have a good life: plenty of work and plenty of booze and a piece of skirt every month till I'm ninety. Brenda and Winnie were out of his reach, penned in by Jack and Bill, but there was always more than one pebble on the beach" (p. 198). Beneath this bravado, however, he realizes that that this is more than just another beating. "He sensed that though he had merely been beaten up by two swaddies — not a very terrible thing . . . he felt like a ship that had never left its slipway suddenly floundering in mid-ocean" (p. 197).

Much to his consternation, Doreen arrives to find him in this passive state. He is flustered and defensive when Doreen comes into his bedroom. "When wounded he liked to be alone in his lair, and felt intimidated by her visit, as if he would have to pay for it with his life" (p. 200). She persists, showing concern for him while calling him out on his rationalizing (p. 201). "But I'm glad you came to see me," he said cheerfully. "I think I'd've stayed down in the dumps for good if you hadn't" (p. 203) — and the two of them proceed to have a further hour of chatting.

Arthur is still in his funk as Christmas rolls around, but spending the holiday at Aunt Ada's, where he feels very much at home, changes his mood. Arthur finds this family event revivifying — "feeling strangely and joyfully alive, as if he had been living in a soulless vacuum since his fight with the swaddies. He told himself that he had been without life since then, that now he was awake once more, ready to tackle all obstacles, to break any man, or woman, that came for him, to turn on the whole world if it bothered him too much, and blow it to pieces" (p. 219).

It is in this frame of mind that he yields to Doreen, becoming her "young man" and, thus taking the first ambivalent step towards matrimony and domesticity. She makes no bones about her determination to make him her husband — denying him sex until their relationship is made permanent (p. 223). He protests. "I'm courtin' now, can't you see" (p. 224). She is, however, adamant and for good measure critical of Arthur's drinking. He understands that she is trying to keep him "in check" and halfheartedly protests while taking comfort from her concern. "I like to see you arguing and telling me off" (p. 226). She makes no effort to hide her intentions: "'You think you're the cock o' the walk,' she said, implying: 'But I'll tame you, you see if I don't'" (p. 227). When finally Arthur succumbs to the gravitational pull of domesticity, he is both apprehensive and relieved.

> Arthur was subdued . . . fighting the last stages of an old battle within himself, and at the same time feeling the first skirmishes of a new conflict. But he was good in his heart about it, easy and

confident, making for better ground than he had ever trodden on before (p. 234).

Indeed, they are both overwhelmed by the giant step they have decided to take. On the one hand, they feel as if in making the decision "the weight of the world had in a minute been lifted" (p. 234). On the other, they sensed a "stalemate" in the making, as they struggle to hang onto their individuality in a life together — and "sought relief from the great decision that they had just brought upon themselves" (p. 234).

LAMENT

Does Arthur's knuckling under to domesticity demonstrate that his rebellion was without a cause beyond self-indulgence? Arthur doesn't see it that way. Indeed, he is at his most politically conscious as he contemplates marriage — clearly fearing but determined to evade being coerced or enticed into support of the state.

> Once a rebel, always a rebel. You can't help being one. You can't deny that. And it's best to be a rebel so as to show 'em it don't pay to try to do you down. Factories and labour exchanges and insurance offices keep us alive and kicking — so they say — but they're booby traps and will suck you under like sinking sands if you aren't careful. Factories sweat you to death, labour exchanges talk you to death, insurance and income tax offices milk money from your wage packets and rob you to death. And if you're still left with a tiny bit of life in your guts after all this boggering about, the army calls you up and you get shot to death. And if you're clever enough to stay out of the army you get bombed to death. Ay, by God, it's a hard life if you don't weaken, if you don't stop that bastard government from grinding your face in muck" (p. 220) . . . They shout at you from soapboxes: 'Vote for me, and this and that,' but it amounts to the same in the end whatever you vote for because it means a government that puts stamps all over your phizzog until you can't see a hand before you, and what's more makes you buy 'em so's they can keep on doing it. They've got you by the guts, by backbone and skull, until they think you'll come whenever they whistle" (p. 221).

What are we to make of his determination to remain a rebel or even of this sudden outpouring of political estrangement?

Our only clue comes from the brief chapter with which the novel concludes. Arthur, about to be but not yet married, spends a bucolic day of freedom fishing. He begins to think about himself as a fish who has not yet taken the bait — "had really only licked the bait and found it tasty, that he could still disengage his mouth from the nibbled morsel" (p. 236). However, we know and he probably does as well that he will take the bait because he and Doreen have already gotten down to the nitty-gritty of figuring out how they can make ends meet by living with Doreen's mother (p. 237). Thus, while Arthur may have some reservations, his practical self, mindful of money, is taking charge and his rebel-self is receding.

He has come to the realization that settling down is inevitable for him and for others. "Everyone in the world was caught, somehow, one way or another, and those that weren't were always on the way to it' (p. 236). He catches a fish and "felt mobile waves of hope running the length of its squamous body from head to tail. He removed the hook, and threw it back into the water" vowing to give it "one more chance" (p. 238) — but just one more. He re-baits the hook and says to himself: "This time it was war, and he wanted the fish to take home, either to cook in the pan or feed to the cat" (p. 238). The last line of the book finds him "with a grin on his face" (p. 239), set to land a fish which has taken the bait.

Clearly Arthur has a melancholy longing for his old rebellious self. He reassures himself that "for me it'll be fighting every day until I die. Why do they make soldiers out of us when we're fighting up to the hilt as it is? Fighting with mothers and wives, landlords and gaffers, coppers, army government" (p. 238). He thus reduces war and rebellion to squabbling that he associates with marriage, family, and occasional run-ins with others who cross his path.

For Arthur this adds up to "a good life and a good world, all said and done, if you don't weaken, and if you know that the big wide world hasn't heard from you yet, no, not by a long way, though it won't be long now" (p. 239). We can take Arthur's efforts to rationalize his capitulation to domesticity with a grain of salt. Or we can believe that his anger will continue to smolder. Either way Arthur's discontents are strictly personal. Even the transient traces of *political* discontent have been left behind. The personal has displaced politics, making them irrelevant and political estrangement total.

In the end then, Sillitoe's searing portrayal of working-class anger turns into a melancholy meditation on the capacity of the postwar welfare state to neutralize Arthur's seething rebellion and transform him into a responsible citizen.[42] The transformative event is, of course, the fight in which Arthur is brutally beaten for thwarting social convention. The beating thus becomes a metaphor for the futility of Arthur's broader struggle to maintain his independence from social constraints and the meager comforts of the welfare state.

White Teeth

And so I sat in the centre of this old city that I loved . . . I was surrounded by people I loved, and I felt happy and miserable at the same time. I thought of what a mess everything had been, but that it wouldn't always be that way.

Hanif Kureishi[43]

Zadie Smith recounts the multicultural lives of two families across two generations. The two families, both parents and children, are enmeshed. However, the generations bear sharply contrasting burdens. The older generation lives on something of a cultural island, at arm's length from and in tenuous connection with, the British mainstream. The children's burden is much heavier, in large part because their schooling thrusts them into British culture which they must master if they are to be accepted. In addition, when they reach adolescence they find themselves in the age-old intergenerational struggle to separate from their parents — a struggle that is exacerbated by the determination of their parents to protect them from British cultural imperialism.[44] As the novel proceeds, the cultural terrain becomes still more problematic; modernity takes center stage, adding yet another cultural divide for all to negotiate.

This sounds desperate, and to some extent it is. However, Smith sees multiculturalism as inevitable — indeed, as a fact of British life. Therefore, the novel, punctuated by "Smith's frisky and irreverent comic attack,"[45] depicts multiculturalism less as cleavage than as misunderstanding, more comic than tragic, and unwieldy rather than dire — in sharp contrast, therefore, to the inter-racial black abyss portrayed by African-American writers.

MULTICULTURALISM WITHIN AND BETWEEN GENERATIONS
The multicultural tangle begins very simply with an unlikely cross-cultural friendship between two World War II British soldiers: a clever and strong-willed Bengali Muslim, Samad Miah Iqbal, and Alfred Archibald Jones, stolid, solid and white — a working-class Englishman. The circle of friendship is extended when each marries, and the two families come together. The children are playmates and virtually siblings. The husbands are mates who pass many an hour together at a local pub. The wives — one a Bengali and the other a Jamaican — are commiserating soul mates.[*] The parents have their own cultures to sustain them in their adopted

---

[*] The women condescend to their husbands, with Alsana, for example, complaining that initially she fell head-over-heels in love with Samad but: "Now every time I

country. The children, however, have no idea where they belong, so they are perforce immersed in intrinsically irresolvable cultural and familial contradictions.

The ties that bind Samad and Archie were established when the two soldiers found themselves marooned and alone behind enemy lines in Bulgaria. Their isolation leads them to reach across the cultural divide and to confide in one another in a way that under normal circumstances would have been impossible.

> They knocked around ideas that Archie did not entirely understand, and Samad offered secrets into the cool night that he had never spoken out loud. Long, comfortable silences passed between them . . . In short it was precisely the kind of friendship an Englishman makes on holiday, that he can make only on holiday. A friendship that crosses class and color, a friendship that takes as its basis physical proximity and survives because the Englishman assumes physical proximity will not continue (p. 82).

Their military misadventure ends with what turns out to be a portentous dispute concerning a Belgian doctor who lives very close to where they have been marooned. This doctor has been involved in eugenics research conducted under the auspices of Nazi officials. Samad decides that the doctor is in effect an enemy who must be killed and somehow manages to convince the reluctant and aghast Archie to do the dirty deed. Unknown to Samad for many years, Archie takes the doctor off to kill him but only pretends to do so. This eugenic chicken comes home to roost at the very late-modern culmination of the novel.

It is, however, the postwar years that dominate the novel — beginning with the marriage of Archie to a much younger Jamaican woman, Clara.

When he meets Clara, Archie is in a suicidal funk following the devastating breakup of his first marriage. Archie is stunned by Clara's beauty and captivated by her powerful presence. She has her own reasons for accepting Archie's precipitous proposal of marriage. Her mother, Hortense, is devoted body and soul to the Jehovah's Witnesses and Clara had accepted the religion. At some point Clara managed to recruit the nerdy Ryan Topps, who is smitten with Clara. Responding to his hormonal needs, he accepts conversion, only to drive Clara to distraction. Ryan becomes so religiously pure that he condemns Clara's sexuality — that same sexuality that led to his religious awakening. Largely to escape Ryan

---

learn something about him, I like him less" (p. 68). She considers him a failure for being mired in a poor-paying job in his cousin's restaurant.

and his religiosity, Clara abandons him and the Jehovah's Witnesses and marries Archie. Their multicultural union produces a daughter, Irie. She is thoughtful and shy and has inherited from her mother an un-British, buxom Jamaican beauty that makes her very self-conscious.

Samad and Alsama have twin boys: the irascible and irresistible Millat and the serious and self-contained Magid. Samad's sense of cultural alienation makes it seem vitally important that he pass on to the twins their Bengali birthright. He fears that he has made a "pact with the devil" in bringing his family to "a place where you are never welcomed, only tolerated . . . you belong nowhere" (p. 336). Samad is also bitter about having to earn his living as a waiter in an Indian restaurant, bowing and scraping before customers, and at the mercy of his cousin, the restaurant's owner.[46]

Samad's struggle to keep his boys out of the clutches of English culture puts him at odds with the school system, which is doing its ineffectual best to bridge the cultural gap. The twins and Irie are dispatched by their school for a cross-cultural and intergenerational visit to the home of one Mr. Hamilton. When they arrive at his door he is initially certain that they are there to do him harm.

> I must ask that you to remove yourselves from my doorstep. I have no money whatsoever; so be your intention robbing or selling I'm afraid you will be disappointed (p. 141).

Once they have through great persistence established their good intentions, things only get worse. Even before they are enveloped by cultural outrage, the children stumble into interracial misunderstanding by bringing some little presents of food that suit them but are completely unpalatable to him. The well-intentioned Hamilton proceeds to antagonize them irretrievably.

> When I was in the Congo, the only way I could identify the nigger was by the whiteness of his teeth, if you see what I mean. Horrid business. Dark as buggery it was. And they died because of it, you see?

And when he denies that their "wog" father could have served in the British army, Millat is furious. "'It's the truth!' shouted Millat, kicking over the tea tray that sat on the floor between them. 'You *stupid* fucking old man'" (pp. 144–5).

Things go no better at a public meeting of teachers and parents. Samad brings his grievances and his scheme for righting cultural wrongs. He proceeds to hijack the agenda — denouncing the school calendar and in particular the multiplicity of frivolous school holidays which have only specious connections to Christianity (p. 109). Were these holidays to be struck from the calendar, he argues, there would be more than enough time to introduce Bengali culture and religious traditions into the curriculum without jeopardizing the school's academic mission. In short, Samad wants the school system to balance the surfeit of English cultural influences that he deems are robbing Magid and Millat of their Bengali identities.

Of course, the school curriculum is largely irrelevant to the twins, who are each determined to be accepted by their English peer group. Millat becomes a:

> rudeboy, a badman, at the forefront, changing image as often as shoes; sweet-as, safe, wicked, leading kids up hills to play football, downhill to rifle fruit machines, out of schools, into the video shops . . . He was arsey and mouthy, he had his fierce good looks squashed tightly inside him like a jack-in-the-box set to spring aged thirteen, at which point he graduated from leader of zit-faced boys to leader of women (p. 181).

Magid, while studious and serious, has become "Mark" in order to fit in better with English culture. The name change was "a symptom of a far deeper malaise. Magid really wanted to be in some other family . . . wanted his mother to make the music on the cello, not the sound of a sewing machine; . . . wanted to go on biking holidays to France, not day trips to Blackpool to visit aunties; . . . wanted his father to be a doctor, not a one-handed waiter" (p. 126).* Samad, for his part, seems unable, or too desperate, to grasp the depth of his boys' cultural schizophrenia.

Just after the public meeting Samad's own cultural schizophrenia intrudes suddenly, unceremoniously and irresistibly. On the way out he is complimented for his principled stand by Magid's music teacher, Poppy Burt-Jones. She is the flower of English womanhood. Samad is bewitched by the alluring and willing young music teacher. Their affair develops at a glacial pace, because Samad is guilt-ridden as well as lovestruck. He turns to Islam for respite (p. 115), because he deems himself at "a moral crossroads in my life" (p. 121). Eventually, however,

---

* Samad had seriously injured his arm while a member of the *Indian* army. Thus he had to serve in the British army as an enlisted man rather than as a pilot and an officer — a status more in keeping with his family's military prowess and heritage which he traces back to the great warrior, Mangal Pande (p. 74).

he succumbs to Poppy's charms, all the while fearing for his immortal soul. Thus, although Samad chooses to think of himself as the family's stalwart guardian of Bengali culture and Islam, it turns out that he, just like his sons, is in a multicultural bind — a contradiction that has long been apparent to Millat.* The affair follows its overheated course until a chance meeting between Samad, Poppy and the twins brings Samad to his Bengali senses. He concludes that he is failing not only his religion at the cost of his immortal soul but his duties as a father to his two sons whom he can never hope to save from British cultural imperialism while he is culturally and religiously compromised.

Samad returns to Islam with insufferable vengeance. His embrace of religion is a harmless annoyance to the family. Not so his wacky decision to kidnap the serious and studious Magid and pack him off to India where he would be free of English culture and where he would be reunited with his Bengali origins. The seemingly incorrigible Millat will be left to his own blasphemous devices, but so be it. Samad anticipates Alsana's objections, but he is adamant. She believes that India will put Magid in physical and spiritual danger. India was at the time a very violent place. Alsana is also leery of Bengali culture which is steeped in disaster and too fatalistic for her taste. She fears that Magid will "learn to hold his life lightly" (p. 176).

When Samad goes through with his plan, it transforms their marriage into a pitched battle. Alsana wins virtually all of the confrontations with Samad, including the frequent physical encounters. More devastatingly, she refuses to communicate with Samad. "Whatever the question asked in the Iqbal house, there would never be a straight answer [from Alsana]" (p. 178). When all is said and done, Samad takes himself so seriously that it is difficult for the *reader* to take him seriously. This is true not only of Samad but of virtually all of the characters — thus becoming the book's leitmotif and the touchstone of its ironic humor.

MULTICULTURALISM MEETS THE MODERN PROJECT
After Magid is dispatched to India, the school authorities decide that Irie and Millat need some tutoring. At the request of the headmaster of the twins' school, the widely celebrated Chalfen family agrees with alacrity to mentor Irie and Millat so as to get them on track academically.

---

* Millat sees his father as a hypocrite who "prays five times a day but he still drinks alcohol and has no Muslim friends" — only Archie (p. 277). Indeed he and Archie do repair nightly to their favorite hangout, the multicultural "O'Connell's Poolroom" (p. 153). O'Connell's is a faux replica of a British pub and serves traditional pub food: chips, beans, eggs, tomatoes, mushrooms and toast.

The Chalfens have married across religious lines — he is Jewish, she is Christian — but they share a commitment to science, to rationality and their own insularity. They are dismissive of religion, spirituality and all non-scientific understandings of the world (p. 261). The family is also staunchly Labour, committed to doing good and firm believers in the importance of nurturing the intelligence that they immediately detect in Irie and Millat.

Marcus Chalfen is at the cutting edge of research on recombinant DNA and genetic engineering, with which he is determined to free human beings of inherited diseases that threaten their lives and their well-being (p.347).

His search for answers to these puzzles of mortality has led Marcus to create a disease-resistant mouse, which he is to unveil at a public meeting that becomes the novel's calamitous, culminating event. Joyce Chalfen inflects her modernity differently — anchoring it in developmental psychology and mental health. Whereas Marcus's modern project is directed at solving the life-and-death problems of the species, Joyce's modernity is interpersonal and directed at resolving what she comes to see as Millat's life-and-death issues. Their son Joshua is clearly a chip off the old block, brilliant at math, socially isolated at school, and a classmate of Irie's whom he finds irresistibly attractive but out of his nerdy reach.

Although the Chalfens' mandate is restricted to tutoring, because they are devoted missionaries of the modern project, their influence inevitably becomes much more pervasive and culturally confrontational — especially once Irie and Millat burn their familial bridges. The two post-adolescents break with their parents whom they hold responsible for exacerbating their cultural demons.

> Millat disappeared from home for weeks at time, returning with money that was not his and an accent that modulated wildly between the rounded tones of the Chalfens and the street talk of the KEVIN clan [Keepers of the Eternal and Victorious Islamic Nation]. He infuriated Samad beyond all reason. No, that's wrong. There was a reason. Millat was neither one thing nor the other, this or that, Muslim or Christian, Englishman or Bengali; he lived for the in-between, he lived up to his middle name, *Zulfikar*, the clashing of two swords (p. 291).

When finally Millat is thrown out of his house for calling Samad a cunt, he turns to the Chalfens for shelter. Irie leaves the Jones's household of her own accord and goes to live with her grandmother, Hortense. The event precipitating her departure occurs at a dinner of the Jones and Iqbal families. Irie is exasperated by comments critical of Millat, whom she loves. She punctuates her outraged departure with f-bombs — including "for fuck's sake" and "What possible fucking difference can it make?"*

As the two young people come under the influence of the Chalfen family, they take advantage of their opportunities in dramatically different ways. "Where Irie saw culture, refinement, class, intellect, Millat saw money, lazy money, money just hanging around this family not doing anything in particular, money in need of a good cause that might as well be him" (p. 268). Never mind; they each serve the missionary purposes of the Chalfens. Meanwhile, Joshua is intensely ambivalent about what has happened. On the one hand, he has Irie regularly in his house and his connection to the popular Millat provides him with social cachet at school. On the other hand, "Joshua had not bargained on the power of Millat's attractiveness. His magnetlike qualities" (p. 273). Joshua sees that Irie is smitten and soon discovers that Joyce is heavily invested in Millat.

Irie, taken under Marcus's wing and working as a kind of gofer-secretary (p. 283), does get herself back on track academically. Her A levels improve sufficiently to make a university education and a career in dentistry realistic probabilities (p. 312). Working as Marcus's secretary and gofer, she manages to put his chaotic affairs in order. Millat, however, simply exploits Joyce's good intentions. He continues his wayward disregard for school and more or less ignores Joyce's efforts to deploy the tools of developmental psychology. Nonetheless, because Millat has become her vocation, she is unflagging in her efforts to save him from himself.

If we ask why Irie responds so well and Millat so perversely to the Chalfens, it is because his cultural malaise is deeper and more pervasive than hers. Her problems are largely and typically post-adolescent — albeit exacerbated by cultural dislocation. At school she is self-conscious about the contrast between her buxom Jamaican beauty and the typically "slender, delicate English rose" (p. 222). She feels excluded and is willing to go to ridiculous lengths to alter her appearance — putting herself, to that end, through a punishing and tragically comic hair straightening (p. 229 ff.). Poor Irie, "didn't know she was fine. There was England, a gigantic mirror and there was Irie, without reflection. A stranger in a stranger land" (p. 222). Of course, she has no idea that the shy, brilliant Joshua Chalfen finds her irresistible.

Millat, for all of his social success as a leader of his "crew" with magnetic sexual power, is the most culturally compromised character in the book. He is handsome, sexually irresistible and a master of British popular

---

* "'That girl,' tutted Alsana as her front door slammed. 'Swallowed an encyclopedia and a gutter at the same time'" (p. 200).

culture. "Millat Iqbal's main squeezes were almost all exclusively size 10 white Protestant women aged fifteen to twenty-eight, living in and around the immediate vicinity of West Hampstead" (p. 306). However, he resists shedding his Islamic identity and ambivalently embraces KEVIN. Eventually, he comes to realize that he is living a lie.

He must somehow assimilate KEVIN's ascetic ethos and its determination to reveal the corrupting influence of the West: "*The Right to Bare: The Naked Truth About Western Sexuality*" (p. 308). What was he to do? The "split level" Millat was able to conform in his own loose and Anglo-inflected fashion to the putatively rigid strictures of KEVIN — not by abstaining from alcohol and sex with English women but by moderating his indulgence. "On the scriptural side of things, he thought Muhammad (peace be upon Him!) was a right geezer, a great bloke, and he was in awe of the creator, in the original meaning of that word: dread, fear, really shit-scared" (pp. 366–7). Millat is at sea — unwilling to give up either the gratifications of being an inside-outsider in British culture or his Islamic heritage.

Joyce digs deeply and desperately into Millat's malaise and discovers that "Millat was filled with self-revulsion and hatred of his own kind; that he had possibly a slave mentality, or maybe a color-complex centered around his mother (he was far darker than she), or a wish for his own annihilation by means of dilution in a white gene pool" (p. 311). She can "hardly sleep" for worrying about him (p. 360). She refuses to "just sit back and watch them [Millat and Magid] tear themselves apart . . . just because their parents don't seem concerned . . . I should think I know a traumatized child when I see one" (p. 360). Understandably this puts Joyce on a collision course with Alsana, who thinks of the Chalfens in general and Joyce in particular as intrusive and dangerous — responsible for the defections of her sons.*

In his shrewdly introspective moments Millat comes to his own understanding of these deeply felt needs to act out. His life is constructed around the contradictory and therefore unsustainable expectations of

---

* Of course underneath it all is the distrust of the English Chalfens whom both Alsana and Clara associate with British imperialism. Alsana declares that "A little English education can be a dangerous thing" and, more to the point, "The English are the only people," she would say with distaste, "who want to teach you and steal from you at the same time" (p. 295). As for Clara, her great-grandmother, Ambrosia, was taken under the wing of an English gentleman in Jamaica. He did educate her but he also impregnated her. Ambrosia subsequently (influenced by another Englishman) came under the spell of *The Watchtower* and Jehovah's Witnesses — another black mark as far as Clara is concerned.

others — that the authentic Millat, not unlike Ralph Ellison's nameless narrator, is an invisible man whom others re-imagine to suit their needs.

> Thing is, people rely on me. They need me to be Millat. Good old Millat. Wicked Millat. Safe, sweet-as, Millat. They need me to be cool. It's *practically* a responsibility (p. 224, original italics).

And for all of his ostensible social acceptance, he remains an outsider who "smelled of curry; had no sexual identity; took other people's jobs; or had no jobs and bummed off the state . . . In short he had no face in this country, no voice in this country" (p. 194). He sees in his own tenuous acceptance by the English that he is following in the footsteps of his ineffectual father. "All his life he wanted a Godfather, and all he got was Samad. A faulty, broken, stupid, one-handed waiter of a man who had spent eighteen years in a strange land and made no more mark than that" (p. 419).

Acting out is, then, about being noticed. Well before his religious awakening by KEVIN he took his "crew" (p. 192) to Bradford to burn a book deemed blasphemous of Islam (p. 196). Suddenly, he and other demonstrators were "on every channel and every radio and every newspaper and they were angry, and Millat recognized the anger, thought it recognized him, and grabbed it with both hands" (p. 194). How gratifying then to end up on television[*] and to escape invisibility. How much more gratifying to be associated with KEVIN where acting out is fused with religious principle. Samad denounces the radicalism of KEVIN and thus takes no comfort from Millat's religious awakening.

Magid's return further complicates the multicultural muddle. While away he has grown into "a tall, distinguished-looking young man . . . dressed in a tweed suit and what looked . . . like a cravat" (p. 239). He returns, then, as an out-and-out Anglo-Indian and every bit the *modern* man. Millat, ever more involved with KEVIN, totally rejects Magid as a nonbeliever and refuses to even speak to him. Of course, Samad also rejects Magid who has abandoned his Bengali culture and his Muslim religion.

A bond, however, develops between Marcus and Magid, who is

---

[*] Alsana sees the television coverage of the demonstration and of Millat's participation. When he returns home in the evening, his entire accumulation of "cool" and "secular stuff" has been burned up (p. 197). "'Everyone has to be taught a lesson,' Alsana had said, lighting the match with heavy heart . . . 'Either everything is sacred or nothing is. And if he starts burning other people's things, then he loses something sacred also. Everyone gets what's coming sooner or later'" (p. 197).

fascinated by the DNA research and especially by the mouse experiment. Irie finds this off-putting because she who had served Marcus so success-fully was in effect displaced by Magid. "[S]he was a secretary, whereas Magid was a confidant, an apprentice and disciple" (p. 353). Joshua is also unsettled by the ever closer relationship between his father and Magid. Joshua, already discomfited by Joyce's obsession with Millat, sees Magid as yet another rival for his parents' affections. In reaction, he turns away from his family and becomes increasingly involved with an animal rights group that finds Marcus's experimentation with the mouse unacceptably loathsome.

The ironies abound, confounding the Chalfens, the Iqbals and Clara Jones — if not necessarily Archie, the congenital bystander. The younger generation has taken their parents' rather mild objections to mainstream English life to extremes that vex the elders.

- Joshua's involvement with FATE, a vegetarian as well as an animal-rights group, amounts to open rebellion against Marcus. Speaking of the husband and wife team that heads the organization, Joshua expresses jejune enthusiasm. "They're just . . . incredible. He's a Dadaist. And she's an anarchist. A real one.* Not like Marcus. I told her about Marcus and his bloody Future-Mouse. She thinks he's a dangerous individual. Quite possibly psychopathic" (p. 234). For his part, Marcus voices his disappointment that his own son "was not as Chalfenist as he had hoped" (p. 348).†
- Irie not only wants to attend university but, presumably responding to the broader horizons and do-gooder sentiments of the Chalfens, is contemplating a "gap year" in Africa. Clara is aghast at the prospect: "Malaria! Poverty! Tapeworm!" The result is "three months of open warfare" between daughter and mother (p. 312).
- Samad is appalled by both of his sons. "The one I send home comes

---

* It is by no means incidental that the seductive Joely has stolen Joshua's heart. "It became clear to him in a blinding flash that he loved Joely, that his parents were assholes, that he himself was an asshole, and that the largest community on earth, the animal kingdom, was oppressed, imprisoned, and murdered on a daily basis with the full knowledge and support of every government in the world" (p. 398). Needless to say, he also becomes jealous and contemptuous of Joely's husband and co-leader, Crispin.

† Joyce, who is sick with worry about Millat, greets her son's defection with equanim-ity — dismissing his flight to the animal rights activists as post-adolescent growing pains. "It's perfectly natural for well-educated middle-class children to act up at his age . . . *In the Chalfen lexicon the middle classes were the inheritors of the Enlightenment, the creators of the welfare state, the intellectual elite, and the source of all culture*" (p. 359, italics added).

out a pukka Englishman, white-suited, silly wig lawyer.* The one I keep here is a fully paid-up green-bow-tie-wearing fundamentalist terrorist" (p. 336). While Magid and Samad both reject the lunacies of KEVIN, they disagree on Marcus, whom Samad sees as blasphemous: "It is God's business. If you meddle with a creature, the very *nature* of a creature, even if it is a mouse, you walk into the arena that is God's creation" (p. 396).

In short, virtually everyone is to a greater or lesser extent victimized by cultural myopia. They each contribute to the cross-cultural maelstrom by taking it as a given that they represent cosmic truths — whether the modern truths of the Chalfens, the traditional truths of Samad's Bengali culture or the fundamentalist Christian truths of Hortense.

DIRECT ACTION
Cultural malaise is transformed into cultural maelstrom by the culminating event of the novel: a public meeting is scheduled by Marcus with great fanfare to present his Future-Mouse. In attendance mostly as disinterested observers are the Iqbal and Jones elders. Irie is there as a more interested observer but she is deeply distracted — envying the mice for the simplicity of their world. She is preoccupied by her pregnancy — a pregnancy for which *either* Millat or Magid could be responsible. She has no way of knowing (p. 426).

Also in attendance are the protagonists beginning with the pompous Marcus, his coterie and of course his mouse. An obsequious Magid is included in that coterie. His reverence of Marcus knows no bounds. After all, Marcus is the scientist who has altered the procreative process and "what more is God than *that?*" (p. 405). More ominous is another member of the coterie — none other than the Belgian doctor who was implicated in Nazi eugenics but whose life Archie spared as the war wound down. The doctor is there to be honored because his eugenics research had inspired Marcus. It is left unclear whether the Jewish Marcus is oblivious to, or in the interests of science simply chooses to ignore, the doctor's links to the Nazis or, for that matter, the connections between his own experiments and eugenics.†

---

* Samid complains that Magid is a "clone" not an Iqbal. "One hardly likes to touch him. His teeth, he brushes them six times a day. His underwear, he irons them. It is like sitting down to breakfast with David Niven" (p. 350).

† Marcus is mystified by opposition to his project — complaining about a girl who "had managed to read a book almost entirely concerned with the more prosaic developments in recombinant DNA . . . and emerge from it full of the usual neofascist

Also there to confront Marcus by way of half-baked action plans are FATE, KEVIN, and the Jehovah's Witness warriors Hortense and Ryan Topps. What these organizations have in common is an elemental antipathy to modern science in general and to Marcus's mouse doings, in particular. Joshua, who has been assigned the job of denouncing his father in public, is anxious. "What he was about to do to his father was so huge, so colossal, that the consequences were inconceivable" (p. 412). Millat's responsibilities are even more daunting. He is to shoot either Marcus or the elderly Belgian doctor. Desperately frightened, he has fortified himself with weed. "It was the second day of Ramadan and he was stoned" (p. 413).* Finally, albeit outside the hall, there is the two-person, Jehovah's Witnesses contingent (pp. 421–2). They, unlike the others, are without self-doubt. They will confront Marcus with the scriptural truth of God and challenge him: "Prove to me that you are right. Prove to me that you are more right than God" (p. 422).

As Marcus begins his presentation, he finds himself in competition for the audience's attention with Hortense and Ryan. From outside the hall they sing up a boisterous Christian storm that is loud enough to divert both the audience and Marcus. That disruption is minor compared to the ruckus set off when the stoned Millat begins shooting. Archie, however, rises to the occasion. He throws himself between Millat and his targets; is shot in the leg for his troubles; but succeeds in saving the lives of both Marcus and, for a second time, the scientist who inspired Marcus. In the chaos that follows, the mouse escapes and takes along with it Marcus's bid for both figurative and literal immortality.

Ah, but all is well that ends well. Archie recovers, and although Millat is charged for his feckless gun play, he escapes serious punishment. The witnesses simply cannot tell the twins apart; they each end up doing community service.[47] Similarly, while there is no way to know which of the twins has fathered the little girl that Irie delivers, she grows up free and fatherless but writing "affectionate postcards to *Bad Uncle Millat* and *Good Uncle Magid*" (p. 448, original italics). We are also assured that Joshua realizes his dream when he and Irie become lovers.

And so the novel ends with a remarkably anticlimactic climax. What does it all mean? Future-Mouse abruptly disappears from the stage and

---

tabloid fantasies: mindless human clones, genetic policing of sexual and racial characteristics, mutated diseases, etc." (p. 346).
* Millat is not the only one with second thoughts. Shiva, a fellow waiter of Samad's, prefers the alternative of simply denouncing Marcus, or as he puts it: "Let's just go with Plan B, yeah?" (p. 416).

from the narrative, along with Chalfenism. We are left with the comically ineffectual tactics of the voices of fundamentalist Christianity, extreme Islam and dogmatic environmentalism. All of this clearly conveys the message that a trouble-free "Happy Multicultural Land" (p. 384) is an illusion. Successful multiculturalism necessitates mutuality, and resistance comes not just from embattled whites but also from the cultural outsider. "Because this is the other thing about immigrants ('fugees, émigrés, travelers): they cannot escape their history any more than you yourself can lose your shadow" (p. 385). But neither is it possible to escape multiculturalism.

> This has been the century of strangers, brown, yellow, and white. This has been the century of the great immigrant experiment. It is only this late in the day that you can walk into a playground and find Isaac Leung by the fish pond, Danny Rahman in the football cage, Quang O'Rourke bouncing a basketball, and Irie Jones humming a tune . . . Yet despite all the mixing up, despite the fact that we have finally slipped into each other's lives with reasonable comfort . . ., despite all this, it is hard to admit that there is no one more English than the Indian, no one more Indian than the English. There are still white men who are *angry* about that; who will roll out at closing into the poorly lit streets with a kitchen knife wrapped in a tight fist . . . But it makes an immigrant laugh to hear the fears of the nationalist scared of infection, penetration, miscegenation, when this is small fry, peanuts, compared to the immigrant fears — dissolution, *disappearance*" (p. 272, original italics).

White Teeth's bittersweet portrayal of immigration stands in stunning contrast to the deadly perils of immigration that doom the boat people in *Continental Drift*. Even as Zadie Smith's characters are to one degree or another haunted, indeed tormented, by their divided cultural loyalties, Smith invokes a detached humor that enables the reader to simultaneously enter into and stand outside these cultural dilemmas that are intrinsic to the evolution of a multicultural society that defines for her the late twentieth century.

Thus, in good humor and with ironic detachment, the novel exposes the foibles of all of the characters while stressing the obstacles that they must surmount and their efforts to do so. Smith thereby provides a cheerful but deadly serious inquiry into the contradictions of multiculturalism — its painful and never definitive struggles to resolve these contradictions. There is no gainsaying the culturally defined, dauntingly complex and mutually incomprehensible racial discontinuities and racial boundaries that must be negotiated. However, the lives of her characters also reveal multiple avenues of access into the mainstream for both first and second generation South Asians and Caribbeans.[48]

But most of all, this novel is about the inevitability of multiculturalism, which for all of its problems is intrinsic to, and enriching of, British culture. The contrast with the conflict-ridden portrayal of race relations in American novels is striking. In the United States African-Americans are depicted as the eternal Other — forever destined to be in mortal conflict with the American mainstream. Put another way, South Asian and Caribbean immigrants who immigrated voluntarily to the United Kingdom are portrayed as responding to its opportunities more like European and Asian immigrants to the United States than like African-Americans who were sold into slavery and treated as chattel for hundreds of years.

Saturday

Ian McEwan's novel revolves around the actions and reflections of Dr. Henry Perowne, the narrator. Perowne leads a well-ordered life centered on his medical practice as a skilled, successful neurosurgeon, and his family: his wife Rosalind, a media lawyer; their daughter Daisy, a promising poet; and their son Theo, an equally promising blues musician. The novel is set in London in the vicinity of University College where Perowne practices and where he lives in a spacious and comfortable house.

He cherishes Saturdays for their relaxed tempo: sleeping in, sex with his wife to whom he is devoted, a game of squash with his American colleague and anesthetist, Jay Strauss, the comforting reassurance of a gracious home, and even running errands in his "luxurious, silver Mercedes S 5000 with cream upholstery" (pp. 74–5). Awakening *this* Saturday at 3 a.m., he gazes out of the window and takes somewhat puzzled note of his own "*distorting* euphoria" (p. 4, italics added).

> Standing here, as immune to the cold as a marble statue, gazing toward Charlotte Street . . . Henry thinks the city is a success, a brilliant invention, a biological masterpiece — millions teeming around the accumulated and layered achievements of the centuries as though around a coral reef, sleeping, working, entertaining themselves, harmonious for the most part, nearly everyone wanting it to work. And the Perowne's own corner . . .; the perfect square laid out by Robert Adam enclosing a perfect circle of garden — an eighteenth-century dream bathed and embraced by modernity, by street light from above and by fibre-optic cables, and cool fresh water coursing down pipes, and sewage borne away in an instant of forgetting" (p. 3).

Euphoria, yes; but why distorting? Henry is well aware of the city's and society's darker story — much darker than his own mood as he looks forward to Saturday's respite following an usually stressful work week (p. 4).

His apprehension is fully warranted. On this Saturday things go awry almost immediately and spin ever more wildly out of control for the ensuing 24 hours. His day ends with emergency surgery on Baxter, a young London tough who has invaded Perowne's home, humiliated his daughter, manhandled his father-in-law and terrified the entire family.

PREMONITIONS

Immediately after his euphoric reaction to his cocooned corner of London and his privileged place within it, Perowne observes an airliner on fire heading for Heathrow. Figuring out whether this is an act of terrorism remains unsettled and unsettling during the night and well into the next day — prefiguring the transformation of terrorism, hitherto experienced almost entirely as an abstraction, into an excruciatingly intimate intrusion into his own life. As the day begins, however, the impending Iraq war is the more portentous and insistent presence, because a clamorous anti-war march will disrupt Perowne's route to his squash match; lead to a minor but fateful traffic accident; and conclude with a disastrous termination of a much anticipated family reunion.

Perowne views the anti-war rally with condescension. "The scene has an air of innocence and English dottiness" (p. 60). However, he also has come to conclusion that Saddam Hussein's regime is despicable — particularly given the terror it inflicts on Iraqis in general and in particular on Iraqi surgeons who have refused to engage in mutilations ordered by the regime (p. 72). Still, he views Iraq's problems as somebody else's and the anti-war demonstrations as an irksome intrusion into his well-ordered life. He is therefore annoyed by the demonstrators' "cloying self-regard [which] suggest[s] a bright new world of protest, with the fussy consumers of shampoos and soft drinks demanding to feel good, or nice" (p. 71). He is, however, unaware just how precarious is his own grip on the rationality which he thinks of as the stable core of his being.

PRIMORDIAL MAN

Perowne's determination to get to his squash game on time leads to a legally suspect crossing of the route of the anti-war march, and in his hurry to do so he gets into a minor fender bender (pp. 81–2). Road rage ensues. "Above all there swells in him a peculiarly modern emotion — the motorist's rectitude, spot welding a passion for justice to the thrill of hatred . . . The only person in the world he hates is sitting in the car behind, and Henry is going to have to talk to him, *confront* him" (p. 82, italics added). The other car is occupied by Baxter and two "subordinates, sidekicks" (p. 85) — Nark and Nigel. "Here are the guys, the strangers, whose self-respect is on the line" (p. 87). Baxter seizes the initiative — asking for an apology. Henry is unwilling to provide it. The resultant conflict escalates to Baxter's demand for "seven fifty" (presumably 750 pounds) to get his mirror replaced — and to Henry refusing.

The confrontation ends unsatisfactorily for both Perowne and Baxter. Perowne is injured as well as insulted during a brawl, and he strikes back by exposing a crippling nerve disease that he, the neurosurgeon, detects in Baxter's problems with balance and coordination as well as in his emotional lability. Baxter seems well aware of his medical problem and its bleak prognosis. Because this is his "secret shame," he is unwilling to have it exposed in front of Nark and Nigel. Accordingly, and much to their disgust and puzzlement, Baxter calls things off before they can figure out what Perowne is talking about.

Baxter cannot however resist the opportunity for a consult with Henry, leading to a role reversal. "[He]'s accepted Perowne's right to interrogate. They've slipped into their roles and Perowne keeps going" (p. 97). However, the consultation ends abruptly when Baxter concludes that Henry can't help. The three of them return angrily to their damaged BMW and, in the short run at least, Perowne's problem is solved. He is, however, left ill at ease both for losing his cool and for deploying his professional knowledge in a thoroughly unprofessional way. "Did he, Henry Perowne, act unprofessionally, using his medical knowledge to undermine a man suffering from a neurodegenerative disorder?" (p. 113).

He takes his resentments and the affront he has suffered to the squash court. His disquiet has an impact on the course of his match with Jay Strauss, who moves him around the court almost at will. "Only he can go wrong in quite this way, and only he deserves to lose in just this manner" (p. 108). Perowne is taken aback at his own single-minded determination to turn the tide of the game.

"There is only one thing in life he wants. Everything else has dropped away. He has to beat Strauss" (p. 109) . . . This is, he decides simply "the irreducible urge to win as biological as thirst" (p. 115).

With renewed energy, he manages to regain his footing and is on the verge of victory until a disputed point. Henry gives in because according to the rules of the game he must honor Strauss's call for a let. Henry loses the replayed point and two points later the match. Driven by primordial impulses, Henry refuses to yield graciously and punctuates the end of their match with a decisive "Fuck you, Strauss" (p. 118).

"Here he is for the second time this morning sifting through the elements of a darker mood" (p. 125). The pre-dawn euphoria is gone and largely forgotten. Traveling down Harley Street he reflects on the "botched cases" his hospital has had to treat — "cases botched by the elderly over-paid incompetents around here" (p. 124). "Cities and states beyond repair. The whole world resembling Theo's bedroom" (p. 123). He broods about the Chinese state's brutal response to the Falun Gong, which, despite "beatings, torture, disappearances and murder . . . now outnumber the Chinese Communist Party" (pp. 122–4). He brings much the same arm's length sentiments to Baxter's "predicament" which strikes Henry as both "terrible and fascinating — the tough-guy street existence must have masked a longing for a better kind of life even before the degenerative disease showed its first signs" (p. 149). Meanwhile, Baxter — who may or may not be trailing Henry on his shopping trip — is plotting to transform Perowne's ambivalent unease into profound misery.

FAMILY: SUSTENANCE AND SANCTUARY

As the day progresses, Perowne's mood improves. He attends a rehearsal of his son's band and is transported by the music and by his son's talent. "There are these rare moments when musicians together touch something sweeter than they've ever found before in rehearsals or performance . . . when their expression becomes as easy and graceful as friendship or love. This is when they give us a glimpse of what we might be" (p. 176). Henry enthusiastically embraces this moment of transcendence: "He can go for miles, he feels lifted up . . . He doesn't want the song to end" (p. 177) — thus belying his self-perception as strictly a man of science unable to fully experience the musical and poetic passions of his children. He takes this new buoyancy home with him — further enhancing the pleasure of pre-paring dinner for the family reunion. "What he likes about cooking is its relative imprecision and lack of discipline — a release from the demands of the [operating] theatre" (p. 181).

However, despite a comforting anticipation of preparing dinner for the "three people he . . . most loves, and who most love him" his malaise returns (p. 186). He is depressed by the news of the day and even more so by his own failure to do anything about it.

> He's a docile citizen, watching Leviathan grow stronger while he creeps under its shadow for protection . . . Does he think he's contributing something, watching news programmes, or lying on his back on the sofa on Sunday afternoons, reading more opinion columns of ungrounded certainties? Does he think that his ambiva-lence — if that's what it really is — excuses him from the general conformity? (pp. 184–5).

Things go from bad to worse once a distracted Daisy arrives and they begin to quarrel about the impending war in Iraq which Daisy opposes in no uncertain terms and about which he, as we have learned, is of two minds.

She berates him both for his failure to understand what is manifestly at stake and for his failure to turn out for the anti-war demonstration. She participated, while for Henry it was an unwarranted incursion into the pleasures that he takes from normal Saturdays (see pp. 192–8). Their bitter and angry words end with her "back . . . firmly turned on him" (p. 198). He reflects that he somehow had virtually the same argument with Jay Strauss earlier — although then he was a "dove" and Strauss was the "hawk" (p. 198).

How could things go so wrong so fast with his beloved daughter? Why had he felt compelled to indulge his "adversarial' inclinations (p. 195)? Things go further awry when Grandfather Grammaticus arrives — expansive with pride about his granddaughter's about-to-be published first book of poetry. He wants praise and gratitude from Daisy, whose affinity and talent for poetry Grammaticus discovered and nurtured. She, however, is in no mood to stroke her grandfather's ego and a minor tiff develops.

Despite this rocky start to the evening, Perowne's mood begins to change for the better. An implicit truce develops between granddaughter and grandfather. Perowne begins to relax into the moment (p. 211). His spirits are also lifted by the return of an exuberant Theo, the apple of Grammaticus's eye. The two come together warmly, and at Grammaticus's insistence, Theo and he listen to the new song that had so moved Perowne at the afternoon's rehearsal.

PRIVILEGE VIOLATED

This interlude of familial bliss ends abruptly when Baxter and Nigel force their way into the house. Nigel is looking for booty, but Baxter's motives are darker. He comes in anger, determined to square accounts with Perowne, not only for the events of the day but for the privileged existence that the family enjoys — in unbearable contrast to Baxter, who is afflicted by a terminal disease and by inescapable poverty. Baxter, wielding a knife with menacing intent, initiates a ritual of degradation in which Daisy is forced to disrobe completely in front of her father, mother, brother and grandfather. It is at this inopportune time that everyone discovers the source of Daisy's petulance — her pregnant condition revealed by "the weighted curve and compact swell of her belly and the tightness of her small breasts" (p. 226).

The dominant theme of this encounter for Perowne is desperation and a complete loss of control. "The scale of retribution could be large" (p. 213).

> Within [Baxter] are the unique disturbances, the individual expression of his condition — impulsiveness, poor self-control, paranoia, mood swings, depression balanced by outbursts of temper, some of this, or all of it and more, would have stirred him as he reflected on his quarrel with Henry this morning (p. 217).

Perowne imagines tactics to overpower the knife-wielding Baxter, but understands that he is largely powerless. "He's only ever taken a knife to anaesthetized skin in a controlled and sterile environment. He simply doesn't know how to be reckless" (p. 221).

However improbably, everything changes when Baxter, with a knife at Rosalind's throat, forces the terrified and embarrassed Daisy to read from her book of poems. Baxter is enthralled by the poem which it turns out is not her own but Matthew Arnold's "Dover Beach." Baxter does not know this and decides on the spur of the moment, much to Nigel's disgust, that the only thing he will take from the house are the proof pages of her book. He is stunned by her achievement, but Perowne interprets Baxter's mood change in strictly neurological terms:

> It's of the essence of a degenerating mind, periodically to lose all sense of a continuous self, and therefore any regard for what others think of your lack of continuity. Baxter has forgotten that he forced Daisy to undress, or threatened Rosalind. Powerful feelings have obliterated the memory (p. 232).

Baxter then turns the knife on Henry, demanding that he be taken up to Henry's study to see for himself the evidence of a promising clinical trial of a treatment protocol for Baxter's disease. As they enter the study and Henry launches into a bogus account of the trial, they hear the door slam. An angry Nigel has fled — thus opening the way for Theo to rush up the stairs, and the two of them, father and son, manage to throw Baxter down the stairs.

Gazing at Baxter's inert body and staring eyes, Henry's social conscience kicks in:

> [H]e thinks he sees in the wide brown eyes a sorrowful accusation of betrayal. He, Henry Perowne, possesses so much — the work, money, status, the home, above all, the family — the handsome and healthy son with the strong guitarist's hands come to rescue him, the

beautiful poet for a daughter, unattainable even in her nakedness, the famous father-in-law, the gifted, loving wife; and he has done nothing, given nothing to Baxter who has so little that is not wrecked by his defective gene, and who is soon to have even less (p. 236).

Upon further reflection amidst the family trying desperately to grope towards normalcy, the anger begins to well up in Henry. He fixates on the havoc wrought by Baxter and Nigel to the point that "he almost begins to regret the care he routinely gave Baxter after his fall" (p. 439).

In a final perverse reversal of fortunes, the angry Perowne is summoned to the hospital to attempt life-saving surgery on Baxter. However, once inside the hospital, Henry's persona is transformed. He becomes strictly professional — devoid of any concern for social justice as well as personal animus.

Once a patient is draped up, the sense of personality of an individual in the theatre disappears. Such is the power of visual sense. All that remains is the little patch of head, the field of the operation (p. 255).

The operation is delicate, demanding and ultimately successful. It calls for every ounce of Henry's skill and remarkable powers of concentration. "For the past two hours, he's been in a dream of absorption that has dissolved all sense of time . . . In retrospect, though never at the time, it feels like profound happiness. It's a little like sex" (p. 266). Baxter will live "a diminishing slice of life worth living, before his descent into nightmare hallucinations begins" (pp. 287–8).

NOBLESSE OBLIGE: THE RESTORATION OF PRIVILEGE
Throughout *Saturday*'s trials and indeed in Perowne's day-to-day existence, his one constant refuge is not, first and foremost, his family, but the operating theatre where he is in charge, and which symbolizes the breathtaking achievements of modernity. "At every level, material, medical, intellectual, sensual, for most people it [life] has improved" and he recalls words by Medawar, a man he admires: "To deride the hopes of progress is the ultimate fatuity, the last word in poverty of spirit and meanness of mind" (p. 77).[49] The narrative is replete with evidence of the excruciating delicacy of his surgical interventions into the traumatized and diseased brains of patients. Their lives are utterly dependent on his consummate diagnostic and manual skills.*

---

* His love affair with neurosurgery and his future wife began when a young Henry

However, over the course of *Saturday* Henry discovers how easy it is for the man of science to yield to the elemental — for better and for worse. For better when he is overcome with emotion by his son's performance. For worse when he succumbs to the wretched anger of road rage and to the competitive vanity unleashed during the squash match. Only in the surgical theatre, a controlled environment, a sterile field — unsullied by the cacophony of social, cultural and political life — can Perowne reliably maintain his devotion to reason.

With some success, however, he almost succeeds in coming to terms with his divided self.

Before leaving the hospital, he returns to Baxter's bedside. Holding his hand, Henry "attempts to sift and order his thought and decide precisely what should be done" (p. 271). Done about what? The question is whether Baxter should be prosecuted, and when he returns home, Rosalind, still both frightened and angry, makes it clear that she wants punishment for what "[t]hat vicious, loathsome man . . . did to John [Grammaticus], and forcing Daisy . . . and holding the knife against me, and using it to force you to go upstairs. I thought I might never see you alive . . ." (p. 274).

Perowne, however, is moving towards an entirely different resolution — towards, that is, getting "a colleague or two, specialists in the field to convince the Crown Prosecution Service that by the time it comes around, Baxter will not be fit to stand trial" (p. 288). He feels more than slightly responsible for the whole mess — partaking as he did in the road rage incident between the two alpha males.

But there is more, much more, to Henry's conviction that Baxter's disease is punishment enough. To begin with, "Baxter heard what Henry never has, and probably never will . . . Some nineteenth century poet — Henry has yet to find out whether this Arnold is famous or obscure — touched off in Baxter a yearning he could barely begin to define" (p. 288). The closest he can come to this apotheosis emerges from the sharing of intimacies with Rosalind — intimacies of family love that were at the mercy of Baxter's knife and his lunacy. Henry goes on to muse about how precious and fleeting are the gentle pleasures of family ties and how vitally important, therefore, to put family at the center of one's life.

Matthew Arnold's poem, reprinted in its entirety in an unpaginated

---

observed a particularly tricky and successful surgery on "a beautiful woman suffering a pituitary apoplexy." The operation saved Rosalind's life — thus lending a poignant note to Henry's supremely clinical appreciation of the surgery. "The elegance of the whole procedure seemed to embody a brilliant contradiction: the remedy was as simple as plumbing, as elemental as a blocked drain . . . And yet the making of a safe route into remote and buried places in the head was a feat of technical mastery and concentration" (pp. 44–6).

endnote, is a brooding reflection on the perfidious character of what is worldly and a tribute to the redeeming power of loving relationships:

> Ah, love, let us be true
> To one another! for the world, which seems
> To lie before us like a land of dreams,
> So various, so beautiful, so new,
> Hath really neither joy, nor love, nor light,
> Not certitude, nor peace, nor help for pain;
> And we are here as on a darkling plain
> Swept with confused alarms of struggle and flight,
> Where ignorant armies clash by night.

In the closing pages of the narrative, it is precisely these truths of Matthew Arnold which resonate with and illuminate what Henry identifies as the human condition: the impermanence of life and its felt certainties and grievous harms inflicted by political leaders with utopian dreams: "the young boys . . . [lost] at the Somme. And what of the body count, Hitler, Stalin, Mao? . . . Beware the utopianists, zealous men certain of the path to the ideal social order" (p. 286).

In the end, then, the accomplished man of science and hitherto the voice of modernity bemoans its false promises. Baxter has made him, albeit briefly, not a detached observer but a resident in a strange land — and sensitized him to the dispossessed and the chasm that divides him and others of his ilk from "the various broken figures that haunt the benches" on the square just beneath his windows. Perowne has also become more keenly aware not only of his privilege but of his civic inadequacies. He observes social and political injustice with detached disapproval and at a safe distance. Is there any reason to believe that a new Henry will shoulder civic responsibility? Not bloody likely. It has taken Baxter's home invasion and his violation of the Perowne sanctuary to unsettle Henry's civic lethargy which seems to be imprinted into his social DNA. Absent the extreme, it is hard to envisage the public and political trumping the private and the professional.[50]

3. Conclusions

It goes without saying that the unfulfilled promises of contemporary democracy pale in comparison to the catastrophes of total war, Nazism and the Holocaust. However, both the "then" of earlier chapters and the "now" of this chapter are part and parcel of continuing narratives of political estrangement. In the novels of the interwar era, the transformation of democracy into tyranny is traced to the contradictory pairing of the fledgling democratic and modern projects. The post-World War II novels find analogous oppositions at work in the mature democratic and modern projects of the United States and the United Kingdom.

These novels all tell tales of insufficient civic engagement to sustain robust republican democracies. The affluent, cloistered and self-interested bourgeoisie — most notably McEwan's remarkably skilled surgeon, Henry Perowne, and Roth's paragon of upward mobility, Swede Levov, are portrayed as absorbed by the private (the everyday concerns of earning a living, sustaining a family, realizing a sense of fulfillment and self-worth) and estranged from the political. The onus falls particularly heavily on science and scientists, who are portrayed as sequestered and out of touch — Perowne, the neurosurgeon, the Chalfens with their commitments to biological and behavioral science, and even the Marxian science of the Brotherhood. Society's losers are forced into a precarious netherworld of the dispossessed Baxter in *Saturday*; the downwardly mobile Bob Dubois in *Continental Drift*; the cultural Other in Ralph Ellison's *Invisible Man*; as well as to a lesser extent the South Asian immigrants in *White Teeth*. The losers are antagonized by and at the mercy of forces and structures that they neither understand nor believe they can influence. With the marginalized deprived of voice and the privileged uninterested in its exercise, citizenship and thus democracy are portrayed as imperiled from above and below.

While, therefore, both in the US and UK, novelists identify political estrangement among society's winners and losers, the textures of estrangement are strikingly different on the eastern and western shores of the Atlantic. There is a powerful undercurrent of anger in the American novels stemming from exclusionary practices that set race against race and the privileged against the marginalized. This anger is palpable in each of the three American novels which depict life as a zero-sum struggle in which winners profit at the expense of losers. Put another way, the novels strongly suggest that a competitive ethos, in combination with the pervasive commodification of civic culture, tends to shatter social solidarity.

In contrast, novelists in the UK tend to express a sense of promises partially redeemed by the welfare state and sustained by a political culture of social welfare biased toward inclusion. Perowne is not a grudging but a willing supporter of the welfare state. Perowne also regrets his predilection to privilege the private and marginalize the public — in this respect altogether unlike Swede Levov who is largely clueless and unable to figure out "[w]hat on earth is less reprehensible than the life of the Levovs?" (p. 423). Even for the South Asian Other, the social order is depicted by Zadie Smith as permeable rather than permanent and multiculturalism as inevitable rather than unattainable. And while Sillitoe depicts the working class as more or less immobile, his is a tale of co-optation by the benefits of the welfare state, rather than of exclusion and deprivation. Only Baxter is doomed.

When all is said and done and for all of the cultural contrasts, there is no gainsaying a sense of mourning within the Anglo and the American literary communities for the failure of both the US and the UK to provide settings in which engagement trumps estrangement. With accountability, agency, social mobility and social solidarity all attenuated, especially in the United States, it follows that republican democracy is imperiled. Thus, the literary imagination once again turns out to be at odds with many liberal, neo-liberal and social welfare intellectuals who see the pairing of the democratic and modern projects as mutually constitutive.

6 Re-imagining the Twentieth Century, Remembering the Twenty-First

The tremendous world I have inside my head.

Franz Kafka[1]

This book is about what *novels of political estrangement* tell us retrospectively about the twentieth century and prospectively about the twenty-first. Two interrelated but analytically distinct narratives capture and define these inquiries. *Narratives of betrayal* reveal how the institutions and ethos of modernity which were to have enhanced political agency, and thus democracy, have instead subverted them. *Narratives of estrangement* reveal the corrosive impact of the subversion of agency on *political engagement*.

The literary imagination provides access to, and breathes life, meaning and diversity into betrayal and estrangement by creating characters and exposing them to the defining calamities of the twentieth century. The novelist then registers the impact of calamity on the characters' interior lives. The interior lives resonate precisely because they are woven into the fabric of the multiple outrages of the terrible twentieth century. Because the literary imagination takes us into lives scarred by incomprehensible and inaccessible forces, we are empowered to re-imagine the twentieth century and to a limited extent to anticipate the twenty-first.

1. Re-imagining the Twentieth Century
Betrayal and estrangement emerge as two sides of the same coin — both attributable to the contradictions of modernity with its stunning technological achievements, its successes in creating new configurations of power, and its control over the production of knowledge. All of this plays out across the diverse settings of Chapters 2–5 and reveals multiple, subtle and often counterintuitive iterations of betrayal and estrangement — varying from time to time, place to place, and calamity to calamity.

Narratives of betrayal: the subversion of agency
While I have indicated that the narratives of betrayal vary from time to time and place to place, they are all the product of aggregations of power

that are intrinsic to, and made possible by, the achievements of the modern project. The technological triumphs of modernity led to a sea change in the *modes of warfare* that became ever more destructive and impersonal over the course of the twentieth century. Similarly *modern organizational techniques* made it possible to construct ruthlessly efficient institutions governed by the relentless logic of bureaucratic self-aggrandizement. These opaque, incomprehensible and unaccountable bureaucracies were then invested with extensive authority over everyday life. Finally, by gaining control over the *production of knowledge*, the modern project managed to impose new truths on political discourse and in so doing destabilized long-settled understandings of the boundaries between right and wrong, sanity and madness, the intelligible and the incomprehensible.

OVERPOWERING AGENCY

The sites where agency was simply crushed were the wartime military and the Nazi terror against the Jews. As warfare became more and more destructive over the course of the twentieth century, agency, always precarious for both soldiers and civilians, was robbed of any meaning. To begin with, the technological achievements of modernity came to serve purely destructive purposes. This process was already under way in World War I, although trench warfare was decidedly low tech. Subsequent triumphs of technology produced ever more powerful, more frightening and more impersonal modes of warfare — the Nazi blitzkrieg, the waves of bombers dropping blockbusters on both military and civilian targets, nuclear weapons and so on.

The victims included both helpless civilians and soldiers who were traumatized, robbed of their humanity and turned as much as possible into killing machines. This is especially true of the World War I novels. The loss of agency by members of the military begins, Remarque tells us, with a dehumanizing training regime directed at making them cogs in the machinery of war and killing. Trench warfare also subjected the adversaries to foul living conditions; to hunkering down as artillery shells exploded all around them; and to going over the top to face withering fire from a well-entrenched enemy. As Dr. Rivers notes in *Regeneration*, "The war that promised so much in the way of 'manly' activity had actually delivered 'feminine' passivity, and on a scale that their mothers and sisters had scarcely known" (pp. 107–8). The World War I militaries were, in short, trapped in no-win situations without any meaningful capacity to control their own destinies.*

---

* For Heinrich Böll and Gerhard Lenz, it is not modernity or even total war which suppresses political agency but the authoritarian militarism which is deeply embedded

As for World War II, Kurt Vonnegut's Billy Pilgrim found himself a prisoner of war ominously housed with other prisoners in slaughterhouse-five — available only because "all the hoofed animals in Germany had been killed and eaten and excreted by human beings, mostly soldiers. So it goes" (p. 152). When he emerged after the firestorm he discovered nothing but death all around him. In the post-firestorm strafing Bill saw fighter pilots shooting at anything that moved. Billy seemed to shake off this dehumanizing experience, but it came back to haunt him many years later — estranging him not so much from politics as from his entire postwar identity. Joseph Heller in *Catch 22* and Vonnegut both savor parody, cynicism and the metaphor of mental illness. However, Heller has less to say about the dehumanizing horrors of war than about the forces, bureaucratic and material, that transform war into unparalleled opportunities for self-aggrandizement.

The Holocaust was, of course, a product of Nazi terror unleashed against Jews. They were herded into ghettos, rousted out by the SS with dogs, subjected to beatings, and transported long distances under inhuman conditions which led to sickness and death along the way. Consigned either to extermination or to slave labor camps, they were either murdered immediately or had the life squeezed out of them by brutal working conditions, meager food, non-existent sanitary conditions and the denial of medical treatment — with the toxic exception of debilitating and disfiguring medical experiments. Jews were, in short, hostages robbed of hope or options. Among the novels that bear witness to all of this carnage and terror are Imre Kertesz's *Fateless* and Ian McMillan's *Village of a Million Spirits: A Novel of the Treblinka Uprising*. The Jewish prisoners in *Fateless* are indeed portrayed as hostages without hope or options. However, as McMillan's subtitle suggests, the Treblinka prisoners were able to summon up the strength and the determination to mount an uprising. And although the uprising was doomed to failure, it gave meaning to, and was redemptive for, those who stood up to the terror of Treblinka.

THE LOGICS OF BUREAUCRATIC SELF-AGGRANDIZEMENT
The power exercised by opaque and non-accountable modern bureaucracies is found throughout these novels — sometimes, as in the Holocaust

---

in German culture. Modernity is not left entirely off the hook, at least for Böll, who is troubled by the failure of the respectable professional classes to stand their ground against the Nazis. Both authors agree that it is those who stand outside the society who are best able to understand Nazism and militarism for what it is. Grandmother Faemel locks herself away in an asylum to maintain her sanity, and the artist, Max Nansen, maintains his emotional and moral equilibrium by casting his artist's eye over the insanities of the Nazi regime.

novels, in combination with terror, and other times as in *The Trial* as a shadowy presence that puts meaningful choice, indeed any choice at all, out of reach. Heller's account of the US Air Force in World War II is built around an all-powerful, self-serving and self-perpetuating military bureaucracy sustained by a seemingly irresistible process of co-optation. For the cynics and the opportunists, agency is not so much suppressed as corrupted. The official bureaucracy is dedicated primarily to advancing at all costs the military careers of ambitious officers. In parallel, Milo Minderbinder creates a rival bureaucracy for enlisted personnel dedicated to material acquisition and thus to enhancing at all costs the syndicate's bottom line. Both bureaucratic organizations were ready, willing, able and anxious to subordinate the war effort to their own self-aggrandizing motivations.

A much more ominous exercise of bureaucratic power, albeit in combination with SS terror tactics, was the Nazi organization of the Holocaust. One of the messages to be taken from the Holocaust is that the Nazis created a powerful bureaucratic machine without which the massive job of identifying Jews and transporting them over hundreds and hundreds of miles would have been clumsy, inefficient and much less thorough. The bureaucratic process began with a series of measures which legally and physically isolated Jews and made them readily available to those, perhaps most notably Adolph Eichmann, who were organizing their transportation eastward. This in microcosm is the story of *Badenheim 1939* which recounts the incremental steps that led to the nullification of Jewish citizenship. Jews were initially forced to register; their entry to and egress from the city were blocked; their activities within the city were increasingly confined "to the hotel, the pastry shop and the swimming pool" (p. 55). Then the water was shut off and the guests were thus deprived of the diversion of the swimming pool. These measures continued through the arrival of dispossessed Jews (pp. 121–2) and eventuated in the final deportation. Much the same story is told in other Holocaust novels — perhaps most notably by Imre Kertesz in *Fateless* in which we see the naïve and clueless Georg being ever more constrained — ending up much to his surprise in Auschwitz.

THE TRANSFORMATION OF CONSCIOUSNESS

In a modernist setting, knowledge is power. A monopoly of professional knowledge is represented in the novels by the pioneering psychoanalyst Dr. William Rivers and the supremely skilled neurosurgeon Henry Perowne. Neither of them has any interest in wielding power. Indeed both of them do their best to deploy professional knowledge for humane purposes and to use their privileged positions to listen to and learn from their patients. It is, however, an uphill struggle.

Rivers finds himself caught in two searing contradictions: one related to his vocation and the other to his military responsibility to use psychoanalysis to treat war fatigue. Barker portrays a doctor-patient struggle over memory, which the doctor is trying to help the patients recover, but which is being repressed as a consequence of the traumas of the trenches. Insofar as Rivers is able to successfully treat war neurosis, he dooms his patients to a return to the trenches — the cure that kills. To make matters worse, he discovers that one of his patients, the poet Siegfried Sassoon who refuses to return to the trenches is not mentally ill as the military would have it. In an extended psychotherapy session Rivers learns that Sassoon is not afflicted by war neurosis but by "a very powerful *anti*-war neurosis" (p. 15).

The real insanity, Barker tells us, is to be found among those who precipitate war and fight it so stupidly and wastefully, not among those who are unable to bear the unbearable afflictions visited upon them. In addition, Barker reveals that professional knowledge, a cornerstone of the modern project, does at least as much to suppress agency as to liberate it. In effect, all of the characters, whatever their level of insight, are victims of their circumstances, not masters of their fates.

Dr. Henry Perowne's plight is different, but still deeply troubling. He thinks of himself as a man of science who is able to put his expertise at the disposal of his patients — curing their illnesses, relieving their suffering and thus making a singular contribution to his society. So far, so good! But with his back almost literally to the wall — being strong-armed by the London hoodlum Baxter — he discovers that he can deploy his diagnostic skills to neutralize Baxter and shame him in front of his sidekicks. To make matters worse, Henry comes to understand that he contributed to the road rage that led to the physical confrontation between him and Baxter. Still, when Baxter invades Perowne's home, humiliates his daughter and terrorizes the household, Perowne takes one more liberty — deliberately lying to Baxter about promising treatments for his neurological deficits. His professional knowledge is power and is indeed the only power that he has available to defend himself and his family against the brutal Baxter.

Baxter is finally overcome in a physical struggle with Henry and his son Theo. In the process, however, Baxter suffers a brain injury and Henry is called in to perform emergency surgery. He does so with consummate skill — there in the operating theatre which is entirely under his control and where Baxter is no longer Baxter. "Once a patient is draped up, the sense of personality, an individual in the theatre, disappears. Such is the power of visual sense. All that remains is the little patch of head, the field of the operation" (p. 255). The operation is delicate, demanding and ultimately successful — although only insofar as it will buy Baxter some time before the underlying disease turns his life into a "nightmare" of "hallucinations" (pp. 287–8).

But what is to be done with Baxter? Should he be prosecuted as Perowne's wife Rosalind insists? Perowne decides instead that the prognosis for his disease is punishment enough and that the best course of action is therefore to enlist his colleagues in a plan based on the inference that once he recovers from the surgery he will, because of the disease, be unfit to stand trial.

Henry has come to understand himself much better as a result of his run-in with Baxter and several other events of that fateful *Saturday* — how easy it is for the man of science to yield to the elemental in the worst possible ways. He also comes to understand how limiting is his scientific identity — how he is largely impervious to the aesthetic and the emotional side of life. He is struck by the way in which even Baxter is brought to tears by poetry, which Henry can appreciate, but not be absorbed by.

More insidious and more characteristic of these novels is the manipulation of truths by political elites who mobilize the media — deploying advances in behavioral psychology to colonize the intellect and dehumanize the soul. It is not by chance that madness figures so prominently in these novels but because madness is woven into the fabric of modernity. *The Trial* offers an instance in which Joseph K's rationality is subverted by an ethos in which nothing is at it is expected to be: the courts, the law and problem solving prove frustratingly futile. This is, of course, as much a commentary on Joseph K's modernist belief in the power of the intellect to solve problems as it is a commentary on the institutions of modernity, which turn K's world inside out. In other words, although represented as an agent of rationality, the institutions of modernity are unable to cope with the problems that they create. Over and over again, we see examples of the imposition of the overwhelmingly irrational rationality on modern life.

The theme of madness recurs repeatedly in these novels, whether as a metaphor or as a clinical diagnosis. In *Badenheim 1939* the world of assimilated Jews is turned upside down as the Nazis incrementally suppress their agency. As they are being increasingly confined, travel posters begin to appear urging Jews to appreciate the beauty of Poland and the virtues of work.

> Labor Is Our Life . . . The Air in Poland is Fresher . . . Sail on the Vistula . . . The Development Areas Need You . . . Get to Know the Slavic Culture (p. 43).

When Trudi, the pharmacist's wife, senses the danger, she is dismissed as a hysteric. Her husband Martin believes she is emotionally unstable because their daughter has made a bad marriage and fled Badenheim and because of Trudi's isolated upbringing in the mountains deprived of savvy to understand the ins and outs of polite society. As it turns out, it is the *assimilated* Jews who are in deep denial and rationalize their peril.*

Vonnegut's Billy Pilgrim, exposed to the purposeless slaughter of the Dresden fire bombing, manages to repress his emotional trauma for decades. When the trauma breaks through in fantasies of alien abduction, Billy's sanity is called into question. To Vonnegut it matters not whether Billy has or has not been abducted, because Billy comes back from outer space able finally able to understand the fire bombing, and by extension total war, for what it truly is — namely that which masquerades as rationality and precipitates madness in those who wage it. Yet only those who are thus afflicted can detect the madness of war itself. It is the supposedly delusional Billy who is truly sane.

SOCIAL DESTABILIZATION AND THE FLIGHT FROM AGENCY
The political agency of adult Germans in the 1930s was not subverted but willingly abandoned. It was subordinated to fascist truths by the true believers and traded by ordinary Germans, along with republican values and political accountability, for meager material benefits and/or modestly enhanced social status. In contrast, it is readily acknowledged by novelists that to German youth who grew up during the Nazi era, political agency had no meaning or relevance, because civil society had been destroyed — leaving the Nazi state with total control over education, political discourse and popular culture.

Then there is the older generation who did knowingly forfeit political agency. Böll, Grass and Lenz, while in general accord, point the finger of blame in different directions. They agree that the problem is buried deep within German culture and pre-dates but is connected to modernity. For Böll, the cultural culprit is traditional Junker militarism. For Lenz it is the deep well of insular nationalism and an obsession with order and duty. For Grass, anti-Semitism looms large, not so much as a first-order cause but as a symptom of the intrinsic corruptibility of the German soul.†

It is Christa Wolf who reveals the breathtaking capacity of the Nazi

---

* Awaiting the train that will take them eastward to oblivion, one of the characters purchases a financial weekly and another character advises the musicians among them to be certain to submit the proper form for claiming travel expenses. And when the train arrives, its squalid condition suggests to another of the deportees that they do not have far to travel.

† Consider Oskar in *The Tin Drum*, who is determined at a high personal cost to maintain his purity despite the rampant hypocrisy and corruption of the adult world. In

state to create true believers among the German youth who were saturated in Nazi truths. Thus, even well after the end of the war and the fall of the Nazis, Nelly in *Patterns of Childhood* can recall the Fuhrer as sweet pressure in the stomach area (p. 45) as well as the "delirium of joy" among the Viennese as the Nazis marched in Austria — a delirium "which moved Nelly's inner depths" (p. 164). Because of the pervasive messages of anti-Semitism,* of Hitler as a demigod, of the glories of joining the Nazi movement and participating enthusiastically in Nazi spectacles, Nelly is infuriated by her mother Charlotte's anti-Nazism and shattered by the German surrender at the end of World War II.

In short, the Nazi experience casts a particularly ominous shadow over the prospects for democracy in times of crisis when people are beset by cultural malaise, political turmoil and economic deterioration — all arguably consequences of the dislocations of an emerging modernity. However, the Nazi experience led to postwar soul-searching by Germans who came of age under the Nazi regime and by their progeny. Among the Germans who bartered their political agency, forgetting clearly trumped learning.

JUST OUT OF REACH: AGENCY IN LIBERAL DEMOCRACIES

In the well-established liberal democracies of the United States and the United Kingdom, agency is taken as a given — an intrinsic entitlement that is inalienable. The result is that in the United States the illusion of agency survives even as it moves further out of reach. This loss of agency tends to be interpreted as a personal failing rather than as a structural barrier. This is particularly true of Phillip Roth's *American Pastoral* and Russell Banks' *Continental Drift*. In *American Pastoral* the Swede finds that his life has spun out of control, robbing him of all sense of agency. How can that be — given his hitherto charmed life and his full-blown realization of the American dream? In contrast, Bob Dubois has always been on the outside looking in and confounded by his failure to take charge of his life — as he believes (incorrectly) his go-getter friend and his own brother have. It's not clear that either Bob or the Swede ever get it — namely that they are, each in his own way, victims of forces over which they have virtually no control. In contrast, Ralph Ellison's nameless narrator finds his

---

the long run, however, Oskar cannot resist feathering his own nest and readily, even enthusiastically, joins the harvest of forbidden fruits.

* "A German girl must be able to hate, Herr Warsinski [Nelly's teacher] said: Jews and Communists and other enemies of the people. Jesus Christ, Herr Warsinski said, would today be a follower of the Fuhrer and would hate the Jews" (pp. 128 and 130).

authenticity and his identity appropriated by others who in the end deny him a respectable niche in American society. In a tortured and dubious ending, Ellison portrays the resolve of the nameless narrator to convert his outsider status into a politically inspiring and efficacious role. He calls attention to the way the exclusion of American blacks has empowered them to serve as the conscience of the nation because they recognize how white society has betrayed its own ideals.

In Alan Sillitoe's portrayal of the post-World War II working class, Arthur Seaton chooses to think of himself as a rebel with subversion in his soul and his agency intact. However, as Sillitoe peels away the layers of blather that Arthur finds so reassuring, it turns out that Arthur's agency is indeed illusory. He comes off a creature of the British welfare state and a hollow exemplar of the hard left in the UK. While Arthur fancies himself fighting the good fight, Sillitoe leaves no doubt Arthur is not exercising agency but feeding his insatiable hunger for self-indulgence at the expense of others. He has neither any sense of civic responsibility nor working class solidarity.

In the end, then, Sillitoe's searing portrayal of working-class anger turns into a melancholy meditation on the capacity of the postwar welfare state to neutralize Arthur's seething rebellion and transform him into a responsible citizen. The transformative event is a fight in which Arthur is brutally beaten for thwarting social convention. The beating thus becomes a metaphor for the futility of Arthur's broader struggle to maintain his independence from social constraints and from the meager comforts of the welfare state.

Zadie Smith's *White Teeth* is a striking exception to the trend of the other novels. Not only is a sense of personal and social agency realized, it is inextricably linked to modernity. Smith does not gloss over the inertial resistance of Islamic fundamentalism nor the instinctive resistance of mainstream English society to South Asian immigrants. Indeed, she portrays the first-generation immigrants as mostly leading socially and culturally insular lives, because they want to protect their traditions against the all-too-familiar English cultural imperialism that threatens to engulf second-generation immigrants. The second generation, however, embraces modernity because, particularly in contrast to traditional Islam, it promotes an inclusive society.[2] *White Teeth* thus reads more like a modern novel of hope than a late-modern novel of despair, but it also moves us towards a seminal twenty-first century issue: the worldwide clash between traditional and modern societies, to which we will return at the conclusion of this chapter.

The late-modern novels, each in its own way, reveal how the institutions and the ethos of modernity have worked at cross-purposes to agency. In some cases, modernity's mechanisms for suppression of agency are straightforward — the product of brute force. In other cases, bureaucracy represses agency by the imposition of order. Finally, modernity imposes the tortured logic of abstract rationality in ways that work at cross-purposes to common sense and destabilize the boundary that divides sanity from insanity, thus leading its victims to lose touch with reality. In brief, late-modern novels reveal that agency is subverted in a variety of contrasting ways that destabilize truths, alter identities and discourage political engagement. Whether and under what circumstances the subversion of political agency leads toward or away from *political learning* is the focus of the next section.

Narratives of estrangement: disengaging from politics

Late-modern novelists consistently express a profound antipathy to totalitarian politics and serious misgivings about democratic politics. The twentieth century was rife with states behaving badly — making war, engaging in genocide, betraying their citizens, countenancing corruption and on and on. In so doing, states made a mockery of governing by consent, safeguarding rights and maintaining accountability. The novelists help us understand the *several ways* in which people who were thus deprived of personal and political agency and of any semblance of control over their lives became estranged from politics.

Over and over again, the characters in these novels turn their back on political solutions to what are arguably political problems. Instead, they eschew the political and find widely divergent avenues for adapting to their proscribed circumstances. In each instance the adaptation represents a kind of learning, but not always in a good way — leading towards replicating rather then re-imagining the past. The nature and extent of the learning reflects the conditions of the characters' oppression and tends to break down along generational lines — thus accentuating intergenerational conflict with important implications, not just for re-imagining the past, but for remembering the future.

REPRESSING AND REPRODUCING THE PAST

In these novels examples abound of burying the past rather than remembering it. Particularly in *Dog Years*, Gunter Grass presents a cast of characters roughly divided between those like the profoundly conflicted Matern and the congenitally opportunistic (and odious) Nettlinger. Nettlinger's motivations are simple: he is determined to conceal his compromising association with the Nazis so he can resume a position of privilege in the Federal Republic. This was not much of problem, because so many of the postwar elite were similarly compromised.[3] Matern, because he is so deeply conflicted, is a more interesting, sympathetic and important character. He is tormented by the emotional turmoil generated by his love–hate relationships with the putative Jew Eddi Amsel — at one and the same time Matern's best friend and his *bête noire*. Like Germany itself, he can neither live with *his* Jew nor live without him, and accordingly reconciliation is not possible.

Eddi complicates the picture even further. Driven out of Nazi Germany by anti-Semitism and envy, he becomes a kind of self-fulfilling prophesy. As the consummate outsider Eddi is able to see into the German soul. He puts that insider/outsider knowledge to work to exploit German character weaknesses — whether as the wartime impresario or the post-war proprietor of trendy night clubs that indulge the moral failings of the re-emergent wartime elites. He then moves on to become a mining magnate whose scarecrow factory deep in the bowels of German soil illuminates the corrupt foundations of the Federal Republic. Thus Eddi not only survives, but triumphs by becoming the supreme opportunist in a sea of opportunism.[4] Of course, it is reasonable to conclude that Eddi's opportunism has been forced upon him — fighting fire with fire, so to speak.

The anti-war novels, like the anti-Nazi novels, underscore the stultifying impact of self-involved, tunnel-vision military leaders who are represented as congenitally unable and unwilling to learn from the past — irrespective of the consequences for the soldiers that they command. This is the major theme of the novels of both the first and second World Wars. Denied voice and choice, rank-and-file soldiers tend to be left without any good options. The victims of trench warfare who do not die on the battlefield bear the emotional costs of repressing what they cannot bear to remember, and are beset by shame for not being manly enough to shrug it all off. The poet Siegfried Sassoon who is unwilling to go along is vilified as a coward and a traitor.

Joseph Heller's characters in *Catch 22* also divide between a self-serving military leadership and rank-and-file soldiers. The latter are unable to alter the course of World War II, but they learn from their commanders how to take advantage of the opportunities afforded by the wartime military. For the officer corps, war is a golden opportunity for careerism, which takes unquestioning precedence over the war effort as such. The savvy enlisted personnel portrayed by Heller have no interest in a military career but they are obsessed by the promise of building capital for their postwar, post-military lives. Heller's poster boy is the obsessive war profiteer Milo Minderbinder, who creates a vast, well-coordinated black market syndicate — even going so far as to make deals with the

Germany military. These are deadly serious fun and games dedicated to enhancing at all costs the syndicate's bottom line.

In the end, M&M enterprises may well subvert the military hierarchy but they also affirm America's most squalid impulses. These are Americans at their worst, but who are under the all-too-plausible delusion that they represent America at its best. Milo and his enterprising fellow war profiteers appropriate whatever they can to pursue their American dream of material acquisition and upward social mobility. Thus Heller represents the wartime military as a hyper-microcosm of American life.

SEEKING REDEMPTION, MAKING AMENDS

While most of the wartime generation was obsessed with forgetting, the surviving Faemels in *Billiards at Half-Past Nine* sought redemption for the family's longstanding involvement with the wars of Germany's military aristocrats.

Under the tutelage of its devout and forceful matriarch, Grandmother Faemel, the family unites across the generational lines to lead exemplary lives — thus demonstrating through their contrition how German society can be redeemed. What brought the family together were its terrible losses through the two wars of the twentieth century together with the realization that the family had betrayed its religious values and its civic responsibilities — most egregiously with respect to the sons, who became zealous Nazis, but also by its complicity through the years with Germany's authoritarian nationalists.

In contrast to the Faemels, Christa Wolf's Nelly and Siegfried Lenz's Siggi portray the generation that came of age during the Nazi era and were engulfed by Nazi culture. It might seem counterintuitive that these children who were arguably victims of Nazism should be so desperate to make amends. However, the Nazi experience was in retrospect so shattering that facing up to it becomes a moral imperative for both Nelly and Siggi.

Nelly is desperate to understand how she could have fallen under the spell of a regime that she now considers hateful. As she looks back she comes to realize that she was immersed in Nazi ideology at an especially vulnerable age. However, she cannot let herself off the hook, because she is also aware that she ignored both her mother's warnings and her own second thoughts about Nazi brutality and anti-Semitism. Worse, she did so largely because to do otherwise would have deprived her of the approval and status available only to those whose loyalty to the Fuhrer was enthusiastic and without reservation.

As befits the complexity of her inquiry and her own unflinching honesty, moral clarity evades her. In the final pages of the book, she wonders whether in her effort to re-imagine the past she is has simply "proven . . .

that it's impossible to escape the mortal sin of our time: the desire not to come to grips with oneself" (p. 406). But of course her searching inquest into the past and the part she played has awakened Nelly's conscience and impressed upon her that it is essential that she make amends both for her own peace of mind and for the sake of her relationship with her judgmental daughter Lenka.

In contrast to Nelly, Siggi in *The German Lesson* was a witness to, not a participant in, Rugbull's culture of blood, soil and duty. He is implicated only through his parents. They, like most of Rugbull, clung to a parochial view of the world. They denigrated the cosmopolitan and humane values that attracted Siggi and were represented by the painter, Uncle Nance, who takes Siggi under his wing. While Siggi's allegiance is thus clear, he is consumed by the mystery of how and why his parents and the other residents of Rugbull are so much in thrall of hatred of the Other. After the war, he is appalled to see that Rugbull culture is unchanged and indeed that his father remains intent on destroying Uncle Nance's paintings. Siggi reacts by stealing and sequestering Uncle Nance's paintings to protect them, but in so doing is in effect going against all that Uncle Nance stands for.

After he is caught and incarcerated, he takes advantage of postwar Germany's progressive penal practices. He is promised his freedom if only he will write an essay on, of all things, the joys of duty. Paradoxically, Siggi does learn, if not the joys of duty, then that he must be guided by his conscience. This draws him back to Rugbull where he can exemplify an alternative to the narrow and hate-filled local culture. Siggi has no reason to believe that Rugbull will be receptive to the counterculture that he represents. Indeed in a worst-case, but utterly plausible, scenario, Siggi could actually succumb to, rather than transform, the culture to which he is returning. After all, Siggi is drawn back to Rugbull not only by his sense of moral responsibility but also because of the gravitational force of blood and soil. Nonetheless, his return to Rugbull is clearly about redemption and indeed civic responsibility.

HIDING FROM HISTORY

The novels of Christa Wolf, Gunter Grass and Bernard Schlink reveal the destructive impact on the postwar generation of an ill-considered and self-serving decision by postwar German leaders. Encumbered by their own checkered past, they were determined to put the Nazi experience behind them and beyond the nation. They created a school curriculum that failed to address in anything approaching its full complexity Germany's embrace of Nazism and its devastating consequences in death and destruction for the German people. The postwar generation therefore never got beyond the horrible things that the Nazis had done and the part played by their parents, who were in one way or another accessories to the crimes of the state. When, for example, Konni submits a school essay, "The Positive Aspects of the Nazi Organization Strength through Joy," it is not even given a reading.

However, without subjecting the Pandora's Box of Nazism to robust public discourse or parental guidance and classroom scrutiny to help young people get to the bottom of things, they were left to their own devices. Konni is deprived of all three and left to the half-truths of his manipulative and nationalistic grandmother Tulla. Small wonder then that Konni became a neo-Nazi. Lenka, for undisclosed reasons, lurches leftward but she is not interested in an explanation, only in condemnation. Even the thoughtful and well-educated Michael in *The Reader* admits that he and his fellow law students were completely uninterested in learning and went to Hanna's war crimes trial in eager anticipation of a guilty verdict. In the end Michael eschews the comforts of moral certainty. His escape from this dead-end is idiosyncratic — a consequence of his tangled relationship with Hanna. Their relationship forces him to see Hanna as a whole person, and in looking back he also becomes acutely aware of his own shortcomings.

Broadly speaking, this postwar generation is left angry, guilty and resolutely judgmental about having to live with the indelible stain of Nazism and with their parents' inability to have prevented it all from happening.

REKINDLING LIFE, RENEWING JUDAISM

It can be taken as a given that the Holocaust imposed the most crushing burden: destroying millions of lives and obliterating modernity's promise of citizenship. Late-modern novels help us understand in the most elemental way the social alchemy that somehow transformed death into a source of spiritual renewal for Holocaust victims and succeeding generations. This life-affirming legacy of the Holocaust was, however, hard won and contingent — dependent, that is, on sources of spiritual strength — the product of both religious and secular epiphanies.[*] Both

---

[*] The clear exception to this generalization is the unmitigated negativity of Siegelbaum's seemingly endless journey on Aaron Appelfeld's *Iron Tracks*. Siegelbaum's quest is to avenge the murder of his parents by Nachtrigel and to salvage relics of Eastern European Jewish culture. Both of these missions, despite their apparent success, turn to ashes in Siegelbaum's mouth. He realizes that the preservation of artifacts cannot restore life to a now-vanished culture. Similarly, the murder of Nachtrigel, while a justifiable act of vengeance, is reduced in Siegelbaum's mind to a largely meaningless confrontation between two superannuated and hollowed-out adversaries. But

the religious and the secular epiphanies underscore the healing power of traditional Judaism.

Elie Wiesel's *The Oath* offers a Talmudic understanding of this healing power in the post-Holocaust world. The Talmud, according to Wiesel, enables us to see that an affirmation of life can be drawn from death and destruction. Wiesel's main character, Azriel, has been told of a devastating pogrom that took place in the distant past in the town of Kolvillag. The pogrom, like the Holocaust, Azriel points out to a Holocaust victim contemplating suicide, was the work of the Exterminating Angel who has been the agent of darkness through the ages. He deals in death, and in choosing suicide over life, the boy is *ipso facto* making common cause with the devil: "Just as every murder is a suicide, every suicide is a murder" (p. 65).[5]

In Ann Michael's *Fugitive Pieces*, Jakob, an orphaned survivor of the Holocaust, is sheltered by Athos, a secular scientist. Judaism is a presence in Michael's narrative, but for the wisdom that can be gleaned from it as an element of culture, not as a repository of faith. As a scientist, Athos looks to the redemptive power of natural catastrophe rather than to religious faith.[6] His primary message to Jakob is that he not think of the Holocaust, for all of its butchery and barbarism, as *sui generis*, but as part of the inexorable flow of history.[*]

For redemption, it is necessary to leave the dead in peace. "To remain with the dead is to abandon them" (p. 170). But neither should they be abandoned. To resolve that paradox, it is necessary to find meaning in their shattered lives. Jakob, of course, finds such meaning in the "cosmology of cataclysm." The book concludes not with Jakob's renewal, but with him passing on the redemptive message of the cosmology of cataclysm to Ben, the child of Holocaust survivors — to, that is, the next generation.

The next generation is also the focus of *Second Hand Smoke*. Duncan Katz, the son of Holocaust survivors, has become an avenging angel as a result of his mother Mila's determination to make him one tough and

---

nothing embitters Siegelbaum more than the evidence he uncovers in his travels that the Holocaust was a success for the anti-Semites who wanted to purge Eastern Europe of Jews and Judaism and have been able to do so. Perhaps the explanation for the pervasive hopelessness of *The Iron Tracks* is somehow connected to Appelfeld's portrayal of the cultural bankruptcy of the pre-war fixation on assimilation and thus on the flight from Judaism.

* Recall Athos' specific formulation: "At that moment of utmost degradation, in that twisted reef, is the most obscene testament of grace. For can anyone tell with absolute certainty the difference between the sounds of those who are in despair and the sounds of those who want desperately to believe? The moment when our faith in man is forced to change, anatomically — mercilessly — into faith" (p. 168).

fearless Jew. The second-hand smoke that permeates his childhood is both the product of Mila's nicotine addiction and a metaphor for Mila's obsession with vengeance. Duncan enthusiastically builds his career around a relentless determination to ferret out and prosecute anti-Semitic war criminals. Indeed, it might be said that under Mila's tutelage it is hard to distinguish Duncan from Wiesel's exterminating angel of death.

The obsessively driven Duncan is so preoccupied with death and revenge that he is unable to live — making himself miserable and estranging him from life, from love and thus from his wife and child. On a visit to Poland (of all places) he finds a spiritual alternative to a life of hate from the example of his half-brother, Isaac Borowski. Duncan's spiritual awakening begins when the gentle Isaac easily defuses an angry confrontation between Duncan and some young Poles. Duncan's tough-Jew, Mila-inspired credo is shaken by Isaac's capacity to achieve what for Duncan is the unachievable. Slowly Duncan is drawn into Isaac's life, which is devoted to preserving and restoring what remains of Judaism's Polish heritage by working as a caretaker at the Jewish cemetery in Warsaw. Duncan prays in the synagogue, but following Isaac's lead also finds solace and spiritual sustenance in Catholicism, yoga and Zen Buddhism. *Second Hand Smoke* is thus another tale of how spiritual and religious engagement can bring forth life from death.

THE MALAISE OF DEMOCRATIC POLITICS

The post-World War II late-modern novels all tell tales of insufficient civic engagement to sustain robust republican democracies. The affluent, cloistered and self-interested bourgeoisie — most notably McEwan's remarkably skilled surgeon, Henry Perowne, and Roth's paragon of upward mobility, Swede Levov, are portrayed as absorbed by the private (the everyday concerns of earning a living, sustaining a family, realizing a sense of fulfillment and self-worth) and estranged from the political. Society's losers are forced into a precarious netherworld of the dispossessed: Baxter in *Saturday*; the downwardly mobile Bob Dubois in *Continental Drift*; the cultural Other in Ralph Ellison's *Invisible Man*; and the illegal Haitian immigrants fleeing to the United States. In search of a better life, they find that they have become reviled symbols for divisive inequalities and blocked upward mobility. The losers are antagonized by, and at the mercy of, forces and structures that they neither understand nor believe they can influence. With the marginalized deprived of voice and the privileged uninterested in its exercise, citizenship and thus democracy are portrayed as imperiled from above and below.

Both the US and the UK novels reveal pervasive estrangement — an obsession with the personal and a lack of civic, much less political, engagement. However, the US novels exude despair, with the characters too mired in the false promises of the American dream to look beyond, much less to transcend, their illusions. The nameless narrator in *The Invisible Man* ends up living underground in New York City — exiling himself from a society that excluded him and put his American dream out of reach. Bob Dubois and Swede Levov seem incapable of learning from their estrangement. The bewildered Swede tries desperately to figure out why everything has gone wrong for the Levovs, but he does not have a clue: "And what is wrong with their life? What on earth is less reprehensible than the life of the Levovs?" (p. 423). Bob Dubois does see that in search of material well-being, he has betrayed the Haitian refugees and his family while dishonoring himself. Still, he dies because he is unwilling to yield his ill-gotten gains to Haitian toughs. His last words tell it all: "This money is mine" (p. 363).

In contrast, the UK novels are much less bitter and hopeless. When Perowne reflects on his life, he is profoundly troubled by the way he has marginalized civic engagement and privileged his family and his profession. While his confrontations with Baxter go from bad to worse, by the end of the book he has come to see Baxter as a sympathetic character struggling against both his terrible illness and the losing hand he has been dealt. In short, Perowne has a civic conscience. He has not given up on himself or his country. Alan Sillitoe's Arthur Seaton likes to think of himself as a political rebel — bitter and alienated. We learn, however, that this is all bluster and that Arthur, just like his father and mother, is neither politically engaged nor alienated. He is only too happy to become a family man and to make a separate peace with the welfare state. Zadie Smith's second-generation South Asian immigrants are classic outsiders in Britain's tight little island and they manage through perseverance to find promising social niches. While their first-generation parents tend to be estranged, it is in large part by choice — that is, by a determination to preserve their Islamic cultural heritage. It is unclear whether the second generation will become politically engaged or will devote their energies to upward mobility and social acceptance. Either way, to think of them as estranged would miss the mark.

In short, the British novels celebrate the imperfect solidarity of the welfare state, while the US novels mourn exclusionary practices that divide the races, and the zero-sum struggle that pits winners and losers against one another. Still, politics is the absent presence in the novels of both countries — implying that republican democracy is at risk even in its most receptive and well-entrenched settings.

2. Remembering the Twenty-first Century

> *The sophistic distinctions we draw today in our war on terror — between the rule of law and "exceptional" circumstances, between citizens (who have rights and legal protections) and non-citizens to whom anything can be done, between normal people and "terrorists," between "us" and "them" . . . are the self-same distinctions that licensed the worst horrors of the recent past: internment camps, deportation, torture and murder.*
>
> Tony Judt[7]

What does it mean to remember the twenty-first century, which is just barely under way? The prelude to remembering is re-imagining the twentieth century — taking stock of its destructive blunders. To that end, the narratives of betrayal and estrangement that drive late-modern political novels have been summarized and synthesized in the previous section. They provide the foundation for re-imagining the twentieth century as we project its lessons onto the twenty-first in this section of the chapter. What we readily discover with the help of Tony Judt is that, on the one hand, political leaders are *unwilling or unable to re-imagine the twentieth century.* They are oblivious to its lessons and afflictions and, not surprisingly, are repeating rather than re-imagining the twentieth century. On the other hand, because the circumstances of the twenty-first century are not precisely the same, its narratives of betrayal and estrangement are inflected in subtle but significantly different ways.

It is, however, important to keep in mind that much of what follows is speculative — inferred from a necessarily provisional understanding of the twenty-first century and its literature. Put another way, what follows is a kind of heuristic down payment — laying the basis for a research agenda. In the spirit of remembering the future I will focus on the twenty-first-century iterations of the thorniest frustration of the earlier era: war, genocide and modernity. We will then turn to literary knowledge to better understand the impact of the conditions and circumstances of the emerging new century on political agency and political estrangement.

New century, old transgressions

Tony Judt warns us that the political leaders of the new century seem to have learned so little from the past that they are well on the way to recreating its destruction and its despair. While the twenty-first century has not, at least not yet, subjected us to total war, the unlimited war on terror is a clear and present danger. Arguably terrorism is about power — the struggle to obtain it and to protect it, but terrorism is also driven by a revealing struggle between modernity and tradition — part and parcel of the culture wars between the north and the south, between the developed and developing world.

As formulated by the Bush Administration, the war on terror is power-driven. Judt's reading is confirmed by the experiences of Jack Goldsmith and the research of Kim Scheppele. Goldsmith characterizes George W. Bush's administration as a "terror presidency — a presidency fueled by terror which it hyped and then exploited to silence critics while it was engaging in manifestly unconstitutional practices."[8] Goldsmith served the Bush administration for only nine months. He resigned once it became unequivocally clear that the line between the legal and the illegal was meaningless to those, like most notably David Addington, who were at or near the top of the White House hierarchy. Scheppele looks beyond the United States to resolution 1373 of the UN Security Council that ordered all member states to create a crime of terrorism, to monitor terrorist activities, and to take specified affirmative action against terrorists and terrorism. The result has been a globalization of states of emergency, working at cross-purposes to constitutionalism and human rights.[9] Once again the issue is power, with resolution 1373 amounting to an open invitation to autocratic regimes around the world to rationalize silencing their opponents. More broadly, while there has been no repeat of the Holocaust, there have been multiple examples of ethnic cleansing and genocide which, while preceding the war on terror, have been validated by the distinction it draws between "us" and "them" — "between citizens (who have legal rights and legal protections) and non-citizens (to whom anything can be done)."[10]

It is, however, not just civil, political and human rights that are casualties of the war on terror. In addition, according to Judt, the war on terror leads to the "abstracting of foes and threats from their context." In effect, we create an enemy which is a figment of our imagination. As a consequence, complex variations among those who commit terrorist acts are ignored, and terrorism is reduced to the work of "'Islamofascists,' 'extremists' from a strange culture who dwell in some distant 'Islamistan,' who hate us for who we are and seek to destroy 'our way of life.'"[11] These labels tend to be affixed to *adversaries* of the United States while terrorist acts by *allies* are overlooked. The result is a kind of self-fulfilling prophecy in which our disregard of difference and our expressions of hostility tend to unite Islam against the US in particular and the West in general.[12]

Last but not least, the tactics of terror and the tactics of its suppression are not only about power but expressions of cultural conflict. Terrorism in today's world reflects in large part a struggle between traditional modes of authority — the autocratic, the theocratic and insular — and modernity with its promise of democracy, its embrace of the secular and its privileging of cosmopolitan values. This cultural struggle has meaning and significance in both theocracies, like Iran, and in secular Israel. In both settings, secularism and democracy are embraced by Western-educated and Western-influenced segments of society but challenge the religious orthodoxies which control the state in Iran and challenge the state in Israel.[13] This conflict between the secular and theocratic has spilled over from the third world to Europe and the United States where immigrants desperate to escape endemic poverty find themselves adrift between the cultures of their adopted country and their traditional cultures which provide solace — especially, but not exclusively, to those who are marginalized culturally and economically from the mainstream. This influx of refugees has frequently led to cultural warfare against immigrants, the ethnic Other, who are seen as outsiders in, for example, Germany, the United States and France. Thus, in France, the wearing of the *burqa* and the head scarf has been curtailed because they are deemed threats to indigenous French culture.[14]

Literary knowledge

In this context it seems clear that literary knowledge is particularly useful and to some extent predictable. So much of the past is being repeated by political leaders of the new century who seem to have learned next to nothing from the past. We are thus well on the way to recreating the destruction and despair of the twentieth century. It is therefore reasonable to infer that, at the very least, late-modern literary sensibilities dominated by narratives of betrayal and estrangement will continue to be consonant with the prevailing zeitgeist.

In addition, Tony Judt's analysis of the widespread ramifications of the war on terror suggests how and why literary sensibilities are likely to prove at least as essential to understanding the twenty-first century as they were for the twentieth. Insofar as political discourse indiscriminately stigmatizes all terrorism by Muslims as Islamo-terrorism and as part of a worldwide conspiracy against the West and liberal democracy, novelists can help us get to the bottom of things. Without understanding in all their glorious complexity the hopes, fears and motivations driving and dividing Muslims, there is no way to understand the impact of autocratic regimes, both secular and theocratic. Will the suppression of agency lead to political estrangement and/or to concerted political resistance, and under what circumstances? There are, of course, examples of both kinds of responses and there may well be political novels, most probably with a late-modern inflection, that reveal the hearts and minds of the downtrodden and help us understand how these questions, likely to become increasingly prominent as the twenty-first century unfolds, will be answered.

A related issue concerns the long-term impact on combatants of their wartime experiences. As I suggested in Chapter 2, this seems to be matter touched on by, but only ancillary to, the anti-war novels — whether waged in the trenches of World War I, the sea, land and air battles of World War II, or through insurgencies in which combatants are largely indistinguishable from the civilians as in the Vietnam, Iraq and Afghanistan wars. As wars continue to be waged, it is clear that there has been a failure the world over to learn "how war brutalizes and degrades winners and losers alike."[15] When combatants return to civilian life, they bear "battle's latent scars"[16] and frequently fall into self-destructive behavior leading sometimes to suicide and predictably to problems maintaining intimate relationships and family life.

Finally, in settings where tradition and modernity are at odds with one another, modernity tends to be associated with democracy rather than the betrayal of democracy. Recall that Bauman traces the Holocaust to the stresses and strains of modernity rather than to anti-Semitism. More broadly, Bauman and virtually all late-modern novelists measure modernity against its own acknowledged ideals and find it wanting. When, however, modernity is refracted through autocratic, theocratic and repressive regimes as well as through the lives of those who struggle against them, modernity becomes a lifeline, with its virtues far outweighing its vices.

3. Democracy and Modernity

The late-modern political novels of the twentieth century underscore how modernity was consistently at odds with democracy — undermining political agency, fomenting political estrangement and in general driving society's losers, like Bob Dubois, and its winners, like Swede Lvov, to turn away from collective political action. They, together with other casualties of modernism, were forced to adapt to their plight and did so in a variety of ways. Sometimes these adaptations were learning experiences — individuals searching their consciences for spiritual, religious and moral solace and redemption. At least as often, adaptation was about burying the past and crafting opportunistic survival strategies at the expense of others. Collectively, these personal quests added up to a re-imagining of the twentieth century. Political engagement was seen as futile and democracy as undependable — likely to create more problems than it resolves.

The searching inquiries of late-modern novelists also provide some tentative clues about what is likely to transpire as the twenty-first century develops. Briefly put, there seems little prospect that the political will come to trump the personal. This is because political leaders continue to repeat the blunders of the past rather than learning from them. They betray the public trust by waging destructive wars, demonizing the ethnic Other, and more broadly visiting suffering on those in society who are least able to protect themselves. So much for continuity between the centuries!

The twenty-first century is generating its distinctive adaptations to the subversion of political agency. The developing conflict between the poor and the rich countries, the so-called north-south divide, is arguably a new phenomenon.* These days immigrants flow into the prosperous countries of Western Europe and the United States — often from former colonial states. They come bearing ancient and more recent grievances and proudly, one might say defiantly, committed not just to their religions but to a traditional way of life that is often at odds with the cultures of their not very welcoming new countries.

Is this a recipe for hope or for despair? It may be either, depending on the political, economic, social and cultural circumstances and on the willingness and determination of immigrants to fit in. *White Teeth* is all about hope, but there are most certainly twenty-first-century novels of despair to be written, perhaps already written. Consider also the traditional societies that are in effect using emigration to export poverty and social unrest and consequently have no interest whatsoever in stemming the outflow of emigrants. In these societies, autocracy and theocracy trump modernity and democracy. However, even in the most closed of traditional societies modernity is intruding and being embraced by opponents of the established regime as the only avenue to liberation.[17]

In these twenty-first-century settings, twentieth-century assumptions about the contradictions between modernity and democracy will surely be reexamined and revised, and the literary imagination is well suited to contribute to our understanding of how all of this will play out. Through literature we learn how the lives and fortunes of individuals are caught up in, and scarred by, overarching events and calamities: wars, revolutions, genocide and the like. Accordingly, one key to understanding the complexities introduced by the circumstances of the twenty-first century would be an inquiry into its political novels. My expectation is that this inquiry would build upon and adapt to what is useful in my effort to re-imagine the twentieth century while correcting the shortcomings of my

---

* Of course, mass migration from the poverty-stricken countries of Western Europe to the United States was one of the dominant features of the nineteenth and early twentieth centuries. But in that era, the need for labor to settle the continent and perhaps a more generous and hopeful public discourse tended to moderate the hostility between earlier generations of immigrants and the new arrivals.

research — shortcomings which are always part and parcel of honest and productive intellectual exchange. This is especially the case, I will add, in a venture that reaches across the contested intellectual terrain that tends to put literary, historical, and political modes of inquiry at odds with one another.

Notes

Notes to Chapter 1: Novels of Political Estrangement: Subversion of Agency in the Twentieth Century

1 *The New York Times*, 27 December 2009.

2 *The New Yorker*, 18 January 2010: 48.

3 The prerogative state also overrode the normative state — thus subverting legal agency as well as political agency. See Ernst Fraenkel, *The Dual State: A Contribution to the Theory of Dictatorship*. Translated from the German by E. A. Shils, in collaboration with Edith Lowenstein and Klaus Knorr. New York: Oxford University Press, 1941. xvi, 248 pp. Reprinted 2006 by The Lawbook Exchange, Ltd.

4 Edward P. Jones, *The Known World*. New York: Amistad, 2004.

5 Stuart Hall, David Held and Toney McGrew, eds, *Modernity and its Future*. Cambridge: Polity Press, 1992: 2. See also Christopher Crouch, *Modernism in Art, Design, and Architecture*. New York: St. Martins Press, 1999: 10.

6 Anthony Giddens, *The Consequences of Modernity*. Stanford, California: Stanford University Press, 1990: 1.

7 Crouch, 1999: 15.

8 Giddens, 1990: 71.

9 Hall, Held and McGrew, 1992: 3.

10 Crouch, 1999: 86.

11 Crouch, 1999: 129.

12 Crouch, 1999: 129.

13 Crouch, 1999: 131.

14 Crouch, 1999: 128.

15 I will also draw upon Robert Boyers who shared Howe's views and introduced them into the analysis of post-World War II novels. *Atrocity and Amnesia: The Political Novel Since 1945*. New York: Oxford University Press, 1987.

16 Quoted in Jesse Matz, *The Modern Novel: A Short Introduction*. Oxford: Blackwell Publishing, 2004: 7.

17 Matz, 2004: 4.

18 Matz, 2004: 16.

19 Other novelists, Matz tells us (see Chapters 2 and 5), deployed modernist techniques to look beyond the interior of individual lives. To name only a few: Conrad and Forster on British imperialism; D. H. Lawrence and Edith Wharton on social class and money; John Dos Passos on war; Zora Neale

Hurston on race; Virginia Woolf on feminism; and Christopher Isherwood on fascism. However, their status as masters of the modern novel rested entirely on their contribution to capturing the tempos of modern life and the impact of those tempos on the inner lives of their characters — on what Matz refers to as a "passion for aesthetic justice," which he speculates might be "incompatible to doing justice to the real world" (Matz, 2004: p. 16). In any case, these were not political novels according to criteria developed by Howe. With the exception of Dalton Trumbull's *Johnny Got His Gun*, these examples are drawn from Matz, 2004.

20   Howe seems to be out of fashion these days — hardly surprising given the privileging of technique and the marginalizing of the political.

21   Irving Howe, *Politics and the Novel*. Chicago: Ivan R. Dee, 2002: 92.

22   Howe, 2002: 206.

23   Howe, 2002: 222.

24   Howe, 2002: 239.

25   Howe, 2002: 24.

26   Howe, 2002: 239.

27   As Howe sees it, the "twentieth-century political novel moves along a line of descent, an increasingly precipitous fall into despair. To turn from the revolutionary ardor of [Malraux's] *Man's Fate* to the rebellious doubt of [Silone's] *Bread and Wine*, and from these to the symbolic triumph of Stalinism in [Arthur Koestler's] *Darkness at Noon*, is to see in miniature a history of our epoch" (2004: 227). He notes a similar defect in Dostoevsky's "Kirillov . . . one of most brilliant ideological projections but not, I think, an entirely successful one. Is it really true, as Dostoevsky seems to assert, that the highest expression of the will is suicide? One would suppose that a higher heroism of the will might be a choice to live" (Howe, 2002: 67).

28   Howe, 2002: 204.

29   Howe, 2002: 208.

30   Howe, 2002: 213.

31   Howe, 2002: 211.

32   Howe, 2002: 226.

33   Howe, 2002: 226.

34   Howe, 2002: 223.

35   Howe, quoted by David Bromwich — from his introduction to Howe, 2002: 5.

36   Howe, 2002: 5.

37   Bromwich, in Howe, 2002: 3.

38   Howe, 2002: 20.

39   With respect to Orwell's *1984*, on the other hand, Howe dismisses critics who complain about "the gritty and hammering factuality" of his prose and the absence of "'three-dimensional' characters" (2002: 237). Indeed, he sees these elements of Orwell's novel as authentic expressions of the nature of the twentieth-century totalitarian regime, which, in effect, obliterates "individual consciousness, psychological analysis and the study of intimate relations" (2002: 236). This symmetry between style and substance

emerges as strength rather than weakness — providing "a model of the totalitarian state in its 'pure' or 'essential' form and a vision of what this state can do to human life" (2002: 239).

40 Howe: 2002: 5.

41 Howe, 2002: 71.

42 Howe, 2002: 60.

43 Tony Judt, "Review of *Interesting Times: A Twentieth Century Life* by Eric Hobsbaum," *New York Review of Books*, vol. L, no. 18 (20 November 2003): 43–5.

44 Tyrus Miller finds late modernity in "the writings and related works — visual, critical, political, and cultural-polemical of Wyndham Lewis, Djuana Barnes, and Samuel Beckett." *Late Modernism: Politics, Fiction, and the Arts Between the Wars.* Berkeley: University of California Press: 5.

45 Franz Kafka, *The Trial.* New York: Schocken Books, 1998. Henry Sussman, *The Trial: Kafka's Unholy Trinity.* New York: Twayne Publishers, 1993: 5.

46 Zygmunt Bauman, *Modernity and the Holocaust.* Cambridge: The Polity Press, 1995.

47 Bauman, 1995: 13. Italics in the original.

48 Bauman, 1995: 1.

49 Bauman, 1995: 2. The latter way of thinking has led, as Bauman sees it, to social science research aimed at "disclosing the peculiar combination of psycho-social factors which could be sensibly connected . . . with peculiar behavioral tendencies displayed by the 'dirty work' perpetrators" (1995: 7).

50 Bauman, 1995: 7.

51 Bauman, 1995: 10.

52 Bauman, 1995: 13.

53 Herbert C. Kelman, "Violence Without Moral Restraint," *Journal of Social Issues*, vol. 9 (1973): 29–61.

54 Bauman, 1995: 21. Italics in the original.

55 H. H. Gerth and C. Wright Mills (eds), *From Max Weber.* London: Routledge & Kegan Paul, 1970: 214, 215.

56 Bauman, 1995: 22. In a move reminiscent of the controversy generated by Hannah Arendt's *Eichmann in Jerusalem: A Report on the Banality of Evil* (New York: Viking Press, 1963), Bauman also paraphrases the findings of Holocaust historian Raul Hilberg. He asserted that the institutions and ethos of the SS bureaucracy led not only ordinary Germans but also Jewish victims, albeit on German orders, to an obedience "with dedication verging on self-abandonment" (Bauman, 1995: 22).

57 Bauman, 1995: 25.

58 Bauman, 1995: 26.

59 Bauman, 1995: 27.

60 Tony Judt, "What Have We Learned, If Anything," *The New York Review of Books*, May 1, 2008: 16. See also his *Postwar: A History of Europe Since 1945* (New York: Penguin, 2005).

61 Judt, 2008: 16.

62 Judt, 2008: 16.

63 Also see Jack Goldsmith's view from inside the administration: *The Terror Presidency: Law and Judgment Inside the Bush Administration* (New York: Norton, 2007). More broadly, Kim Schepple has called attention to the emergence of "international security law" as the result of Security Council Resolution 1373, passed in the aftermath of 9/11 and requiring all member states to create a crime of terrorism, to monitor terrorist activities and to take specified affirmative action against terrorists and terrorism, which has led to a kind of globalization of states of emergency which work at cross-purposes to constitutionalism and human rights. K. L. Scheppele, *The International State of Emergency: Challenges to Constitutionalism after September 11*. Working Paper, Law and Public Affairs Program, Princeton University, 2006: 3, 15.

64 Judt, 2008: 20.

65 Judt, 2008: 18.

66 Judt, 2008: 20.

67 Judt, 2008: 18.

68 Brooke Allen, "Review of *Isherwood: A Life Revealed* by Peter Parker." *New York Times Book Review*, 19 December 2004: 20.

69 This approach serves my purposes but only scratches the interpretive surface of the riches that have been unearthed by Kafka scholars. For a penetrating introduction to the multiplicity of Kafka, see Henry Sussman, *The Trial: Kafka's Unholy Trinity* (New York: Twayne Publishers, 1993).

70 Malcolm Feeley, *The Process is the Punishment: Handling Cases in a Lower Criminal Court*. New York: Russell Sage Foundation, 1979.

71 Sussman, 1993: 4. I do not mean to suggest that Sussman's reading of Kafka is definitive or authoritative. I was, for example, taken by an ingeniously constructed and compelling psychoanalytic interpretation of *The Trial*, in which the events and the ethos of the novel become an externalized realization of Kafka's inner demons. René Dauvin, "*The Trial*: Its Meaning," in Angel Flores and Homer Swander, eds, *Franz Kafka Today*. Madison: University of Wisconsin Press, 1964. I see each of these interpretations as equally valid and persuasive but Sussman's focus on Joseph K.'s vulnerability to social forces rather than inner demons serves my purposes without prejudicing Dauvin's.

72 Sussman, 1993: 73.

73 The painter who spends his time painting virtually unrecognizable drawings of justice — unrecognizable largely because he portrays "Justice and the goddess of Victory in one" (p. 145). When K. expresses his doubt about the compatibility of justice and victory, the painter claims that he is "just following the wishes of the person who commissioned it" (p. 145).

74 Sussman also detects premonitions of postmodernism in Kafka. "To the degree to which *The Trial* joins and dramatizes the insufficiency of logical superstructure, it also anticipates movements of twentieth-century philosophy known as phenomenology, as exemplified by Martin Heidegger,

and deconstruction, a variegated set of textual attitudes assembled by Jacques Derrida. Sussman, 1993: 17.

75 Sussman, 1993: 9.

76 Sussman, 1993: 3.

77 Patricia Ewick and Austin Sarat, "Hidden in Plain View: Murray Edelman in the Law and Society Tradition," *Law & Social Inquiry*, vol. 29, no. 2 (Spring 2004): 453. See also Timothy Mitchell, "Everyday Metaphors of Power," *Theory and Society*, 19 (1990): 569.

78 David Riesman, *The Lonely Crowd: A Study of Changing American Character*. New Haven: Yale University Press, 1950.

79 I am grateful to Christine DiStefano for calling my attention to this way of distinguishing agency from freedom.

Notes to Chapter 2: Anti-War Novels in the 20th Century: An Anti-Modern Drift

1 Raymond Aron, *The Century of Total War*. Boston: Beacon Press, 1968:18.

2 Aron, 1968: 21.

3 Aron identifies precursors of total war in the eighteenth and nineteenth centuries — for example, the American Civil War with its "relentless mobilization of national resources and the competition over new inventions." Aron, 1968: 21.

4 As Elizabeth Kier put it in a private communication: "Total war is different from, for example, limited war in its scope (time and geographically) and intensity (number of individuals, mobilized for the war effort) — both soldiers on the battlefield and civilians consumed by economic mobilization at home). Intensity would also refer to the absence of restraints — strategic bombing and the targeting of population centers for example. Some observers see the French Revolutionary war as the first — not only with the introduction of universal military conscription, but also because of the mobilization of the home front and the harnessing of science to the war effort. World War I and World War II are commonly seen as total wars though not for all countries. For example, I think it's arguable whether World War I was a total war for the US."

5 Recall Irving Howe's modernist claim that the mission of a political novel is to illuminate the shortcomings of the prevailing political order and to identify how best to correct it.

6 The increasing prominence of asymmetrical conflict would perhaps alter the mix of factors that denote total war and warrant some new characterization, but would it change the underlying message and late-modern trajectory of anti-war literature? This is terrain that deserves attention.

7 Margot Norris, "Introduction: Modernisms and Modern Wars," *Modern Fiction Studies*, Vol. 44.3 (1998): 505.

8 Ewick and Sarat, 1990: 569.

9 Dewey Ganzel argues that *A Farewell to Arms* is neither a love story nor a war novel. As to the latter, he writes: "The associations which accrue from that label — the fear of violent death, the carnage of battle, the monotony

of routine activity, the debasement of idealism — topics which permeate other 'war novels' of the twenties are not central to *A Farewell to Arms*." Dewey Ganzel, "*A Farewell to Arms*": The Danger of Imagination," *The Sewanee Review*, Vol. 79, No. 4 (Autumn, 1971): 576.

10   For a contrasting view, see Robert Merrill, "The Tragic Form in *A Farewell to Arms*," *American Literature*, Vol. 45, No. 4 (January, 1974): 571–9. According to Merrill, the novel has all the elements of tragedy including not just Catherine's death but the context in which the enemy "*is* the universe, that dark and destructive context for all that happens," 1974: 578.

11   Note the way in which Henry "caresses" the "Austrian sniper rifle with its blued octagonal barrel and the lovely dark walnut" (p. 11). It is strictly an ornament, as are helmets (p. 28).

12   She too romanticizes the military — imagining that they will have a son who will become a Lt. Commander (p. 141).

13   He rejects glory or honor (pp. 184–5) as abstractions but clings to them as ideals that bind him to those with whom he serves and those for whom he fights.

14   Sarah Cole cites and then goes on to reject B. H. Liddell Hart's "image of a devastating war redeemed by the intimacy nourished among its combatants." "Modernism, Male Intimacy, and the Great War," *English Literary History*, Vol. 68, No. 2 (2001): p. 470. Instead, she argues, "comradeship did *not* function as the culture demanded," and that "this failure generates a particularly resonant form of anger and bewilderment" (2001): 470.

15   Modris Eksteins claims that the book should be taken more as "a comment on the postwar mind, on the postwar view of the war, than an attempt to reconstruct the reality of the trench experience." "*All Quiet on the Western Front* and the Fate of a War," *Journal of Contemporary History*, Vol. 15, No. 2 (April, 1980): 351. Eksteins goes on to note that "traditionalists" rejected its pacifism, but he concludes that the novel's great success was because of its "passionate evocation of current public feeling, not so much about the war as about existence in general in 1929. It was a poignant cry of 'help' on behalf of a distraught generation" (1980: 362).

16   Yuval Noah Harari argues that in rejecting the heroic and romantic image of war, World War I writers not only "reacted to a changing technologic reality" but also "unmask[ed] war's eternal face." "Martial Illusions: War and Disillusionment in Twentieth-Century and Renaissance Military Memoirs," *The Journal of Military History*, Vol. 69, No. 1 (2005): 128.

17   This seems not unlike immigrants to the United States these days who join the army to get on the fast track to citizenship.

18   Richard M. Zaner notes that Joe's deep-seated sense of himself as a sentient human being is validated by the nurse who "realizes that Joe is in that mangled body." "Sisyphus without Knees: Exploring Self-Other Relationships through Illness and Disability," *Literature and Medicine*, Vol. 22, No. 2 (2003): 197. She stands in stark contrast to his other caregivers: "Joe's nurses and doctors, who are locked in to *pre*–interpreting

Joe as merely a biologically ongoing set of neural reactions without the density of bodily wherewithal or human purpose" (p. 200). Of course, even less unbearably incapacitating wounds of war can lead caregivers, albeit unconsciously, to treat patients as if they are less than whole human beings.

19 Jonathan E. Abel calls attention to the willingness of the "left-leaning Trumbo" to collude in self-censorship. "[D]uring the height of the war [World War II], as fascist groups with the U.S. called for reprints of the book as anti-war propaganda in favor of a quick peace with Hitler, Trumbo and his publishers decided against further pressings." "Canon and Censor: How War Wounds Bodies of Writing," *Comparative Literature Studies,* Vol. 42, No. 1 (2005): 79.

20 Margot Norris sees Barker's trilogy as an exception to "the complacent amnesia of the century's bloody beginning." She goes on to point out that "[w]ith its compelling blend of fiction, history and scholarship — and its compassionate focus on the intersection of psychiatry, poetry and politics — this literary phenomenon is just one sign of a recent growing movement to marshal intellectual and artistic resources to address the unredressable psychic wounds of such events as the Jewish Holocaust, Hiroshima, the Rape of Nanking and the countless other atrocities of this century" (Norris, 1998: 508).

21 Rivers is also struck by a kind of reversal of gender roles in wartime. The men are expected to passively await enemy fire or to advance into it with unquestioning obedience. Women in contrast (exemplified in the novel by Prior's girlfriend) are exchanging the constraints of domestic service for the relative freedom of factory work (p. 90).

22 John E. Talbott notes that Rivers' understanding that "combat trauma . . . could alter young men's lives forever" contrasted with the doubts expressed by other psychiatrists who treated the emotional disorders of the battlefield as due to the purely physical — to "shell shock" or to "a form of malingering." "Soldiers, Psychiatrists, and Combat Trauma," *Journal of Interdisciplinary History,* Vol. 27, No. 3 (Winter, 1997): p. 444. Also in contrast to Rivers' approach was that of medical officers who regarded the emotional disorders as a reaction to the immediate trauma. Rivers' vision was both more expansive and "more attuned to clues from the culture and the environment" (Talbott, 1997: 446). Talbott traces Rivers' sensibilities to his work as an anthropologist and to his Freudian-like appreciation of the unconscious. Barker's own understanding of Rivers is more elemental. "I think Rivers has a real fascination with the intuitive, the irrational, the so-called primitive, and I think he knew perfectly well that the source of creativity is in that area. The epicritic can dress it up, but the goods are delivered by the protopathic." John Brannigan and Pat Barker, "An Interview with Pat Barker," *Contemporary Literature,* Vol. 46, No. 3. (Autumn, 2005): 382.

23 "He was getting all the familiar symptoms. Sweating, a constant need to urinate, breathlessness, the sense of blood not flowing but squeezing

through veins. The slightest movement caused his heart to pound. He was relieved when dawn came and it was possible to summon the orderly" (p. 139).

24   It is clearly not incidental to Barker's narrative that Sassoon, the one open and articulate opponent of the war, is a homosexual, a certified war hero and free of war neurosis.

25   Prior's fate plays out in the subsequent two volumes of Barker's trilogy, *The Eye in the Door* and *The Ghost Road*.

26   As Keith McKean points out in his review of *Slaughterhouse 5*, this is a story without villains, because it reveals "human beings . . . completely subject to incalculable forces over which they have no control." *The North American Review*, Vol. 254, No. 3 (Fall, 1969): 71.

27   Unlike Barker's war whose origins were enveloped in clouds of ambiguity, Vonnegut's narrative plays out on the ostensibly unambiguous moral terrain of World War II — universally understood as an honorable crusade against the aggressive iniquity of fascism. Note that Vonnegut calls attention to the literary device (a novel without characters and almost without dramatic confrontation), which he deploys to convey his late-modern political message. The contrast with Barker's linear, logical and conventionally constructed narrative could hardly be clearer.

28   Keith McKeon notes that Vonnegut sees no satisfactory way of accounting for the horror of it all: "better, just to shrug your verbal shoulders . . . with the curious phrase: 'So it goes'" (McKeon, 1969): 70.

29   See C. B. Macpherson, *The Political Theory of Possessive Individualism: From Hobbes to Locke*. New York: Oxford University Press, 1964.

30   Clearly Heller is echoing the claim of a General Motors president, one "Engine" Charlie Wilson, who notoriously said the same thing about the fortunes of the giant car maker.

31   In a review of Sanford Pinsker's *Understanding Joseph Heller* (Columbia, South Carolina: University of South Carolina Press, 1991), Stanley Trachtenberg underscores Pinsker's account of Yossarian's moral transformation: "Pinsker traces Yossarian's progress from self-absorption to a position of moral responsibility . . . Leaving open the question of how Heller can endorse Yossarian's separate peace . . . Pinsker shows its defining moment hinges on the personalizing of life's indiscriminate injuries. 'They're trying to kill me,' Yossarian cries out, and it is no solace that the violence is impersonal. Indeed, that impersonality is what Heller finds both funny and devastating and resistance to it, finally, the basis of sanity." *Modern Fiction Studies*, Vol. 38, No. 2 (Summer, 1992): 489.

32   Moreover, if *Catch 22* and *Slaughterhouse 5* are essentially indistinguishable, does it follow that *Slaughterhouse 5* is, at least for my purposes, derivative in that it was written long after *Catch 22*, which is generally recognized as an icon among late twentieth-century anti-war novels?

33   But see George Packer, "Embers: Letter from Dresden," *The New Yorker*, February 1, 2010, pp. 32–9.

34   Ira C. Eaker, Foreword to David J. C. Irving, *Apocalypse 1945: The Destruction*

of Dresden. Cranbrook, Western Australia: Veritas Publishing Company, 1995.

Notes to Chapter 3: The Alchemy of Catastrophe: Seeking Spiritual Solace in the Ashes of the Holocaust

1 *Fugitive Pieces*: 101.
2 Zygmunt Bauman, *Modernity and the Holocaust*. Cambridge: Polity Press, 1995: 58.
3 Thus, my undertaking stands in sharp contrast to Efraim Sicher's painstakingly thorough and searching account of *The Holocaust Novel* (New York: Routledge, 2005). While I do draw on Sicher's insights, our projects are distinctively different from one another — his primarily literary and mine political.
4 One of the novels that I had initially included but then decided against, Primo Levi's *If Not Now, When?* (New York: Summit Books, 1985), is an exemplary exception to Holocaust novels of political estrangement. This novel, which is about a Jewish resistance group in Eastern Europe, is a tribute to political action and to the possibility of agency even under seemingly hopeless conditions. It is thus a book in which the literary and the political converge in precisely the way envisaged by Irving Howe — resulting in an affirmation of politics, both the resistance politics of World War II and the regenerative politics of Israeli statehood.
5 David C. Jacobson argues that Appelfeld's account "of the transformation of Badenheim into a ghetto . . . differs significantly from historical accounts of the Nazis' war against the Jews . . . Compared to those accounts, the experiences that the Jewish victims of the novel undergo are relatively benign. As in a work of fiction by Kafka, the absurdity of Nazi evil is portrayed by the author and perceived by the victims as a manifestation of everyday reality" (David C. Jacobson, "'Kill your Ordinary Common Sense and Maybe You'll Begin to Understand': Aharon Appelfeld and the Holocaust," *AJS Review*, Vol. 13, No. 1/2 (Spring-Autumn, 1998): 139. Appelfeld is frequently linked to Kafka by literary critics.
6 Closing lines from *Badenheim 1939*.
7 *Badenheim 1939* and Appelfeld have been subjected to searching inquiries that offer intriguing variations on the meaning of assimilation for Appelfeld. For his most insistent critics it is all pretty simple. They see Appelfeld's assimilated middle-class protagonists and perhaps Appelfeld himself as mired in "Jewish self-hate" (Gershon Shaked, quoted in Stanley Nash, "Critical Reappraisals of Aharon Appelfeld," *Prooftexts*, Vol. 22, No. 3, Fall 2002: 339). In sharp contrast, David C. Jacobson argues that the assimilated Jewish victims were easily diverted from their dire predicament, because of a profound need to interpret the "absurdity" of the Nazis in terms that were more comprehensible to them, more consonant with their understanding of the world and also that gave them some hope. As Jacobson puts it, Appelfeld portrays "the process whereby the absurd invaded the everyday life of the victims and elicited a natural human

tendency toward optimism that interfered with the victims' full understanding of their fate" (Jacobson, 1998: 138).

8   In the same vein, Sicher calls our attention to the way in which voices from
the past intrude on the increasing sense of social malaise. "A wonder child,
a 'yanuka,' appears and sings in Yiddish. Forgotten ghosts are awakening"
(2005: p. 75).

9   Jean-Paul Sartre, *Anti-Semite and Jew*. New York: Schocken Books, 1995.
That is not to say that Appelfeld is influenced by, or sympathetic to, Sartre's
views. However, *Badenheim 1939* certainly reveals the toxic entanglements
that inextricably link the fates of Jews and anti-Semites.

10 Sicher, 2005: 77.

11 The last line of Jurek Becker's *Jacob the Liar*.

12 Sanders Gilman, "Jewish Writers and German Letters: Anti-Semitism and
the Hidden Language of Jews," *The Jewish Quarterly Review*, New Series,
Vol. 77, No. 2/3 (October, 1986–January, 1987). The reference is to a young
girl that Jakob has taken under his wing.

13 John P. Wieczorek, "'Irrefuhrung durch Erzahlperspective?' The East
German Novels of Jurek Becker, *The Modern Language Review*, Vol. 85, No. 3
(July, 1990): 651.

14 The crushing toll taken by this normalization of death in the camps thus
prefigures the post-Holocaust struggles of survivors and their descendants
that are considered later in this chapter.

15 Imre Kertesz, "Who Owns Auschwitz?" Translated by John MacKay, *The
Yale Journal of Criticism*, Vol. 14, No. 1 (2001): 268.

16 From the citation of the Swedish Academy in awarding Kertesz the Nobel
Prize for Literature. Quoted in Alan Riding, "Nobel for Hungarian Writer
Who Survived the Death Camps," *The New York Times*, published October
1, 2002.

17 When he becomes aware of the pervasive smell of death, he asks himself:
"Is the epidemic really so great that there are this many dead?" (p. 79).

18 His own physical transformation confirms his Jewish fate. One day as he
looks around, he realizes that he is being physically transformed in ways
that make him resemble all too much the prisoners he reviled on his arrival
at Auschwitz. He is astonished that he and his fellow workers "have rotted
away" and notices that death becomes ever more common. "I would have
never believed, for instance, that I could be transformed into a dried-up
old man so quickly" (p. 121).

19 Sicher, 2005: 48.

20 "Gyorgy's story is of the kind learned from Kafka . . . Thus our protagonist
emerges as the ultimate heir to Camus' alienated hero: he is exempt from
any attachment to his Jewish heritage, his country, or any family member,"
Clara Gyorgyvey, Review of *Fateless*, *World Literature Today*, Vol. 74, No. 3
(Summer, 2000): 612.

21 MacMillan's understanding of his own mission is to help rescue the
Holocaust from those who deny that it ever happened (p. xii). Note that
he also sees the death camps as the last stage "of a process that began with

denial of human rights, went through the theft of wealth, then murder" (Ibid.).

22 See also Gila Rarras-Rauch,"Aharon Appelfeld: A Hundred Years of Jewish Solitude," *World Literature Today*, Vol. 72, No. 3, Hebrew Literature in the 1990s (Summer 1998): 493–500.

23 Michiko Kakutani, "Surviving the Past Through the Power of Words," *The New York Times*, March 7, 1997.

24 As Efraim Sicher puts it, Michaels wants to preserve rather than purge time and space and does so by way of Athos' archaeological geology in which "the past is never past but a layer of the present geology of time and space" (2005: 187). Michaela instinctively recognizes Athos' geological truth of past and present inextricably intertwined and of cataclysms that are not only survivable but also regenerative.

25 The Zohar, most likely of medieval origin, is believed to be "a traditional work standing beside the Bible and the Talmud as the three pillars of Jewish faith and ancient tradition [and] has become an article of faith in modern Orthodox Judaism." Joseph Dan, *Kabbalah: A Very Short Introduction*. New York: Oxford University Press, 2006: 29.

26 Sicher, 2005: 185.

27 Sicher, 2005: 185. Sicher also notes on the same page that Nadine Fresco, a French psychologist, thinks of this very much like the physical sensation of "an amputated limb that makes itself felt in some phantom pain."

28 Dalia Kandiyoti acknowledges Jakob is empowered to "make meaning out of his own cataclysms," but she denies that Athos has provided redemption. "'Our Foothold in Buried Worlds'; Place in Holocaust Consciousness and Anne Michaels's 'Fugitive Pieces,'" *Contemporary Literature*, Vol. 45, No. 2 (Summer, 2004): 322. Indeed, there are those like Saul Friedlander who believe that redemptive moments subvert Holocaust literature, which should be confined to portraying trauma. See Donna Coffey, "Blood and Soil in Anne Michaels's *Fugitive Pieces*: The Pastoral in Holocaust Literature," *Modern Fiction Studies*, Vol. 53, No. 1 (2007): 32.

29 The book is dedicated to the author's parents.

30 Efraim Sicher, "The Future of the Past: Countermemory and Postmemory in Contemporary American Post-Modern Narratives," *History and Memory*, Vol. 12, No. 2 (2001): 67.

31 Duncan "belonged to the generation that was born in the shadow of shame, memory, and nightmare — foot soldiers conscripted into a trembling army of 'Never Again!' placard holders, where no draft dodging was possible because there was little choice but to serve" (p. 53).

32 Duncan goes to Poland because he is urged to do so by his "uncle" and guardian angel, Larry Breitbart, a leader of the Jewish Mafia in Miami. Breitbart is deeply concerned about the way that Duncan's life and his personality are disintegrating under the pressure of his own hatred and his separation from his wife and daughter. "It's time for you to see a psychiatrist (p. 61) . . . I don't know whether there is a twelve-step rage recovery program, but if there is you should be in it" (p. 62). One of Breitbart's

European operatives has discovered Isaac, and Breitbart concludes, correctly as it turns out, that a meeting with his half-brother will prove a step in the right direction.

33   He is helped along the way by getting a posthumous letter from Maloney who has "gassed himself" and confides in Duncan: "I missed our visits. Maybe we are both free . . . P.S. Hold on tight to the pysanka [a Ukranian easter egg]. Eggs bring good luck at this time of year." (p. 296).

34   Sicher, 2005: 142.

35   Dan, 2006: 78.

36   Wiesel's account of the Kolvillag pogrom, first published in 1973, anticipates the problematic of assimilation and fragmentation which are so prominent in later novels. One of the very first to sense the peril of Kolvillag is the scribe who chronicles the Jewish community, and thus understands via history and tradition what is at hand (p. 113). Others in the community see the chronicler as living in the past and thus unable to apprehend the present. As Braun, the lawyer, puts it, "we are no longer living in the Middle Ages. Really!" (p. 212). He is married to a Gentile, has converted, and therefore believes that he is bullet proof. Similarly, Davidov, the President of the Jewish community, believes that he and the community are safe because of his mutually beneficial relationships with the Prefect (p. 115). At the other end of the social order, Avrom the Wise is not afraid because "logic" (p. 203) tells him that the Gentiles envy, and are a threat only to, the rich (p. 204). And so it goes: endless dithering with some arguing that it is important for the community to stick together; others hoping to take advantage of their exceptionalism, and still others preparing to take up arms. In the end, they all perish in the inferno sparked by the pogrom.

37   "The Jewish people have two options at this moment in history. They may give in to their memory of hurt, let the fear of future pain become the driving motivation; and, overwhelmed by anxiety, they may scramble to fashion ever more elaborate neurotic defenses against the future. Or alternatively, they may face bravely and openly their undeniable human mortality. In and through this root anxiety of human existence they may seek new ways to hope, hope based not simply on life, but hope founded more deeply in the human spirit." Robert J. Willis, "The Triumph of Humanity: Wiesel's Struggle with the Holocaust," *Journal of Religion and Health*, Vol. 30, No. 2 (Summer, 1991): 175.

38   See Ted L. Estess, "Elie Wiesel and the Drama of Interrogation," *The Journal of Religion*, Vol. 56, No. 1 (January, 1976): 18–35.

39   Dan, 2006: 53.

40   Dan, 2006: 57.

41   Dan, 2006: 58.

42   Dan, 2006: 59.

43   Note that Azriel decides after a brief flirtation with Communism that it is a counterfeit religion making false promises. Initially he is impressed, but in the end, Azriel is overwhelmed by the spiritual power of a rabbi who puts Communism in a religious and historical context. "And so once more

a stranger comes to bring us the good news: salvation is possible and its name is communism . . . That in order to build the future, we must destroy the past? Or in other words, that man will continue his work of destruction until the end of time . . . For us there can be no salvation outside community. Yes, the stranger has just told us that in order to save man, one must annihilate the Jew in man, and that our people must disappear so that mankind may prosper. His mouth betrays his ignorance" (p. 76). "Your communist seems to take himself for the Messiah, right? . . . A messianism without God is like bread without flour, dough without yeast, a body without life, a life without sunshine" (p. 73).

Notes to Chapter 4: Aftermath of Disaster: The Nazi Legacy

1 *Atrocity and Amnesia: The Political Novel Since 1945*. New York: Oxford University Press, 1987: 192.

2 John Reddick concludes that the "savage reality" of the Holocaust "is mirrored with a new and startling intensity" in: *Dog Years. The Danzig Trilogy of Gunter Grass: A Study of The Tin Drum, Cat and Mouse and Dog Years*. London: Secker & Warburg, 1975: 173.

3 For a detailed account of the physical destruction of the Allied bombing, see Jorg Friedrich, *The Fire: The Bombing of Germany 1940–1945*. New York: Columbia University Press, 2006. W. G. Sebald confronts the emotional toll of destruction, occupation and defeat in *On the Natural History of Destruction*. New York: The Modern Library, 2004.

4 Heinrich Böll's *The Silent Angel*, completed in 1950, did address the suffering of Germans in the immediate postwar era, but it was rejected by his publishers and did not appear until 1992 (well after his death in 1985) to commemorate the 75th anniversary of his birth. David Mehegan, "Literature from the Rubble: An Early Work by Heinrich Böll Gives Fresh Insight into Postwar Germany's Idiosyncratic Seer," *Boston Globe*, July 24, 1994: 41.

5 I am grateful to Sabine Lang for first encouraging me to think along these lines.

6 These categories or phases are not airtight. Julian Preece calls attention to references to anti-Semitism in *The Tin Drum* and then there is Heinrich Böll's early *trummer-literatur*. Mehegan, 1994: 41.

7 Gordon Craig, *The Germans*. New York: New American Library, 1983: 213.

8 "Böll," it has been said, by James H. Reid, "does not choose to leave his readers in despair." Cited in Siegried Mandel's review, "*Heinrich Böll: A German for His Time*", *Modern Fiction Studies*, Vol. 35, No. 2, (Summer, 1989): 1045–6.

9 Robert Conrad, *Understanding Heinrich Böll*. Columbia, SC: University of South Carolina Press, 1992: 72–3.

10 "Otto Faemel. Respectable, respectable. Honor and loyalty. He denounced us to the police, and suddenly was the mere husk of a son" (p. 137; see also p. 128). Her daughter-in-law Edith is killed by British shrapnel after

her sister-in-law, Grandmother Faemel's daughter Johanna, has saved her from the Nazis (p. 133).

11 Böll explicitly points out that Schrella is not a Jew.

12 As one reviewer points out, his commitment to playing billiards daily at half-past nine "becomes part of his mind-saving routine," Siegried Mandel, "Sabotage to Assert the Human Spirit," *The New York Times*, August 5, 1962.

13 Conrad, 1992: 74. Not surprisingly, for critics looking for political engagement, Böll's message is deeply flawed. According to Judith Ryan, Schrella's actions do no more than "assuage . . . [his] personal sense of justice." Similarly, Peter Demetz dismisses the attempted assassination, "an act of a trigger-happy grandmother who in so acting has transformed "the absolute purity of the 'lambs'" into "absolute terrorism" (p. 198). Each quoted in Conrad, 1992: 72–3. Of course, Conrad disagrees: "Böll's novel reveals the dead end of solidarity in isolation and implies social change is only possible with a platform, a program and an ideology for change" (Conrad, 1992: 141).

14 Böll is very much driven, as Gordon Craig puts it in comments on a subsequent novel, *Group Portrait with Woman*, by his "preeminently Catholic morality" (Craig, 1983: 222).

15 In his review of *The German Lesson* Ernst Pawel sees this emphasis on the joys of duty as turning Hannah Arendt's celebrated dictum on its head. "[W]hat Lenz sets out to probe is evil of banality." *The New York Times*, April 9, 1972.

16 "My dear, it's a visual age we're living in, all the other senses have lost out . . . For him colour hasn't merely poetic significance, it's metaphorical . . . But he's German to the bone, more than six Pomeranian grenadiers put together" (p. 424). "This work bears testimony to the fact that the sonority of colour can transform an intuitively glimpsed meaning into pure paint" (p. 427). All the while they snicker at Uncle Nance's extravagant and anachronistic garb.

17 Hansi goes on to deride Siggy's "friend Nansen as the very type I regard as a disaster: back-to-the-land and that, visionary, and political" (p. 438). A disillusioned Siggy complains that "condescension or contempt [are] all that you people are capable of where an old man is concerned" (p. 438).

18 In a mixed review of *The German Lesson* Christopher Lehmann-Haupt praises Lenz for capturing the "Third Reich . . . with its prejudices against people not rooted in the land." "Figures in a Dirty Ground," *The New York Times*, April 5, 1972.

19 Quoting an unnamed scholar. "Crybabies: Solving the Colic Conundrum," *The New Yorker*, September 17, 2007: 47.

20 The sinking of the *Wilhelm Gustloff* becomes the central event in Grass's 2002 novel, *Crabwalk*, which will be considered towards the end of this chapter.

21 Patrick O'Neill, *Gunter Grass Revisited*. New York: Twayne Publishers, 1999: 24.

22 Craig (1982: 216–17) also detects a kind of "banality of evil" theme in Oskar's power to drum away the martial ethos of this Nazi. "In Grass's novels, there was nothing either heroic or diabolical about the Nazis. They were bogus strongmen whose posturing was always comic to the clear-eyed observers (like the dwarf Oscar in *The Tin Drum*, whose inspired drumming had the power to dissolve their martial demonstrations into sentimental disorder)." Does this, however, mean that Grass does not see the Nazis as diabolical? Here I think it is important to keep in mind that Grass's focus is on the small-time, opportunistic Nazis, not on the regime, its leaders and its most ideologically committed cadres.

23 In what can be seen as a prelude to *Dog Years*, the corrupted Oskar, "like the West Germany of the *Wirtschaftswunder*, the economic miracle of the immediate postwar years . . . grows rapidly. The expensive suits he is soon able to afford elegantly conceal the misshapen hump he has acquired during his socially inspired growth" (O'Neill, 1999: 26).

24 New York: Harcourt, 2007.

25 Krimmer, 2008: 280–1.

26 O'Neill offers a less dour interpretation rooted in Grass's "unswerving support for democratic socialism." However, O'Neill also acknowledges Grass's sense of "melancholy skepticism" — along with "a profound and similarly growing sense of the fragility of human existence" (O'Neil, 1999: 161).

27 *The New York Review of Books*, May 31, 2007: 4.

28 Julian Preece reports that Karl Schiller learned from Grass himself that *Dog Years* was to be about "the rottenness at the core of the Economic Miracle." *The Life and Work of Gunter Grass: Literature, History and Politics*. New York: 2001: 59.

29 However, the self-righteous younger generation also emerges as resolutely judgmental, morally adrift and no more trustworthy than their elders. "Take the Jewish question. Such a thing could never happen in our generation. We'd have gone on discussing with the Jews until they emigrated of their own free will and conviction. We despise all violence. Even when we engage in compulsory discussion, the conclusion is in no way binding" (p. 491).

30 In his wide-ranging study of Grass's life and work, Julian Preece calls attention to the charges of anti-Semitism that have been leveled against Grass. Although not sharing this view, Preece does concede that: "While Grass sets out to deconstruct the myths and stereotypes of Jewish identity in *Dog Years*, he comes perilously close to reinforcing them" (Preece, 2001: 62).

31 Nazi era schoolteacher, *Patterns of Childhood*, p. 98.

32 Anna Kuhn writes that *Patterns of Childhood* is "autobiographical," — revealing the ways in which Nelly embodies Christa Wolf's life experiences and existential quandaries. *Christa Wolf's Utopian Vision: From Marxism to Feminism*. Cambridge: Cambridge University Press, 1988: 96.

33 The intergenerational tensions that pervade and are entangled in, and yet

distinct from, its politics can be seen in Nelly's determination to avoid "projecting her own needs onto her daughter" as did Charlotte (Kuhn, 1988: 120).

34 Kuhn, 1988: 117.

35 Strauch's *message* was no different from Warsinski's. However, the adolescent Nelly becomes infatuated with Strauch. "Like every lover, Nelly pines for irrefutable proof of requited love" (p. 222). For a dramatic portrayal of just this kind of convergence among adolescent adulation, sexual yearning and political entrapment, see the film version of *The Prime of Miss Jean Brodie*, with Maggie Smith in the title role of a fascist pied piper in an English girls' school.

36 Kuhn (1988: 125) points out that "Bruno Jordan's acquiescence in Nazism conveyed itself clearly to Nelly."

37 She was always fearful whenever she entered the headquarters of the Hitler Youth organization (p. 231). She had qualms about some of the staunchest Nazis in her class like Heinz Blind who seemed a weird loser.

38 Charlotte managed to find Nelly a job as an unpaid clerk in the office of the mayor of a village (p. 337) and through a process of attrition and de-Nazification (pp. 345–6) she, the 16-year-old, becomes (much to her surprise) an influential figure as the village changes hands from the Americans to the British and finally to the Russians (p. 347 ff.). Charlotte's *dutiful* daughter does not so much choose life as simply accept the responsibilities thrust upon her and, characteristically, acquits herself admirably.

39 Even the admirable Charlotte has her blind spots. She professes ignorance of the persecution of Communists — leaving Communist concentration camp victims aghast (p. 332).

40 Lenka's obstinacy should presumably be seen in the context of the palpable continuity that Wolf sees between "the Nazi past and the GDR present" (Kuhn, 1988: 96).

41 Wolf convincingly portrays the intrinsic contingency of Nelly's quest to engage with her different selves as they struggle to cope with generational strife and political sea changes. In so doing she "calls into the question the presumed authority and capacity for self-knowledge." Michael G. Levine, "Writing Anxiety: Christa Wolf's *Kinderheitsmuster*," *Diacritics*, Vol. 27, No. 2 (1997): 107. This web of contingency also makes unequivocally clear why, when all is said and done, Nelly's heartfelt effort to judge her own moral culpability ends in equivocation.

42 Quoted in Kuhn, 1988: 116.

43 *On the Natural History of Destruction*. New York: Modern Library, 2004: 41.

44 Sebald, 2004: 36.

45 Sebald, 2004: 30.

46 Sebald also speculates that the Germans wore their stoicism as something of a badge of honor. "We may also wonder whether their breasts did not swell with perverse pride to think that no one in human history had

ever played such overwhelming tunes or endured such suffering as the Germans" (2004: 44).

47 In the GDR there was, at least officially, no such silence. Citizens of the GDR were urged not to forget the havoc that the Nazis had visited upon them. *Ipso facto* those who governed the GDR were deemed peace-loving, uncompromising foes of the Nazis and thus without any shame or guilt.

48 "Law and Tenderness in Bernhard Schlink's *The Reader*," *Law and Literature*, Vol. 16, No. 2 (Summer, 2004): 181.

49 For an extended analysis of how and why the Germans chose to "lay their dead to rest and find a place in their history for the devastation that World War II brought to Germany," see Robert G. Moeller, "Germans as Victims? Thoughts on a Post-Cold War History of World War II's Legacies (Sensibilities)," *History and Memory: Studies in Representations of the Past*, Vol. 17, Nos. 1–2, (Fall 2005): 147–95.

50 Put another way, this means, as Elisabeth Krimmer points out, that Paul realizes "had he been of age during the Third Reich, he would most likely have been a bystander" — and thus, in effect, typical of those Germans who abetted the Nazis without embracing Nazism. "'Ein Volk von Opfern?' Germans as Victims in Gunter Grass's *Die Blechtrommel* and *Im Krebsgang*," *Seminar: A Journal of Germanic Studies*, Vol. 44, No. 2, (May 2008): 272–90.

51 Krimmer, 2008: 284.

52 Specifically, the *Wilhelm Gustloff* was constructed to serve the Strength Through Joy movement, an important element of Robert Ley's Labor Front, which had absorbed the independent labor unions of pre-Nazi Germany into the one-party, de-unionized Nazi State.

53 On the falling out between Strasser and Hitler, see pp. 205 and 211.

54 This memorial site had been dedicated on January 30, 1995, 50 years to the day after the sinking of *Wilhelm Gustloff*; the day in 1933 when Hitler took over; and, of course, Paulie's birthday as well (p. 96).

55 The captain was also unaware that the *Wilhelm Gustloff* saved English seamen on one of its KDF cruises (p. 62).

56 Predictably, historian Heinz Schon is reviled as a "Russian lover" when in a stunningly ill-advised act of candor he chooses to present the full story at a commemoration ceremony for victims of the sinking. He even explains that the death toll was increased by the blundering failures of the German crew (p. 135; see also pp. 137, 140, 145–6, 158–9).

57 "That's how it goes with monuments. Some of them are put up too soon, and then, when the era of their particular notion of heroism is past, have to be cleared away" (p. 177; more broadly, see pp. 177–81). By way of ironic confirmation of the contingency of political truths and their personification, we learn that it was not until 1990, "forty-five years after the end of the war and twenty-seven years after Marinesko's death" that a monument was erected to this "hero of the Soviet Union" (p. 177). By this time, Alesksandr Marinesko had not only died but has also been consigned to three years of exile to Siberia, courtesy of the NKVD (pp. 179–81). Even had

he been alive, one can only presume that it would have been cold comfort to be honored as a hero of the moribund Soviet Union.

58 Elisabeth Krimmer reads *Crabwalk* differently, given Grass's persistent determination to draw our attention to the dangers inherent in narratives of German victimization" (2008: 274). Accordingly she concludes that: "Konny's story contains a warning not about the danger of repressing stories of German suffering but about the pernicious consequences of a problematic self-perception. If Germans continue to conceive of themselves as victims, they are in danger of repeating the past and of becoming perpetrators again" (2008: 286). These two readings are not, however, mutually exclusive — especially in the context of Grass's indeterminate narratives and his deep suspicion of both the Federal Republic and German culture.

59 The implied equivalence between Michael's and Hanna's transgressions and more broadly the sense of compassion that Schlink's narrative evokes for Hanna has generated intense criticism. While some critics have praised the book, Anthony Quinn dismisses it — vituperatively and gratuitously, in my judgment — as "a clunking fable that flatters German self-pity more than it sharpens German self-knowledge." Quinn goes on to report that: "In her book *The Language of Silence*, the German-born US academic Ernestine Schlant writes off *The Reader* as yet another chapter in a long chronicle of forgetting." Anthony Quinn, "The Art of Memory," *The Independent*, January 2, 2009.

60 Jeremiah P. Conway deplores the privileging of formality by his philosopher father and the judge and their marginalizing of Michael's compassion. Michael has come to "understand Hanna's action *before* he attempts to judge or condemn." But this puts him in direct conflict with "a long legal and philosophical tradition holding that reason operates better, and more clearly and objectively, when distanced from the biases of sentiments." "Compassion and Moral Condemnation: An Analysis of *The Reader*," *Philosophy and Literature*, Vol. 23, No. 2 (1999): 288 and 291, respectively.

61 Another interpretation of her suicide attributes it to the capacity for "self-judgment" gained by the newly literate Hanna from her immersion in the literature of the Holocaust. From this perspective, "Michael's compassion . . . leads Hanna to be more critical and severe with herself than even the legal system deemed necessary" (Conway, 1999: 300). See also John E. MacKinnon's equally penetrating elaboration in "Crime, Compassion, and *The Reader*," *Philosophy and Literature*, Vol. 23, No. 2 (1999): 341–62.

62 Conway, 1999: 284–301.

63 MacKinnon considers the fraught relationships among moral judgment, moral equivalence and legality. (2004): 179–201.

64 As one sifts through the critiques, it becomes apparent that objections to the novel express both political and philosophical differences. Jeremiah P. Conway argues convincingly that the novel probes the tension between compassion and condemnation. Insofar as Schlink's narrative evokes, as it

most certainly does, compassion for Hanna, it is politically objectionable because it seems to let her and others off the hook despite her participation in unspeakable criminality. Conway calls attention to an analogous objection in Martha Nussbaum's philosophy, which concludes that compassion stands in the way of justified moral condemnation. His own view is that *The Reader* reconciles moral condemnation and compassion, most notably Michael's compassion for Hanna, rooted in the understanding he gains of her illiteracy and the "powerful constraining conditions" within which her moral judgments do not let her off the hook (Conway, 1999: 298).

65 Both quoted by Gordon Craig, 1982: 228.
66 Conway, 1999: 298.

Notes to Chapter 5: The Contradictions of Democracy: Political Estrangement in the U.S. and the U.K.

1 Herbert Mitgang, "'Invisible Man,' as Vivid Today as in 1952," *New York Times*, March 1, 1982.
2 *New York Times*, May 31, 1986.
3 *New York Times*, April 15, 1997.
4 Julian Moynahan, "What Life is Really Like in England," *New York Times*, April 19, 1981.
5 Anthony Quinn, "The New England," *New York Times*, April 30, 2000.
6 Michiko Kakutani, "A Hero With 9/11 Peripheral Vision," *New York Times*, March 18, 2005.
7 Princeton: Princeton University Press, 1995.
8 Hochschild, 1995: xii.
9 Hochschild, 1995: xviii.
10 *Another Country*. New York: Vintage, 1993: 423.
11 Writing in 1995 — 43 years after it was first published — Roger Rosenblatt concluded that "improved race relations . . . did not eradicate raw hatred, deliberate ignorance. Underclass crime and the recent resurgence of poisonous phenomena like black anti-Semitism have accomplished the seemingly impossible — made black–white relations worse." Roger Rosenblatt, "Lives Well Lived: Ralph Ellison; Prescience, in Black and White," *New York Times*, 1 January 1995."
12 This socio-political truth, which to me is central, is not the truth that others have read into the novel. Irving Howe and Saul Bellow, who were among the jurors who awarded Ellison the National Book Award, both seemed to believe that the book celebrated the individual and the power of human spirit. Bellow praised the book for this quality, but Howe was critical of Ellison for turning his back on the social and the political. Irving Howe, "Review of Ralph Ellison's *Invisible Man*, *The Nation*, May 10, 1952. Saul Bellow, "Man Underground, Review of Ralph Ellison's *Invisible Man*," *Commentary*, June 1952: 608–10.
13 Ellison was explicit about his rejection of Marxism. "I rejected Marxism because it cast the Negro as a victim and looked at him through ideology. Furthermore, what was written by proletarian writers was so empty that I

could tell they weren't interested in art at all." John Corry, "An American Novelist Who Sometimes Teaches," *New York Times*, November 20, 1966. Irving Howe was critical of Ellison for caricaturing Marxists (1952). More broadly in his article "Black Boys and Native Sons," *Dissent*, Autumn 1963 (included later in *A World More Attractive*, 1963), Howe takes Ellison (along with James Baldwin) to task for failing to understand, as did Richard Wright, "that only through struggle could Black men and all oppressed humanity achieve their humanity." Ernest Kaiser, "A Critical Look at Ellison's Fiction and at Social and Literary Criticism by and about the Author, "*Black World*, December 1970 [a special Ralph Ellison issue].

14 Howe seems to ignore this element of *The Invisible Man*, in all likelihood because in his reading the novel is not a "social document," as Ellison argues but a paean of praise to the unencumbered individual without any political moorings (Rosenblatt, 1995).

15 Quoted in Patrick J. Deneen and Joseph Romance, "Introduction: The Art of Democratic Literature" in Patrick J. Deneen and Joseph Romance, eds. *Democracy's Literature: Politics and Fiction in America*. New York: Rowman & Littlefield, 2005: 6. See Ellison's comments to Roger Rosenblatt, "But in 'Invisible Man' the statement is the literature. The protagonist's story is his social bequest. And I'll tell you something else: The bequest is hopeful" (Rosenblatt, 1995).

16 I agree entirely with Robert Niemi's judgment of *Continental Drift* which "melds the class concerns of New England with the racial politics of the Caribbean, forming a synergistic whole that is much more powerful than the sum of its parts." *Russell Banks*, New York: Twayne Publishers, 1997: 105.

17 Banks asks that we put the Haitian journey in the larger context of third world poverty, drought and endless war leading to the displacement of rural populations to urban areas and from urban squalor and ethnic conflict out of the third world in search of sanctuary and a decent life (pp. 34–6). In linking the American dreams of the Haitians and the Dubois, Banks thus offers, as Robert Niemi puts it, a vision of "human migration as a kind of natural, global process," intrinsic to the future well-being of the planet (Niemi, 1997: 108).

18 Niemi, 1997: 105.

19 Neither Bob nor Elaine shares Eddie's virulent and paranoid animus against people of color, who are for them, along with the multicultural society of south Florida, exotic curiosities. Indeed Bob falls in love and has a brief but intense affair with Marguerite, a black woman. However, as Robert Niemi points out, Banks makes it clear that "Bob's intimacy with a black woman can never result in a separate peace with America's de facto apartheid system" (Niemi, 1997: 111).

20 To the bitter end then, Bob cannot escape. "Like Graham Greene and Robert Stone, Mr. Banks is concerned with moral ambiguities and their consequences on ordinary lives, and his tale of how one man named Bob Dubois went in search of a better life and got in over his head becomes, at

once, a visionary epic about innocence and evil and a shattering dissection of contemporary American life" (Kakutani, 1985).

21   According to Banks, "I wanted his tragedy to be the fact that he causes hers." Janet Maslin, *New York Times*, April 29, 1985.

22   Although Victor regularly drops emigrants off in North Caicos, 60 miles from Haiti, rather than in Miami, he is not blamed. "It was the fault of a baka, an evil spirit, or the fault of the passenger himself, who had [for example] failed to feed the loas adequately" (p. 180).

23   Michiko Kakutani (1985) summarizes, "[Russell Banks'] story of one man's doomed attempts to reinvent his life became a dark mirror of the American dream." The estrangement of Banks' characters is largely unrelieved. They are, as novelist Wesley Brown has observed, "locked in class and race conflict, people with few illusions and even fewer realizable hopes." *New York Times*, September 10, 1989.

24   Saul Bellow, *Mr. Sammler's Planet*. New York: Penguin Books, 1995: 61.

25   Michael Wood, "The Trouble with Swede Levov," *New York Times*, April 20, 1997.

26   Michiko Kakutani, "A Post War Paradise Shattered from Within," *New York Times*, April 15, 1997.

27   Roth thus raises, in the shadow of the Holocaust, the estrangement that is intrinsic to assimilation — one of the dominant themes of the Holocaust novels. "We are made to contemplate the demise of the immigrant dream cherished by men like Seymour's father, the souring of the generational struggle during the 60's, and the connections between assimilation and rootlessness and anomie" (Kakutani,1997).

28   "This reminds us of the cultist aspect of the American revolutionaries of the Sixties, sometimes a small band bound together by their rants, paranoia, and above all the exaggeration of their power and foolish underestimation of the power of society," Elizabeth Hardwick, "Paradise Lost," *The New York Review of Books*, June 12, 1997: 12–14.

29   "Mr. Roth has taken . . . two contradictory impulses in American history: the first, embodied by Seymour Levov, representing that optimistic strain of Emersonian self-reliance, predicated upon a belief in hard work and progress; the second, embodied by the Swede's fanatical daughter, Merry, representing the darker side of American individualism, what Mr. Roth calls ''the fury, the violence, and the desperation'' of ''the indigenous American berserk'' (Kakutani, 1997).

30   *Union Street*, New York: Picador USA, 1984: 213.

31   Stuart Hall, "The Rise of the Representative/Interventionist State 1880s–1990s," in Gregor McLennan, David Held and Stuart Hall, eds, *State and Society in Contemporary Britain: A Critical Introduction*. Cambridge: Polity Press, 1984: 7–49.

32   Christopher Pollitt, "The State and Health Care," in McLennan, Held and Hall, 1984: 134. See also Frank Field, "The Welfare State — Never Ending Reform," *BBC History*. 1999-08-08. uk/history/british/modern/field_01. shtml.

33 Claus Offe, *The Contradictions of the Welfare State*. John Keane, ed., London: Hutchinson, 1984: 19 and 15, respectively.

34 Offe, 1984: 19.

35 Offe, 1984: 15.

36 David Held identified the most vulnerable as "the young (whose opportunities have radically decreased); blacks (whose employment prospects, housing and general conditions of living are becoming ever more difficult); the disabled and sick (who have suffered a deterioration of services due to public sector cuts); the unemployed and poor (who have vastly increased in numbers) and those living in regions that have been particularly hard hit." David Held, "Power and Legitimacy in Contemporary Britain," in McLennan, Held and Hall, eds, 1984: 344. See also Joel Krieger, *Reagan, Thatcher and the Politics of Decline*. New York: Oxford University Press, 1986.

37 Another prominent critique of the welfare state is its intrusions into the lives of those it is supposed to serve. As one of the characters in Pat Barker's novel, *Union Street* (New York: Picador USA, 1999) puts it: "Worse than the Blitz, isn't it? Council's done more in one year than Hitler did in five" (p. 225). See also Mary McIntosh, "The Family, Regulation, and the Public Sphere," in McLennan, Held and Hall, eds, 1984: 38–44.

38 As Malcolm Bradbury put it, "Alan Sillitoe . . . has caught much of the mood of the present-day working class in England — its half-conscious spirit of rebellion, its exploitive laziness and non-cooperation, its uneasy respect for law and order, its secret sympathy for the clever rogue and the army deserter, its sense of a distant "they" which runs life so that you can never win." "Beating the World to the Punch," *New York Times*, August 16, 1959.

39 Psychiatrist Harvey Checkley "isolated sixteen traits exhibited by patients he called 'primary' psychopaths; these included being charming and intelligent, unreliable, dishonest, irresponsible, self-centered, emotionally shallow, and lacking in empathy and insight." John Seabrook, "Suffering Souls: The search for the roots of psychopathy," *The New Yorker*, November 10, 2008: 66.

40 Arthur's resentments against the society that treated his parents so badly in the hard years leading up to World War II have been assuaged by the "good enough life" afforded them by the welfare state (p. 45).

41 Malcolm Bradbury argues that after World War II: "The working class man in England has found a new role for himself since the war — the role of consumer; its wages have risen and mass production has bounded, a carnival of consumption has changed life beyond recognition." *New York Times*, April 16, 1959.

42 While Gilbert Millstein saw *Saturday Night and Sunday Morning* as "a recurrence of the proletarian novel," he went on to point out: "The class conscious writers of the thirties would find him reprehensible — nihilistic, irresponsible and uncomfortably full-blooded, and no man to fit a predetermined thesis." *New York Times*, August 20, 1959.

43 *The Buddha of Suburbia*. New York: Penguin Books, 1991: 284.

44 In *White Teeth*, according to Michiko Kakutani, Zadie Smith "shows not only how one generation often revolts against another — sons against fathers, daughters against mothers — but also how they repeat their predecessors' mistakes, retrace their ancestors' dreams, and in the case of those who are immigrants, commute nervously between the poles of assimilation and nationalism, the embrace of the Other and a repudiation of its temptations." Michiko Kakutani, "Quirky, Sassy and Wise in a London of Exiles," *New York Times*, April 25, 2000.

45 Quinn, 2000.

46 Smith notes the irony that Samad's denunciation of British culture is expressed in ways "betraying the English inflections of twenty years in the country" (p. 336).

47 "Two suspects in a heist at Germany's largest department store have been released because they are twins whose fingerprints and DNA are indistinguishable," *New York Times*, 19 March 2009: A10.

48 Understandably, it can be and has been argued that *White Teeth* expressed "an almost naive confidence that people from different backgrounds could communicate." Daniel Zalewski, "'The Autograph Man': The Quest of a Pop-Culture-Addled Trivialist," *New York Times*, October 6, 2000.

49 This fatuity he attributes to Daisy's university teachers: "young lecturers [who] like to dramatise modern life as a sequence of calamities" (p. 75).

50 I have read *Saturday* as a socio-political narrative. Novelist Zoe Heller, while acknowledging its efforts to probe "the relationship between the private self and the outer world," steers the reader to McEwan's intense concern with "the purpose and value of literature." However, she believes that McEwan has failed to maintain the indeterminacy that is intrinsic to what literature has to offer. For all its "finely wrought and shimmering intelligence . . . it never quite fully submerges its thesis. Its concept is so high and prominent as to disallow the reader the distinctive novelistic pleasure of feeling, rather than coolly registering, the author's intention." Zoe Heller, "'Saturday': One Day in the Life," *New York Times*, March 20, 2005.

Notes to Chapter 6: Re-imagining the Twentieth Century, Remembering the Twenty-First

1 Kafka's *Diaries 1910–1923*. Quoted in Louis Begley, *The Tremendous World I Have Inside My Head, Franz Kafka: A Biographical Essay*. New York: Atlas & Company: 38.

2 Much the same positive portrayal of immigrants finding their way into English society is found in the work of Hanif Kureishi — see, for example, *The Buddha of Suburbia* (New York: Penguin Books, 1990).

3 It is hardly surprising that Nettlinger is more the rule than the exception in *Dog Years* and in other novels as well. Walter Matern's "materniads" lead him from one petty opportunist to another. In *Billiards at Half-Past Nine*, unscrupulous postwar politicians embody the Host of the Beast and are thus deemed mortal enemies of the Faemels.

4   Grass's chronicle of postwar, post-Nazi Germany is full of unprincipled characters who are successfully able to shrug off their shameful past and put their opportunistic instincts to work in the purportedly transformed, but in fact unreconstructed, political culture of the New Germany.

5   Recall the book's Talmudic epigraph: "Had the peoples and the nations known how much harm they brought upon themselves by destroying the Temple of Jerusalem, they would have wept more than the children of Israel."

6   Primarily because he is mindful of Jakob's Jewish heritage, but also because he takes comfort and meaning from old Hebrew sayings, the Psalms and the Zohar, Athos readily incorporates them into Jakob's education (p. 156).

7   Tony Judt, "What Have We Learned, If Anything?" *New York Review of Books*, May 1, 2008, Vol. 55, No. 7: 20.

8   Jack Goldsmith, *The Terror Presidency: Law and Judgment Inside the Bush Administration*. New York: W. W. Norton, 2007.

9   Kim Scheppele, *The International State of Emergency: Challenges to Constitutionalism after September 11*. Working Paper, Law and Public Affairs Program, Princeton University, 2006

10   Judt, 2008: 20.

11   Judt, 2008: 20.

12   See Malise Ruthven, "The Big Muslim Problem!", *The New York Review of Books*, December 17, 2009: 62–5.

13   For example, Michael Slackman reported that the government intends "to purge political and social science departments of professors and curriculums deemed un-Islamic." According to Ayatollah Khamenei, the study of social sciences "promotes doubts and uncertainty . . . Many of the humanities and liberal arts are based on philosophies whose foundations are materialism and disbelief in godly and Islamic teachings." *New York Times*, 1 September 2009.

14   See Steven Erlanger, "Burqa Furor Scrambles Political Debate in France," *New York Times*, 1 September 2009. On orthodoxy in Israel, see Isabel Kershner, "Religious-Secular Divide Tugging at Israel's Heart," *New York Times*, 2 September 2009.

15   Judt, 2008: 20.

16   See "Battle's Latent Scars," *New York Times* editorial, 23 August 2009.

17   See, for example, Claudia Roth Pierpont, "Found in Translation: The Contemporary Arabic Novel, *The New Yorker*, January 18, 2010: 74–80.

Bibliography

Abel, Jonathan E. "Canon and Censor: How War Wounds Bodies of Writing," *Comparative Literature Studies*, Vol. 42, No. 1 (2005), pp. 74–93.

Allen, Brooke. "Review of *Isherwood: A Life Revealed* by Peter Parker." *New York Times Book Review*, 19 December 2004.

Arendt, Hannah. *Eichmann in Jerusalem: A Report on the Banality of Evil*. New York: Viking Press, 1963.

Aron, Raymond. *The Century of Total War*. Boston: Beacon Press, 1968.

Baldwin, James. *Another Country*. New York: Vintage Books, 1993.

Barker, Pat. *Two Novels: 'Union Street' and 'Blow Your House Down.'* New York: Picador USA, 1999.

Barker, Pat. *The Eye in the Door*. New York: Plume, 1994.

Bauman, Zygmunt. *Modernity and the Holocaust*. Cambridge: Polity Press, 1995.

Begley, Louis. *The Tremendous World I Have Inside My Head: Franz Kafka: A Biographical Essay*. New York: Atlas & Company, 2008.

Bellow, Saul. *Mr. Sammler's Planet*. New York: Penguin Books, 1995.

Bellow, Saul. "Man Underground," Review of Ralph Ellison's *Invisible Man*," *Commentary*, June 1952, pp. 608–10.

Böll, Heinrich. *The Silent Angel*. New York: St. Martin's Press, 1994.

Boyers, Robert. *Atrocity and Amnesia: The Political Novel Since 1945*. New York: Oxford University Press, 1987.

Brannigan, John and Pat Barker. "An interview with Pat Barker," *Contemporary Literature*, Vol. 46, No. 3 (Autumn, 2005), pp. 367–92.

Butler, Robert Olen. *The Alleys of Eden*. New York: Henry Holt, 1994.

Coffey, Donna. "Blood and Soil in Anne Michaels's *Fugitive Pieces*: The Pastoral in Holocaust Literature." *Modern Fiction Studies*, Vol. 53, No.1 (2007), pp. 27–49.

Cole, Sarah. "Modernism, Male Intimacy, and the Great War," *English Literary History*, Vol. 68, No. 2 (2001), pp. 469–500.

Conrad, Robert C. *Understanding Heinrich Böll*. Columbia, South Carolina: University of South Carolina Press, 1992.

Conrad, Robert C. *Heinrich Böll*. Boston: Twayne Publishers, 1981.

Conway, Jeremiah P. "Compassion and Moral Condemnation: An Analysis of *The Reader*," *Philosophy and Literature*, Vol. 23, No. 2 (1999), pp. 284–301.

Craig, Gordon. *The Germans*. New York: New American Library, 1983; Boston: Beacon Press, 1968.

Crouch, Christopher. *Modernism in Art, Design, and Architecture*. New York: St. Martins Press, 1999.

Dan, Joseph. *Kabbalah: A Very Short Introduction*. New York: Oxford University Press, 2006.

Dauvin, René. "*The Trial*: Its Meaning," in Angel Flores and Homer Swander, eds, *Franz Kafka Today*. Madison: University of Wisconsin Press, 1964.

Deneen, Patrick J. and Joseph Romance, "Introduction: The Art of Democratic Literature," in Patrick J. Deneen and Joseph Romance, eds, *Democracy's Literature: Politics and Fiction in America*. New York: Rowman & Littlefield, 2005.

Eksteins, Modris. "*All Quiet on the Western Front* and the Fate of a War," *Journal of Contemporary History*, Vol. 15, No. 2 (April, 1980), pp. 345–66.

Estess, Ted L. "Elie Wiesel and the Drama of Interrogation," *Journal of Religion*, Vol. 56, No. 1 (January, 1976), pp. 18–35.

Ewick, Patricia and Austin Sarat, "Hidden in Plain View: Murray Edelman in the Law and Society Tradition," *Law & Social Inquiry*, Vol. 29, No. 2 (Spring, 2004), pp. 439–63.

Feeley, Malcolm. *The Process is the Punishment: Handling Cases in a Lower Criminal Court*. New York: Russell Sage Foundation, 1979.

Field, Frank. "The Welfare State — Never Ending Reform," *BBC: British History in-depth*. See http://www.bbc.co.uk/history/british/modern/field_01.shtml (accessed March 2010).

Foucault, Michel. *Discipline and Punish: The Birth of the Prison*. New York: Vintage, 1979.

Fraenkel, Ernst. *The Dual State: A Contribution to the Theory of Dictatorship*. Translated from the German by E. A. Shils, in collaboration with Edith Lowenstein and Klaus Knorr. New York: Oxford University Press, 1941. Reprinted 2006 by The Lawbook Exchange, Ltd.

Friedrich, Jorg. *The Fire: The Bombing of Germany 1940–1945*. New York: Columbia University Press, 2006.

Fussell, Paul. *The Great War and Modern Memory*. New York: Oxford University Press, 1977.

Ganzel, Dewey. "*A Farewell to Arms*: The Danger of Imagination," *The Sewanee Review*, Vol. 79, No. 4 (Autumn, 1971), pp. 576–97.

Gerth, H. H. and C. Wright Mills (eds). *From Max Weber*. London: Routledge & Kegan Paul, 1970.

Giddens, Anthony. *The Consequences of Modernity*. Stanford, California: Stanford University Press, 1990.

Gilman, Sanders. "Jewish Writers and German Letters: Anti-Semitism and the Hidden Language of Jews," *The Jewish Quarterly Review*, New Series, Vol. 77, No. 2/3 (October, 1986–January, 1987), pp. 119–48.

Goldsmith, Jack. *The Terror Presidency: Law and Judgment Inside the Bush Administration*. New York: W. W. Norton, 2007.

Gyorgyvey, Clara. "Review of *Fateless*," *World Literature Today*, Vol. 74, No. 3 (Summer, 2000), pp. 612–13.

Hall, Stuart, "The Rise of the Representative/Interventionist State 1880–1990s," in Gregor McLennan, David Held and Stuart Hall, eds, *State and Society in Contemporary Britain: A Critical Introduction.* Cambridge: Polity Press, 1984, pp. 38–44.

Hall, Stuart, David Held and Toney McGrew, eds. *Modernity and its Future.* Cambridge: Polity Press, 1992.

Harari, Yuval Noah. "Martial Illusions: War and Disillusionment in Twentieth-Century and Renaissance Military Memoirs," *The Journal of Military History*, Vol. 69, No. 1 (2005), pp. 43–72.

Hardwick, Elizabeth. "Paradise Lost," *New York Review of Books*, June 12, 1997 (Vol. 44, No. 10), pp. 12–14.

Held, David. "Power and Legitimacy in Contemporary Britain," in Gregor McLennan, David Held and Stuart Hall, eds, *State and Society in Contemporary Britain: A Critical Introduction.* Cambridge: Polity Press, 1984, pp. 299–369.

Hochschild, Jennifer L. *Facing Up to the American Dream*. Princeton: Princeton University Press, 1995.

Howe, Irving. *Politics and the Novel*. Chicago: Ivan R. Dee, 2002.

Howe, Irving. "Black Boys and Native Sons," *Dissent*, Autumn, l963, pp. 353–68.

Howe, Irving. "Review of Ralph Ellison's *The Invisible Man*," *The Nation*, May 10, 1952.

Hutcheon, Linda. *The Politics of Postmodernism*, 2nd ed. London: Routledge, 2002.

Irving, David J. C. *Apocalypse 1945: The Destruction of Dresden*. Cranbrook, Western Australia: Veritas Publishing Company, 1995.

Jacobson, David C. "'Kill Your Ordinary Common Sense and Maybe You'll Begin to Understand': Aharon Appelfeld and the Holocaust," *AJS Review*, Vol. 13, No. 1/2 (Spring–Autumn 1998), pp. 129–52.

Jones, Edward P. *The Known World*. New York: Amistad, 2004.

Judt, Tony. "What Have We Learned, If Anything?" *New York Review of Books*, May 1, 2008 (Vol. 55, No. 7), pp. 16–20.

Judt, Tony. *Postwar: A History of Europe Since 1945*. New York: Penguin, 2005.

Judt, Tony. "Review of *Interesting Times: A Twentieth Century Life* by Eric

Hobsbawm," *New York Review of Books*, November 20, 2003 (Vol. 50, No. 18), pp. 43–5.

Kafka, Franz. *The Trial*. New York: Schocken Books, 1998.

Kaiser, Ernest. "A Critical Look at Ellison's Fiction and at Social and Literary Criticism by and about the Author," *Black World*, December 1970 [a special Ralph Ellison issue].

Kandiyoti, Dalia. "'Our Foothold in Buried Worlds'; Place in Holocaust Consciousness and Anne Michaels's 'Fugitive Pieces,'" *Contemporary Literature*, Vol. 45, No. 2 (Summer, 2004), pp. 300–30.

Kelman, Herbert C. "Violence without Moral Restraint," *Journal of Social Issues*, Vol. 29 (1973), pp. 29–61.

Kertesz, Imre. "Who Owns Auschwitz?" Translated by John MacKay. *The Yale Journal of Criticism*, Vol. 14, No. 1 (2001), pp. 267–72.

Krieger, Joel. *Reagan, Thatcher and the Politics of Decline*. New York: Oxford University Press, 1986.

Krimmer, Elisabeth. "'Ein Volk von Opfern?' Germans as Victims in Gunter Grass's *Die Blechtrommel* and *Im Krebsgang*," *Seminar: A Journal of Germanic Studies*, Vol. 44, No. 2 (May, 2008), pp. 272–90.

Kuhn, Anna K. *Christa Wolf's Utopian Vision: From Marxism to Feminism*. Cambridge: Cambridge University Press, 1988.

Kureishi, Hanif. *The Buddha of Suburbia*. New York: Penguin Books, 1990.

Levi, Primo. *If Not Now, When?* New York: Summit Books, 1985.

Levine, Michael G. "Writing Anxiety: Christa Wolf's *Kinderheitsmuster*," *Diacritics*, Vol. 27, No. 2 (1997), pp. 106–23.

MacKinnon, John E. "Law and Tenderness in Bernhard Schlink's 'The Reader,'" *Law and Literature*, Vol. 16. No. 2 (Summer, 2004), pp. 179–201.

MacKinnon, John E. "Crime, Compassion, and *The Reader*," *Philosophy and Literature*, Vol. 23, No. 2 (1999), pp. 341–62.

Macpherson, C. B. *The Political Theory of Possessive Individualism: From Hobbes to Locke*. New York: Oxford University Press, 1964.

Mandel, Siegried. "Review of James H. Reid's *Heinrich Böll: A German for His Time*," *Modern Fiction Studies*, Vol. 35, No. 2 (Summer, 1989), pp. 351–53.

Matz, Jesse. *The Modern Novel: A Short Introduction*. Oxford: Blackwell Publishing, 2004.

McIntosh, Mary. "The Family, Regulation, and the Public Sphere," in Gregor McLennan, David Held and Stuart Hall, eds, *State and Society in Contemporary Britain: A Critical Introduction*. Cambridge: Polity Press, 1984, pp. 38–44.

McKean, Keith. "Review of *Slaughterhouse 5*." *North American Review*, Vol. 254, No. 3 (Fall, 1969), pp. 70–1.

Merrill, Robert. "The Tragic Form in *A Farewell to Arms*," *American Literature*, Vol. 45, No. 4 (January, 1974), pp. 571–9.

Miller, Tyrus. *Late Modernism: Politics, Fiction, and the Arts Between the Wars*. Berkeley: University of California Press, 1999.

Mitchell, Timothy. "Everyday Metaphors of Power," *Theory and Society*, Vol. 19 (1990), pp. 545–77.

Moeller, Robert G. "Germans as Victims? Thoughts on a Post-Cold War History of World War II's Legacies," *History and Memory: Studies in Representations of the Past*, Vol. 17, Nos. 1–2 (Fall, 2005), pp. 147–94.

Nash, Stanley. "Critical Reappraisals of Aharon Appelfeld," *Prooftexts*, Vol. 22, No. 3 (Fall, 2002) pp. 334–49.

Niemi, Robert. *Russell Banks*, New York: Twayne Publishers, 1997.

Norris, Margot. "Introduction: Modernisms and Modern Wars," *Modern Fiction Studies*, Vol. 44, No. 3 (1998), pp. 505–9.

O'Brien, Tim. *Going After Cacciato*. New York: Broadway Books, 1999.

Offe, Claus. *The Contradictions of the Welfare State*. John Keane, ed. London: Hutchinson, 1984.

O'Neill, Patrick. *Gunter Grass Revisited*. New York: Twayne Publishers, 1999.

Pinsker, Sanford. *Understanding Joseph Heller*. Columbia, South Carolina: University of South Carolina Press, 1991.

Pollitt, Christopher. "The State and Health Care," in Gregor McLennan, David Held and Stuart Hall, eds, *State and Society in Contemporary Britain: A Critical Introduction*. Cambridge: Polity Press, 1984, pp. 119–49.

Preece, Julian. *The Life and Work of Gunter Grass: Literature, History and Politics*. New York: Palgrave, 2001.

Rarras-Rauch, Gila. "Aharon Appelfeld: A Hundred Years of Jewish Solitude," *World Literature Today*, Vol. 72, No. 3, Hebrew Literature in the 1990s, (Summer, 1998), pp. 493–500.

Reddick, John. *The Danzig Trilogy of Gunter Grass: A Study of 'The Tin Drum,' 'Cat and Mouse' and 'Dog Years.'* London: Secker & Warburg, 1975.

Riesman, David. *The Lonely Crowd: A Study of Changing American Character*. New Haven: Yale University Press, 1950.

Ruthven, Malise. "The Big Muslim Problem!" *New York Review of Books*, December 17, 2009 (Vol. 54, No. 20), pp. 62–5.

Scheppele, K. L. *The International State of Emergency: Challenges to Constitutionalism after September 11*. Working Paper, Law and Public Affairs Program, Princeton University, 2006.

Schlant, Ernestine. *The Language of Silence: West German Literature and the Holocaust*. New York: Routledge, 1999.

Seabrook, John. "Suffering Souls: The Search for the Roots of Psychopathy," *The New Yorker*, November 10, 2008, p. 66.

Sebald, W. G. *On the Natural History of Destruction*. New York: The Modern Library, 2004.

Sicher, Efraim. *The Holocaust Novel*. New York: Routledge, 2005.

Sicher, Efraim. "The Future of the Past: *Countermemory and Postmemory in Contemporary American Post-Modern Narratives*," *History and Memory*, Vol. 12, No. 2 (2001), pp. 56–91.

Sussman, Henry. *The Trial: Kafka's Unholy Trinity*. New York: Twayne Publishers, 1993.

Talbott, John E. "Soldiers, Psychiatrists, and Combat Trauma," *Journal of Interdisciplinary History*, Vol. 27, No. 3 (Winter, 1997), pp. 437–54.

Trachtenberg, Stanley. "Understanding Joseph Heller," *Modern Fiction Studies*, Vol. 38, No. 2 (Summer, 1992), pp. 489–490.

Wieczorek, John P. "'Irrefuhrung durch Erzahlperspective?' The East German Novels of Jurek Becker," *The Modern Language Review*, Vol. 85, No. 3 (July, 1990), pp. 640–52.

Willis, Robert J. "The Triumph of Humanity: Wiesel's Struggle with the Holocaust," *Journal of Religion and Health*, Vol. 30, No. 2 (Summer, 1991), pp. 161–78.

Zaner, Richard M. "Sisyphus without Knees: Exploring Self-Other Relationships through Illness and Disability," *Literature and Medicine*, Vol. 22, No. 2 (2003), pp. 188–207.

Index